PRAISE FOR BRIAN DOHERTY
AND THIS IS BURNING MAN

"When I received a copy of This Is Burning Man . . . *I trembled. I couldn't wait to open it up and learn who was actually behind an event that I greatly admire and always look forward to attending. This is the rapturous story of the world's great messengers: its artists. It is amazing to follow how the fragile ecosystem of the art world comes together to form the Burning Man, celebrate the Burning Man, and then return him to ashes."*
—Perry Farrell, Lollapalooza founder and activist

"I loved this book! Doherty's writings are a fantastical journey through a world that keeps alive the spirit of a time before September 11, where we were less afraid of each other, more daring, louder, smarter, saner, and able to welcome a kinder terrorism into our culture. It is incredible to know the history of civil rebellion set against the backdrop of intellectual urban unrest, especially in this laugh-out-loud riot of a book."
—Margaret Cho, comedian

"Burning Man is a wondrous topic. The yearning to gather is a primal one, and Burning Man is a magical example. It's based, as Brian Doherty describes, on a love for creating and experiencing: 'The world is a desert. It's up to us to fill it in.' By capturing the people and the wonder of Burning Man, Doherty has contributed to this process.
—Walter Isaacson, author of *Benjamin Franklin*

"This book will teach you many weird things that you ought to be eager to know."
—Bruce Sterling, author of *The Zenith Angle*

THIS IS BURNING MAN

THIS IS BURNING MAN

THE RISE OF A
NEW AMERICAN UNDERGROUND

BRIAN DOHERTY

BENBELLA

BenBella Books, Inc.

Dallas, Texas

BenBella Books
6440 N. Central Expressway, Suite 617
Dallas, TX 75206
www.benbellabooks.com
Send feedback to feedback@benbellabooks.com

Cover design by Frances Yasmeen Motiwalla
Cover photograph by George Post
Cover modified for trade paperback by Melody Cadungog
Front Matter Design and Composition by Melody Cadungog
Printed by Victor Graphics, Inc.

Printed in the United States of America
10 9 8 7 6 5 4 3 2 1

Doherty, Brian.

 This is Burning Man : the rise of a new American underground / Brian Doherty.

    p. cm.

 Originally published: 1st ed. New York: Little, Brown, c2004.

 ISBN 1-932100-86-5

 1. Burning Man (Festival) 2. Performance art--Nevada--Black Rock Desert. 3. Black Rock Desert (Nev.)--Social life and customs. I. Title.

 NX510.N48D64 2006

 394.25'09793'54--DC22

2006014954

For
Jean Poulet
Showman

Without whom . . .

*What is extraordinary about the search for self-fulfillment
in contemporary America is that it is not confined to a few bold
spirits or a privileged class. Cross-section studies of Americans show
unmistakably that the search for self-fulfillment is instead an outpouring
of popular sentiment and experimentation, an authentic grass-roots
phenomenon. . . . It is as if tens of millions of people had decided
simultaneously to conduct risky experiments in living, using the only
material that lay at hand — their own lives.*
— Daniel Yankelovich

*In the form and function of play, itself an independent entity which
is senseless and irrational, man's consciousness that he is embedded in
a sacred order of things finds its first, highest, and holiest expression.*
— Johan Huizinga

*Don't work for my happiness, my brothers — show me yours —
show me that it is possible — show me your achievement — and
the knowledge will give me courage for mine.*
— Ayn Rand

An unintelligible passionate yearning drove them out into the desert.
— T. E. Lawrence

TABLE OF CONTENTS

WELCOME TO BLACK ROCK CITY

It's the strangest thing. I've wiped the dashboard of my '87 Subaru almost a dozen times now, and the white powder filling all its crannies just won't go away. When it's wet, it looks clean, for a minute. But when it dries, the coating is still there.

It wouldn't matter if I got it out of my car anyway. That dust—the residue of the Black Rock Playa, in Nevada—is inside me now. And it's never going away.

Many great faiths have been born in visions arising from the desert. And no desert has ever seen a vision more inspiring of faith than the annual gathering called Burning Man. "Burning Man," wrote journalist Daniel Pinchbeck, with admirable precision, in *Breaking Open the Head,* "is more decadent than Warhol's Factory, more glamorous than Berlin in the 1920s, more ludicrous than the most lavish Busby Berkeley musical, more of a love-fest than Pepperland, more anarchic than Groucho Marx's Freedonia, more implausible than any mirage."

Every year, increasing numbers of pilgrims—more than thirty thousand in 2003—drive down a long two-lane highway, heading about one hundred miles northeast of Reno, Nevada. Their destination is the widest stretch of utter desolation in the continental United States, nearly four hundred square miles of desiccated lake bed. There's no water, no plumbing, no shade, no life—nothing but packed-down alkali dust cracking off to every horizon.

The temperature at this terribly inhospitable wasteland—the Black Rock Playa—can, and probably will, stay well above 100 degrees all day. At night it may well plummet to near freezing. It is frequently beset by unpredictable and brutal windstorms during which the dust rises and coats and blinds you and whatever shelter you've built will very likely be dashed to the ground.

So many people will be there, crammed into such a small space, that the desolation beyond the encampment will seem a cruel tease as the inhabitants live for a week in an impromptu tent city that screams "refugee camp" more than it does "vacation."

Still, almost all of them are more than just resigned to a week condemned to this unpleasant-sounding fate. They are ecstatic. They are at Burning Man.

Burning Man started in 1986 as a little ritual for a couple of buddies and a handful of their friends on a beach in San Francisco—the simple burning of a simple wooden man, for no reason they will specify. They decided to keep doing it every year, and slowly, by accident, this act attracted more and more people, who became dedicated not so much to the burning of a blank icon as to the things that started happening around the fire.

At first it was nothing more than a reason for some friends to gather. Now, a fully functional city—Black Rock City—appears and then quickly disappears around the ritual. This temporary city is complete with a local constabulary, a mainstream daily and an alt-weekly, more than a dozen radio stations, a power grid, thirty-eight miles of roads, and more artistic expressions in more media per square inch than anywhere else on Earth. Journalist Fiona Essa once aptly described the scene as akin to "a war zone where the explosions had left art in their-wake."

Every year on the Saturday before Labor Day, in America's most beautifully forbidding and awesomely empty landscape, a forty-foot statue adorned with lovely neon lighting gets burned. But the burning of the statue is just the MacGuffin, the thing around which the real story gets set in motion, not the theme. The real story is what happens to people—what they do, what it means to them, how it changes them—when they can make a temporary society qualitatively different in many respects from their everyday one. It's a civilization that by the mutual agreement of all attendees has almost no commerce and is dedicated purely to creativity and play, where the standards of normal life can be inverted or ignored in the pursuit of fresh experiences and fresh identities.

People do work at Burning Man—and work remarkably hard—on building ephemeral things for the joy of creation, for the fulfillment of working with others to pull off the grand gesture, for status and bragging rights in their transitory community, pursuing a preindividualist vision of the good life, which at Burning Man is found only in working with and contributing to the polis.

The experience provides so much more than any one person can see, do, or be. Burning Man is not an event or a happening or a theme park or an arts festival, though it has aspects of all those. It is, truly, a city. Black Rock City began as somewhat of a wry gag on the part of the tight-knit group of Bay Area artists and cultural rebels who started it. But it has grown way beyond their control, or anyone's. A true city arises, develops, evolves, catches fire, then disappears, built on a backdrop of nothing, imbuing it with a rich metaphorical resonance and also summoning an extraordinary and ever-shifting visual panorama as the city is constantly either growing or dissolving.

The story of how a handful of people burning a statue on a beach became, in only fifteen years, a temporary civilization of tens of thousands is one of the stories this book tells. While it is a long story, in its way, it is not ultimately very complicated: It happened because people wanted it to happen, people made it happen, and no one stopped them. No one planned for it, ordered it into existence, bought it, or paid for it. It was a spontaneous flowering of a felt need of a free people.

The experience of Burning Man is unique. Aspects of it do resemble older traditions or other gatherings of intentional community. Assembling to burn an effigy reminds one of ancient myths of Celtic sacrifice like the Wicker Man (and the cult movie of the same name based on it), and also of Zozobra, when the Kiwanis in Santa Fe, New Mexico, burn a giant firework-laden effigy in a city park and party all day. The Rainbow Family is another countercultural intentional community that meets on federal land—in national forests rather than a dry lake bed—but a Rainbow Gathering is little more than a get-together, a party for those keeping alive hippie values. Burning Man's unique combination of insistence on active creative participation—in a consciously grim and unwelcoming blankness that becomes a canvas for the largest act of ephemeral collective creativity man has ever known, in an atmosphere largely free of imposed meanings or behavioral norms—has no real parallel.

The event ends up presenting in the starkest possible way the core question of a living being: *What do I do now?* The struggle for survival—sublimated in civilization by going to the office rather than hunting the mastodon—settles that question most of the time: *I-work.* We do what has to be done to make the money to buy the shelter and the food and, if we are lucky, all those other higher-mammal things that make the time when we aren't working go by sweeter. Because everyone puts so much effort into providing flash, entertainment, and bizzarity for the delectation of all, every day at Burning Man is so packed with everything life has to offer—love, freely elected creative work, partying, learning, improvised zaniness, drugs, challenging conversations—that your sense of normal time is shattered. A flood of glorious superfluity washes over you, and each day and each night seem an eternal reoccurrence of everything both wonderful and terrible about life in a human community. Burning Man generates an unspoken and expected bond of mutual dependence, having less to do with any communist vision than with the idea that we are a community of independent, creative adults mutually responsible for making Burning Man work. And Burning Man only works if it's the wildest, most extreme, most unusual experience of anyone's year.

Burning Man is a very American place, frontier expansive and energetic and free, built more on pragmatic experience than any kind of ideology. Like America at its best, it is dedicated to providing the opportunity to pursue happiness and meaning on your own terms. Still, also like America, certain ideas do seem to animate most of the people there. Certain mottoes have been offered up by the organizers and embraced by most of the attendees: "No spectators"—you are encouraged to be creative, adding something to the experience for your fellow citizens; "radical self-reliance"—there is nothing for sale at the playa other than coffee and ice, so you have to bring everything you need to survive in a very harsh environment, including food, water, and shelter, and you are expected to buy and sell nothing. That expectation led to a practice, which in turn led to a new idea that reigns over Burning Man: the notion that it functions as a "gift economy," that with goodwill and open hearts and the abundance of time and energy, we can prosper and thrive together with gracious gifts, freely given.

When combined with those other ideas, it's true, we can. You need to take care of your own survival in a forbidding land where survival is hard. And you are encouraged to act out whatever creativity you may have inside you, to let it bubble forth in this city, as a gift. The gift economy is best expressed not in the proffering of gewgaws but in an expression, a word, a built object, a performance.

Although ideologically driven, to some extent, by the notion of the gift economy (the event is so multidimensional, so chaotic, that pinning it down to any singular meaning is misleading), Burning Man *is* put on by a for-profit limited liability corporation—you do need a ticket to get in, and tickets are priced on a sliding scale ranging from $145 to $250—run by one of the guys who first took that little scarecrow down to Baker Beach in San Francisco, a man named Larry Harvey. While treated as a mock-guru of sorts in the very prankster-filled Burning Man community, Larry cares most, he says, about *immediate experience,* not mystical musings. While Burning Man inspires a level of devotion that could be considered cultish, it has, through most of its history, had no beliefs to sell, nothing to insist on, nothing to order you to do. "I believe there is a way that all of us can be together," Larry Harvey once said, and that is a simple summation of the thread that runs through the story of this event.

☼

I first heard about Burning Man in 1994. I had just moved to Los Angeles and was hanging out with the Los Angeles Cacophony Society, which had been pulling off absurdist fiery pageants at Black Rock already. At the time, the propaganda about the event stressed the rigors of the desert so much that I thought my deskbound, magazine-reporter, bedroom record label–running self would be destroyed by the pitiless desert. So I didn't go in '94.

By 1995, I had heard so much about Black Rock City's functional anarchy that I had to go—anarchy being one of my primary intellectual interests. I showed up early Saturday morning and left Monday morning, so I only got a small taste. It did seem to be a functioning-anarchy for the two days I was there—people living and-getting-along without enforced laws, doing what they pleased, camping where they wished, expressing themselves however they liked—and-everyone seemed, for the most part, content, even thrilled. It indeed held forth the delicious promise that people could get along-peacefully under difficult circumstances without lots of rules and cops.

But why I knew I'd be back had to do with something a little less abstract than that. One afternoon it rained; then it hailed (yes, in late summer in the Nevada desert); then a full rainbow arc appeared, solid and pure. Mud pits formed, and all the lithe and not-so-lithe bodies formed a slippery pile of gray-brown, clambering and sliding around one another—then I saw the dwarf in full bondage gear car-surfing behind a pickup, leather spiked choker and all. The truck was sputtering and catching in the ruts it made, churning thick mud back at the dwarf, who was sliding along, digging little ruts himself, and spitting back tiny chunks of mud with his feet. The world turned to mud, and it wasn't a crisis—it was an opportunity for play and spontaneous shows of spirit and survival—and for a car-surfing dwarf. It was then that I realized I'd be coming back to Burning Man. I've been every year since.

It has only grown more filled with delights and Dada absurdities and breathtaking beauties since that first visit. In 1995, four thousand citizens made Black Rock City; in 2003, around thirty thousand showed up. On any given walk around the semicircular blocks of Black Rock City, you might see an angry milkman in a white boilersuit trolling for milkmaids who can lactate at will; a tether ball on fire, twirling round its pole and then kicking itself back into action; a car dragging behind it a man on a flaming toilet reading the paper; a flyer on a Porta-John warning of an escaped gorilla, only to open that Porta-John and have a kid in a gorilla suit leap out at you, squealing with laughter; two people in harnesses inside a geodesic dome arena leaping and cavorting and bashing at each other with padded poles; people being whipped at the Temple of Atonement or playing chess with their bodies on a block-wide board. You might hitch a ride on any number of fantastical conveyances, from flying carpets to giant heads to bus-sized white whales; laugh at a man in a business suit working frantically using WiFi (the city has WiFi but no cell phone service) in the café, with his water bottle, also wearing a carefully crafted bottle-sized suit and tie, beside him; see a squad of Porn Clowns in a daisy chain with fingers up each other's orifices; stop for some intellectual chat at a free bookmobile; have a lovely stranger stop you to say, "Did you ever believe life could be this wonderful?"; see a group of strangers all flossing off of one thread dangling from someone's chicken suit; have heartfelt and funny conversations with random groups on almost any topic imaginable, from electricity deregulation to Reiki healing to comic books to ancient weaponry to-high-level electrophysics to metallurgy to Eagle Scouting; watch stunningly complex light shows while in the distance people play golf with burning toilet paper rolls; marvel at giant metal lotus flowers spewing flames; and find a jar of mayonnaise sitting by itself, hundreds of yards from anything, with a sign reading FREE MAYO. It's a place for Fitzcarraldan excess and the smallest whimsy. It's a lot of fun.

But it's more than *just* fun. It might sound like a mere indulgent feast for the senses, just sensory flash and silliness. But so many things flood together in that dry lake bed in late summer that the Burning Man gestalt, the nub of what it offers its devotees, can be hard to pin down.

Once, in a twenty-four-hour coffeehouse in Austin, Texas, Tyler Hanson laid out some interesting thoughts for me in an attempt to define that thing that Burning Man supplies in blessed abundance. He calls it the Holy Moment. "It's that moment when you are experiencing what you are experiencing, and you know that it is happening and it should be the way it is. It's the most amazing possible thing that could be happening at the time being, and you are aware of it at that moment."

Despite the fact that it requires reflexive awareness, the moment must sneak up on you at first. "You cannot have any expectations for the Holy Moment. You must be blindsided and only then can you have this epiphany of, here I am and this is what's happening, and the moment before I didn't know but now I know and I will revel in every moment."

The Way of Burning Man, Tyler tells me, is constantly open to reinterpretation because there is no rule book. "So there are thirty thousand reinterpreted reasons as to what is the Way, and really there is no Way—the Way needs to be constantly destroyed and redone again."

This seems a relatively obvious interpretation of the meaning of a repeated burning ritual—every year, it gets destroyed; every year, it gets built again. Lots of other artworks have been burned at the event over the years, inspired by the central ritual, by the general sense of chaotic looseness, and by a yearning for phoenixlike rituals of rebirth, a chance to destroy and transmute in order to make room for freshness, newness—and for the chance to do it all again.

Richard Pocklington, a Stanford anthropologist who's done some fieldwork at Burning Man, pointed out to me that nearly everyone he asked about the meaning of the Burn denied it had any singular one. Still, I always suspect that most people have ideas about the Meaning of It All that they lean toward.

Tyler is no exception, and his interpretation touches on some of the changes that have overtaken Burning Man as it has grown from the hundred who first brought it to the playa to the tens of thousands attracted now: "I think the Way used to be that you had a bunch of people who did everything they did out in the desert when they went home as well. They lived it. They weren't just putting on a costume. But as the numbers increased, there were a lot of people stepping into a form that was prepared already. You always see the people in costumes—gas mask, fairy, robot, naked guy. It's like Halloween with these prefab identities, like goblin, alien, witch.

"Still, for most people that might be the most expression they get in their lives, and hallelujah, we need them. Why Burning Man does work is that it opens that door to whatever freak anyone might have inside of them that they don't get to be at home. For lots of people out there, wearing unusual clothes or being able to talk about—or do—drugs or sexual things might be a big explosion of freedom."

That sense of freedom at Burning Man can manifest itself in the smallest—but most significant—ways. Tyler, for example, likes to talk to most everyone he meets. At Burning Man he does, but in Austin or Atlanta he doesn't, and he wants to know why. "We spend so little time really talking with each other that when it happens it seems this huge important movement, and we dub it neotribalism. Tribalism, wow—it means talking to each other! We're standing around a fire talking to each other again. Wow, really moving up the evolutionary ladder here, people. We're so sophisticated that hanging around a fire talking seems like a genius new step."

That sense of tribal solidarity that Burning Man creates manifests itself in a strange abundance. As Tyler told me, "I'd try to impress on people the idea that everything you ever wanted is here at all times, and if you need it, all you have to do is ask for it. At Center Camp Café, I'd take it upon myself to facilitate this. Whenever I'd hear any-one wanted or needed something, I'd start yelling it out—'Scissors!' Scissors would show up. People would start coming up to me with their requests. 'Well, yell it with me,' I'd say. 'Let's do it together—WATERMELON!!' and the watermelon would appear."

Tyler tells me a few more stories of moments he found especially charming, especially moving, at Burning Man, but then stops himself. He's feeling like they don't really come across verbally, that he can't quite say what it all meant to him. You know—you had to be there. "But 'you had to be there' is an important lesson of the Burning Man experience, actually," he realizes. "What it teaches you is *you have to be there* every moment—have to be alive, alert to possibility, enjoy what the world is offering and what you have to offer the world. It's like, I remember waking up one morning in '97 and seeing a careening couch go out of control and smack into a tent. Behind it-was a lamp rolling along, and that crashed in behind it. And it's like…yeah, coffee? Somehow that becomes the norm—what you are *supposed* to see, what breakfast is *supposed* to be like."

This book tells its story mostly through the voices and reminiscences of Burning Man's organizers, artists, and citizens. An anthropological-/ -sociological approach to the event might be illuminating, though I ultimately concluded that specific human stories had more to say about the topic. I did glean some insights into what might be going on at Burning Man from books like Harvey Cox's *The Feast of Fools,* which explores the need for a revival of wild, sacred festivity in American culture. Johan Huizinga's *Homo Ludens: A Study of the Play Element in Culture* was also helpful. When Huizinga writes that "play may rise to heights of beauty and sublimity that leave seriousness far beneath," anyone who has been privileged to live for a while at Burning Man can only say, "Amen."

For a historical perspective on certain aspects of the Burning Man experience, Marcel Mauss's *The Gift: Forms and Functions of Exchange in Archaic Societies* is useful, discussing what Mauss calls the "purely sumptuous destruction of accumulated wealth" of the potlatch, an ancient custom in which tribes essentially compete through exhibiting how much wealth they can afford to waste. The potlatch cannot help reminding you of how much work and energy and money is turned violently to ash on the Black Rock Playa every late summer, just for the love and joy and entertainment of your fellow citizens.

People attend Burning Man for as many different reasons as there are individuals. And you meet all sorts out there; though it's true most of them are white, a bare majority are from California, and a majority seem to be between twenty-five and forty-five (these are impressions, not scientific demographics). Lots of people come back again and again, but most years, probably somewhere near half might be there for the first time. Burning Man is by no means a youth culture event. Again, lacking scientific demographics, my impression is that about as-many people between forty-five and sixty show up as do those between twenty and twenty-five. Attendees defy easy pigeonholing, and include ravers and techheads, machine artists and hippies, crusty punks and Internet millionaires, underground rebels and suburban parents, academics and carny freaks, book editors and fire-spinners, and every other kind of human seeker from around the globe.

Burning Man can feel decidedly New Agey and/or pagan—there's lots of spookiness and synchronicities and rituals going on around you, camps practicing all sorts of modern healing and "energy move-ment" abound, and, well, all that dancing around the fire can't help but scream "pagan"—but then you can find lots of mockery and parody of all those things at Burning Man too. If someone wanted to-really internalize the farthest potentials of postmodern thinking, they could do a lot worse than hang out and try to grasp Burning-Man.

But uniting every divergent tendency, spirituality, and attitude at Burning Man is a sense that everyday life is missing something: a spark of creativity, a chance for self-expression, some freedom from judg-ment and cold personal relations that one must travel far off the grid to find. Burning Man provides a particularly intense arena in which to play out twenty-first-century America's struggle for meaning and community.

What has been imagined and created at Burning Man is becoming bigger than Burning Man itself, which is why it is worth contemplat-ing even if you never in your life would dream of putting up with the heat, the wind, the noise, the nuttiness. As Burning Man artist Jim Mason observed, the event has "become the reckoning of the identity and self-worth of thousands of people. It's a ritual of inversion, where the standards of everyday society are inverted and suspended, and we don't have that as a national thing. And it's needed, and that-need is being felt and expressed through Burning Man." And not-only through Burning Man; others are finding themselves so enriched by what they think they've learned about life and culture from Burning Man that they are trying to spread it beyond the confines of Nevada's desert.

Larry Harvey presents Burning Man as being in opposition to commodification, which he condemns as a means of alienating people from their own experience, their own essence, and, most important, from each other. Thus, Burning Man has resolutely refused sponsorship and ads—Black Rock citizens are even encouraged to cover corporate logos on their rental trucks.

Many advertisements—particularly of the soft drink or rum variety—try to sell a pale imitation of what Burning Man really delivers: that level of heightened, humming joy and togetherness and the sense that the universe is vibrant and glowing and you are the luckiest person alive to have it pulsing through and around you. Burning Man is just like that, much of the time. I have actually been overtaken by that thought out there: *This is like living in a rum ad.* That I thought of the ad might be sad. The feeling, though, most certainly is not.

Burning Man can shame commodified experience in many ways. Sometimes at night in Black Rock City, the pattern of the colored lights imposed on the stretching, enveloping blackness makes it seem as if you are in a video game. And this is exciting and fascinating—not because the *idea* of being inside a video game is so neat, but because the *experience* of being in a video game is so neat.

In my nine years at Burning Man I've been a roulette dealer, a bass guitarist in a casino house band, star of a confessional TV show, sodlayer, ditchdigger, fireman, pyromaniac, gunman, reporter, furniture mover, painter, welder, driller, hole-digger, rigger. In my life outside Black Rock, I'm a few of those things sometimes, most of them never. Burning Man's hold on me is centered in all the possibilities it has opened—the chances it has given me to pull off fascinating stunts in merry fellowship with amazingly accomplished people. It promises a chance to be more than you've known.

Many people at Burning Man take that idea so far they adopt a fresh identity, known as a "playa name" in the community. This is the ultimate statement of a particularly modern and American freedom:

self-invention. Black Rock City provides a richly inviting place to be whoever you want to be. And as a man named Steven Raspa, whom I met at Burning Man, said to me once: "When people are able to act with joy in doing what they like, it's good for everybody."

This book tells the history of the city that grows and disappears because people want a place to act with joy, and to be together, and to create things for themselves and for their chosen community. It tells stories of what has happened there, what still happens there, and what might be happening in the future because this country, this world, has been fortunate enough to have this city in it, even if it's only for one week a year.

There are stories of danger, absurdity, conflict, mayhem, and even violence. But the portrait of human beings is, through it all, optimistic. I've seen all this and heard all this, and I know that what it amounts to is something strange and wonderful. There's mockery and bad juju, but all in all there are human beings trying their hardest to make life interesting and hilarious and fulfilling and to make a new thing happen.

Burning Man began with a desire to make something and continued in a desire to create communion around such gestures of creation. It grew spontaneously and in many ways accidentally, evolving into something that has become the measure of thousands of people's lives. This book will explain how, who, what, and why.

Welcome to Black Rock City.

A Note on Sourcing

One of Burning Man's principles is "No spectators." I tried to honor that in writing this book. I had been to Burning Man four times before I dreamed of writing about it for public consumption. Back in the midnineties, it still had enough of an aura of "what we do is secret" that keeping it under wraps made a subterranean sort of sense. By 1999, I was convinced that Burning Man was ready for public discussion. (I was a latecomer to this realization, of course.) I wrote a cover feature for *Reason* magazine, mostly about the event's curious and often rocky relationship with government authorities. (The piece, called "Burning Man Grows Up," was the cover story in *Reason*'s February 2000 issue and can be found on the Web at http://reason. com/0002/fe.bd.burning.shtml). That Burning Man was a dream for a writer interested in American culture or the human condition was clear from my first arrival in 1995. But until 1999, all the writing I'd done about the event was private, in letters to friends and in personal journals. But it was abundantly clear by '99 that the gathering was no longer a secret and, in fact, was never intended to be. Letting more people know about it was not doing my new community a disservice. The wave of press was only going to swell and crest further.

I noticed, with a touch of Black Rock townie snobbery, that most of the copious videography of the event was all surface flash that missed the meaning—the human stories that really made Burning Man worthy of documentation; and that most of the newspaper and magazine journalism was written by people who had just shown up in Black Rock City in time to write about it that year. (Some of the resulting journalism was still quite good.) So in early 2000, I decided to write this book.

Many of the stories and observations herein come from events I personally witnessed or lived through. I decided, both before and after choosing to write this book, that I wanted to live Burning Man as deeply and widely as I could. I made it a point to get my hands on as many big art pieces, see as many things, be as many places, and sleep as little as my body could manage. But despite any one man's most manic or impassioned efforts, life in Black Rock City is more vast than any individual can personally experience.

Thus, the stories and observations contained here are a combination of life in Black Rock as I lived it and journalistic re-creations based on stories and reminiscences told to me by the more than one hundred other Burning Man artists, organizers, and attendees I interviewed formally or just lived moments with in Black Rock City and in the larger Burning Man community, both virtual and physical, that has grown up around the event. If I am narrating an event I clearly was not present to witness and am not directly quoting a named source, it is a re-creation based on the best recollections of a person (or persons) who was present.

I should single out Steve Mobia for thanks here; he supplied me with many hours of contemporaneous audio diaries made right after the event each year from 1990 through 1999, giving me the closest thing to a firsthand memory, unmisted by the passing of time, of the early years that I missed in the Black Rock Desert. I have striven for as much accuracy as people's memories allow; do note that there are numerous conflicts in people's memories of what happened and particularly what year it happened in, especially regarding the early years. I have tried to present it all with as much accuracy as the available sources allow.

Black Rock City has existed for more than a decade's worth of weeks; nearly a hundred thousand people have had adventures there that have informed them, moved them, perplexed them, and delighted them. This book obviously and necessarily covers only a sampling of those stories, of those people, focusing largely on the efforts and passions it takes to make the city and its art real—and on what the city's reality means and can mean for countless individual lives and the culture. (The culture is, don't forget, made up of those individual lives.) This sampling is, I think, based on my years spectating and participating at Burning Man, both representative and telling. There are a million stories in Black Rock City, but certain themes and passions dominate. This book is meant to demonstrate and explain them.

Part One

IGNITION

Chapter One

"A SPONTANEOUS ACT OF
RADICAL SELF-EXPRESSION"

When Larry Harvey was a young man, he would stand alone in his bedroom and reach out his arms.

He would imagine his fingers were stretching, extending impossibly far, metamorphosing into a network of thin strands that stretched out of his small room, beyond his rural home on the outskirts of Portland, and into the ether. He could sense them, like telephone wires enveloping the whole world, linking him to everything that exists. It was wonderfully real to him, and he felt a thrill, as if God had plucked him out of obscurity and he was delivered and it was the most inspiring emotion he'd ever known.

Larry Harvey was the adopted child of Dust Bowl refugees who had relocated to Oregon. One day in Nebraska his mother had gone to get laundry off the line and all the sheets were red as blood. She looked up and the sky was a roiling rich crimson. "That's Oklahoma," someone said. It was a disaster that could make one doubt the existence of providence. The land itself blew away, leaving nothing to sink roots into.

Larry's parents, Author Sherman Oliver Harvey (this sonorous, dignified name! His younger brother was simply Jim) and Katherine Langford Harvey, headed west and built a house outside Portland and remained all their lives, in Larry's eyes, nineteenth-century farmers, with all that that implied. "They never really understood the West Coast's soul, and I was raised in Nebraska, essentially. I was an outsider any way you want to look at it, in all my relations with the world." Larry will talk at length, unbidden, about his parents. He will praise them highly for their stern old-world values and ethics, their lack of material pretensions or dreams measured in worldly terms.

But he learned little about how to live as a thinking and feeling human being in relation to other thinking and feeling human beings. He was smarter than his parents; he knew it, and he is pretty sure they knew it too. But they looked on him as something of an idiot savant— bright and creative, but what on Earth was one to do with him? His father was a Freemason, and his brother, Stewart, also adopted, was sent to DeMolay, the fraternal order's youth division. Larry was not. Explains Larry, "They never let me near it. I was the family subversive." In his adolescence, he posted on his bedroom wall a photo of a dead fetus from *Life*. "My mother never said anything. No, no one ever said anything. That was my angst. No one would speak about deeper feelings, certainly not in relation to one another."

Larry spent much of his childhood in a state of hypochondriacal sickness to win the attention of a mother who "didn't seem to love you until you were ready to die." She hid every emotion behind an open newspaper and a refusal to communicate. "You knew the old man had a passion in him," says Larry. "You knew that. But she was elusive—never there in the present." In the middle of Thanksgiving dinner, she would talk about "how nice this was," already having placed the experience in the past.

His father was a builder, but he had no sense of aesthetics. Everything he built, Larry recalls, was pug ugly. Larry remembers his pleasure at even discovering the word aesthetics — "And with an *a* at the beginning! All the better!"

His father was a stoic man and a good man and an honest man, and in many ways, Larry worshipped him. But brother Stewart was five years older, and his father was a Midwestern, midcentury man with a rebellious, intellectual son who bewildered him, so Larry was distant from them both. Thus, any mystic feeling of connection Larry developed was toward the pastures and forests that he could wander in, alone, and into which he could invest his overflowing emotions, which had no thirsty place to spill in the Harvey homestead. One bad day his father made a mistake that adoptive parents sometimes make.

It was regrettable and there was an apology and he didn't really mean it, of course, but it was said. What he said was that when he adopted the boys he thought he was giving them a loving home and family, and now he realized it was the worst mistake of his life. He was proud, so the inevitable apology came through Larry's mother, who wasn't a fountain of loving emotions herself. The pain is still there, and now the only love Larry thinks is worth a damn is the kind of love we feel for a work of art: unconditional love. You don't ask it to do anything to deserve your love, you just contemplate its *isness:* and now, forty years later, Larry Harvey runs an art festival because art tends toward that sacred *pure being* that he seeks, the unconditional reality, the absolute that can't be questioned or changed.

There's a wonderfully tidy redemptive arc to the story that takes this peculiar young man from his loneliness and sense of separation from the world closest to him to his role as majordomo of a thirty-thousand-person intentional community built on nonexclusion. That arc's sense is only retroactive, of course. There was no master plan formed in his troubled adolescent psyche; nor, in fact, could a spontaneous cultural efflorescence like Burning Man *be* planned. But Larry is fascinated with Freud and the unconscious, and likes to think about all the ideas that may have been embedded from the beginning in his first decision to take a wooden scarecrow to Baker Beach on the 1986 summer solstice and burn it. It was a casual decision on the surface, he insists, but one that has changed the lives and shaped the experiences and worldviews of nearly a hundred thousand people so far—and there will, he vows, be more.

Larry left his parents' home to serve briefly in the army in the late sixties. He had some unhappy college experiences on the GI Bill; he loved to read and think but did not love the way his professors would try to belittle and delimit the thoughts of the greats they were supposed to be contemplating.

Larry spent the autumn and spring of love near Haight Street, where, as he recalls, "all you had to do was take your shoes off and you'd be a hippie." Still nursing his alienation, he felt in the scene but not of it. He never believed in the hippie dream. Well, maybe for a brief period one day, on a substance that should remain unnamed, he could accept that all this lovely energy and freedom were going to roll out from the San Francisco Bay in a glorious wave and change the world merely because they were there living the way they were living, so un–hung up and groovy. "Then, after twenty minutes, I said, 'Nah.' I had my parents' common sense," says Larry.

In the early seventies Larry ended up living with a woman named Janet Lohr in Coquille, a small town in Oregon, where she taught elementary school. Larry remembers that town as being close to paradise, really, with more things growing per square inch than anywhere else he'd seen—anywhere else in the world, he imagined. On weekends, he and Janet would go explore some new sight, some new delight they'd missed before. Eventually, they found themselves planning a weekend excursion to a gravel pit they'd heretofore somehow neglected. Larry realized it might be time to move on.

He had already been taking buses to Coos Bay, the nearest town with a substantial library, to feed his hunger for books and ideas. Larry's literary references are never postmodern or even modern; he loves Freud and post-Freudians like Kohut and lards his talk with references to the British masters like Shakespeare and Dickens and, if he's feeling contemporary, E. M. Forster.

On those cultural excursions, he would frequently find copies of the *San Francisco Chronicle* jammed beside the bus seat, reminding him of the things he was missing in his quiet Oregon paradise. He and Janet moved together to San Francisco around 1978 and remain friends, although their romance gradually faded out. She supported Larry financially throughout their time together. After they broke up, "I was suddenly faced in my thirties with the most embarrassing task of trying to support myself—which I had never done."

This was the early eighties. He fell into odd jobs, whatever came along for the conventionally uneducated and unambitious. This included grilling hot dogs at a legendary San Francisco punk rock club, the Farm, and bike messengering. Larry loved the jester's privilege that bike messengers claimed—the ability to enter the citadels of commerce and power, smelly and unkempt, as the joshing underminer of the office way of life. He hurt himself one day when he missed his pedal with his foot. His supervisor had to think for a minute about whether they could spare any gauze to staunch his bleeding. Larry decided to try driving a cab. "People are prone to say, 'Oh, you must meet such interesting people driving a cab,'" he notes. "Not necessarily."

Later, a minor inheritance from an old companion of his grandmother's allowed him to buy a truck and launch the "career" he is most apt to mention in official documentation of his past: landscape gardener. He created his own niche: catering to lower-middle-class clients who didn't care about keeping up with the Joneses but were willing to go with any cockamamy idea that suited their own sense of individuality.

"They'd line the driveway with golden bowling balls. Want to use red ground cover to make it look like Mars? Cool. The problem is, they can't afford something as elaborate as they'd like," Larry explains. Larry wanted to build things. "Just adorning plants, who cares? I didn't want to create a comfy, cozy space. I wanted to create *Mars*." Larry sees it all adding up, experiences coalescing to create a firm surface from which he has climbed to where he is today. The Burning Man's figure, to his eyes, is basically a glorified pergola.

Larry's landscaping company was called Paradise Regained, and he had a partner named Dan Richman. Richman gave Larry—a habitué of no scene—access to a milieu of intellectual workingmen. Latte carpenters, Larry grew to think of them, who liked to gather at Dan's house and discuss ideas and art and music and play guitar and enjoy the fellowship that is the glory of the city. One of their number was a builder and contractor named Jerry James.

Jerry was an air force brat. When his dad settled down in Jerry's adolescence, he chose "that colorful Mecca," as Jerry refers to it, of Boise, Idaho. "After I finished high school and a couple of years of college," Jerry says, "I escaped Boise to the slightly more interesting environs of San Francisco. This was in 1980. Things were loose, socially and lawfully. You could drive down the streets and do U-turns. People smoked pot in nightclubs. I thought, *This is great*. It's not like people were on the streets shooting each other, but this level of lawlessness I enjoyed. I don't need cops giving me tickets for jaywalking. I know how to cross the street."

Jerry was a workingman with two children and, like Larry, had an interest in arts and ideas but no real entrée to a world in which such passions could be comfortably indulged. It was the eighties in San Francisco, and the city was coasting culturally on the fumes of past glories, in flux, its identity ill defined. These two hesitant, alienated men soon began, unwittingly, a ritual that helped both focus and define the cultural energies that would characterize San Francisco's next decade.

Larry had married a Jamaican woman named Patricia Johnson in the early eighties, and she bore him a son named Tristan, though his relationship with his wife was such that he never lived in the same apartment with her. Jerry also had a young son and a tenuous relationship with his son's mother. The two men became fast, best friends, regularly going on dad double dates that often involved building things with the boys—like wooden guns.

"We'd make it participatory," Larry remembers. "Don't buy some cheap plastic—make your own guns. 'Why, if more people in this country made their own guns, then things would be all right!' One day, at a battery near Marin, off the bridge, we're running around shooting at each other with wooden guns. There was no way to confuse them with the real thing. We didn't even paint them. That would ruin the aesthetic. These are not metal guns. These are wooden guns! A woman saw us and was outraged—this *was* Marin—going on about how she can't believe we're teaching that lesson to our children. So we all turned toward her. And we shot her.

"Thinking back, building the first Man came out of that same impulse. It was one of those wood projects. The kids could help; hand them a glue gun. They couldn't get in the way too much."

I'm talking to Larry about all this seventeen years down the line, and it has all become so much more than he could have thought or hoped on that first summer solstice day. That first Burn comes up in almost all of our conversations, usually at my prompting, as I continually try to get some fresh and sudden illumination about what this whole phenomenon meant from the beginning. Whether we are talking in Burning Man's airy and attractive Third Street office in San Francisco or at restaurants in the Haight or in Larry's almost frighteningly dank, messy, cluttered, and claustrophobic kitchen in the Alamo Square neighborhood, I'm always seeking a fresh perspective on the origin story. Wherever we are, Larry is usually wearing his iconic Stetson, in honor of the hat his father wore. When he takes it off, as he did once in his kitchen, he reveals a Caesar haircut and a face of Roman handsomeness and solidity that is somehow shadowed by the hat, a face with heavy-lidded eyes and a thick, serious mouth, contrasted with teeth aptly described in *Time* as "like a colonial graveyard."

Larry is openly weary, though—and possibly wary—of discussing too openly and in too detailed a way that First Time. Really, it doesn't matter in the end, does it? "To seek the source of things in that way," he explains, "to affix great significance to the first act, is like looking for the tiniest trickle of a tributary that eventually flows down into the Mississippi and confusing *that* for the Mighty Mississip. In fact, it's the sum of a thousand tributary waters."

When reporters, or other curious citizens, ask about the hows and whys of that first burn, what they are asking for, Larry says, is a myth: "They want first causes in a mystical sense, as if everything radically emanated from some singular and unconditionally real event—a just-so myth that explains things like how the nightingale and the cricket entered our human realm."

He can offer only suggestive hints toward an answer: "There were all these things that led to that simple act in the beginning and disposed us to continue acting in certain ways. The problem with this question"—Why did they burn a Man on the beach on the summer solstice in 1986, and then why did they do it again, and again, and again?—"is that the answer becomes my entire life story."

So that's what I get, his life story, in such a flood that anything I might say or ask becomes a small pebble around which the water of his words flows. Interviewing Larry is generally not so much like a-conversation as it is like being a singular audience to a usually compelling one-man monologue. A wild ride, but not really very interactive.

Larry is an awkward man, and he shakes as he raises a continuous series of Camels to his mouth. He talks a lot about the importance of human warmth and community, yet his shyness manifests itself as a long-lasting guardedness. Most of his old friends and associates agree he's a great talker but a poor listener.

What, then, were some of the ideas and influences that fed into what he insists was a largely unplanned, unmotivated act? Dan Richman and the working-class intellectuals around him "gave me permission, I who had idealistic ideas of the perfect thing I was inwardly embarrassed to accomplish. They seemed to give permission to express, to leap off the ladder and just do it."

Then there is Mary Grauberger. Mary is a handsome woman with a strong, sane face and deep-set light eyes, her hair straight and long, and colored a lively rich silver. She is the direct inspiration for what became Burning Man. The Burning Man she immediately inspired, though, was not as detailed and full and multifaceted as what she did. The Burning Man of today, though, has become much more.

Mary was a sculptor who befriended Larry's girlfriend Janet Lohr while attending one of Lohr's ceramics classes in the midseventies at San Francisco Community College at Fort Mason. Grauberger had come to the Bay Area from faraway Kansas City in 1964, attracted by news and rumors of the Free Speech Movement at Berkeley. She pursued her previously planned career of teaching Spanish after graduating from Berkeley, but only for a while. Then that sixties spirit overcame her, and she began pursuing her bliss as a sculptor. She still makes her living that way, teaching some, picking up the odd grant, and mostly avoiding the gallery system. She sells her pieces by word of mouth and out of her own trunk.

In the late seventies, after her experience helping some heavy dudes set up Unity Fairs—post–Be-In groovy gatherings to bring the Tribes together in celebration—Mary began hosting a series of-spontaneous art-party happenings down on San Francisco's Baker Beach. Baker is a cove frequented by area nudists, pinched off at both ends by cliffs, nearly beneath the Golden Gate Bridge.

It was, Grauberger remembers, "just a bunch of nude freaks going down to the beach to hang out. I was a sculptor and I'd get bored sitting around the studio, so I'd pick up stuff washed up on shore and build sculptures. We'd stay 'til the evening and cook, and then it seemed natural to torch the sculptures. It was a personal thing, for fun."

Larry would come down at times. Says Mary, "It hit him that you could be free and not have an institution and create this incredible art and burn it. The burning part, it really affects people. Some of us would burn everything we had—blankets, clothes. Sometimes I'd spontaneously billow a blanket out and let it settle on the fire. It would really bother people.

"I liked everything to disappear quickly. The need for people to have something permanent of their creation leaves all this junk sitting around. It's more beautiful to have people experience it and then it's-gone."

She'd create with rope, tires, big hunks of driftwood, sometimes things as simple as cigarettes butts formed into a cone. Once, she and her friends stuck an old car seat in a big hole in the sand and torched it along with a pile of old clothes. It looked like some unspeakable accident. To challenge herself, she'd use only what she found washed ashore. "I'd work with what the sea gave, then give it back."

It would be difficult for the sociologist, the art historian, to define Mary Grauberger and her friends, what impulse they represented, how to categorize them. She herself loves Andy Goldsworthy, but she was doing this nature-supplies-the-materials routine before she heard of him. She explains, "We were nurses, ex-convicts, professional artists. The guy straight out of prison was best for heavy dragging. He had a ball. He thought it was the greatest thing that ever happened to him. Doing these things in a group, it gives you license for your own whims and desires to come out." There would be spontaneous happenings going on up and down the beach. "It would blow people's minds who didn't know about it and stumbled upon it."

She'd often do it on the summer solstice, but not always. Sometimes she'd do it at other times. She stopped around the mideighties— she doesn't remember exactly why. She's watched Burning Man grow and has attended a few times. But she doesn't much care that it's in many ways a continuation of what she had been doing all those years ago, when she had no idea anyone was taking permanent notice, when it all seemed for the moment, the direct experience of the creation and the cold and the fire. The notion of Burning Man as something that has become the subject of cultural historians does not excite or even bemuse her—it doesn't seem to mean anything at all to her. "The difference between me and Larry," she says, "is that Larry needs to be famous and feel that he has moved society in some way. I don't need that at all. It's a difference between men and women, I think. I see a lot of men who if you asked them what they want more than anything would say to be famous. I admire Larry because he got what he wanted. Most people would have dropped out when Burning Man just seemed like a piddling daydream. But he was sure of it, and he was right. People seem to need [Burning Man], and they come from all over the world. But I know it's hard on Larry's health, and I have no desire for it. Women can have children—fame is like a man's own child."

It was 1986 and the summer solstice came around and Mary wasn't doing her thing anymore, so Larry approached Jerry and with no specific reason or motive suggested they build a figure of a man, take it to Baker Beach, and burn it. Jerry, being a carpenter, was ready and willing to oblige. "It was a spontaneous act of radical self-expression," Larry says. That's their story, and they are sticking to it.

There are other myths and rumors, some sparked by things Larry himself told reporters when pressed to plumb the depths of his soul for reasons that explain that first burn. He's enough of a Freudian that he won't completely dismiss unconscious explanations—maybe there *were* things motivating him that he never consciously recognized. But despite stories that spread because of careless words spoken to a reporter long ago, words that hinted the burn might have had something to do with sorrow over a woman, Larry insists now that commemorating or expiating any lost love by destroying an effigy of the woman, the woman's new boyfriend, or himself was not his intended purpose at the time. (Some old Burning Man associates swear, though, that such a story was Larry's official line for many years in the early nineties.)

The figure of the Man was built by Jerry with some help from Larry in the "dismal basement garage" of Larry's old girlfriend Ellen Into, the daughter of Whittaker Chambers, the tragically troubled ex-Communist turned conservative predictor of Western decline and doom, famous for fingering his old comrade Alger Hiss for having been a Communist agent while Hiss worked for the U.S. State Department.

"What turned out to be most important," Larry says, "was that we happened to choose to do it in a public space. It was done impetuously as a pure gesture. That was part of the culture [surrounding Dan Richman and the 'latte carpenters'] I had absorbed, the culture of the self-expressive gesture, this bohemian notion that you could manifest your spirit by acting on creative impulse and have the courage—real courage for me, being so shy—to do it in a public way. It was a sort of spiritual extravagance."

Larry and Jerry went down to the ocean with their kids—Tristan, four, and Robin, five—who brought with them, Larry remembers, a wooden dog they had built, an act they failed to repeat, providing Larry with a stern fatherly example of the importance of follow-through for his son (no one remembers the Burning Dog now). A handful of other friends also came along—whom, specifically, neither Larry nor Jerry remembers for sure. The attendance number in the Burning Man organization's official time line is eight.

It was a blustery, chilly, foggy San Francisco dusk. They stood this fragile figure up in the sand against the ocean horizon and doused him with gasoline. Jerry lit a match, and suddenly it became a burning man though not yet *the* Burning Man—Larry didn't name their ritual for a couple of years. The Man was really drenched in the volatile, fast-burning fuel (so volatile and fast-burning that they switched to kerosene for future burns) so that "when it went up, it exceeded our expectations," Larry remembers. "Although burning the Man is a ritual and it's very meaningful to us, it is a species of showmanship. The trick is to always exceed audience expectations. If you can lead them to the point that they expect something, but that what they experience exceeds what they expect, it will cause an intake of breath. It will move them and transport people."

Aesthetically, the figure was a poor cousin to the streamlined asexual alien articulated with neon that is the Man today. "It was just a crude thing stuck in the sand," Larry says. "It wasn't a work of art, really, by any normal standard. You *might* see something like that in one of the cruder, simpler, more backward theme camps [at Burning Man] today. But even those sort of camps would blush to do something so slapdash."

Looking at pictures of that first Man, you can see the ancestral relationship to today's Man. The ribs look similar, if not as plentiful and even; the head is spiked with wild hair, instead of shaved like today, but still a familiar inverted pyramid; the legs are the same orthopedic device–looking sheaths. His flesh and viscera were burlap.

Larry recalls, in what is an almost perfect myth of the passing of his pre–Burning Man life and the beginning of the new, that he and Jerry, by coincidence, saw Dan Richman and a date as they were walking their Man down the beach, and that Dan scoffed uncomprehendingly at their queer little ritual.

Well he might have scoffed, Larry understands. "You have to see it from the subjective to understand what it meant. Or what it felt like. Not only in release of natural energy did it exceed our expectations— it practically blew up!—but poised against the broad Pacific, it was theatrical in a whole other sense. Backed by this long, low horizon, though only about two feet taller than us, it seemed to gain great stature. William James said something about how the needs of religion merely require that you feel inwardly connected to something both other and larger than your conscious self. The combination of fire being such a primal element, and having made the thing and carried it, and seeing it exceed us in so dramatic a fashion, it took us beyond ourselves.

"And then the most significant thing happened: Strangers ran and joined us. Suddenly the crowd doubled or tripled. The Man was near the waterline, so the people formed a small half circle around him and they too were delighted by the flaming humanoid form. It was darkening toward night, as I recall. I could see everyone's face lit by the flame. We were moved, as one is moved by the enthusiasm of strangers for something you've done. Something about the kindness of strangers, unconditional love. It was touching. And then a woman I didn't know ran up and held his hand—the wind was blowing the flame all in one direction. Just as a lark. She was touching it as if in awe of it, but also companionably, like it was something you could lean against. Ah—participation!

"And a guy played a song about fire, improvised it on the spot. Kind of a hippie guy. I've never been a sitting-around-the-campfire-singing-songs kind of guy. I didn't grow up on that, and I'm not inclined to it. But in that instant, that gift—it was moving.

"Those acts of impulsive merger and collective union were what made it so special. I'm very much of the conviction that we would never have done it again if those circumstances had not happened and helped us be so moved by what we'd done."

Larry is contemptuous of those who deny unconscious motivations, who are maddened with a hubristic certainty that they, the conscious they, are always in charge. When struggling, as I tried to make him do, to get to the deepest bottom of *why?*, he remembers a time in his life around the beginning of the Burning Man ritual in which he would quiet his mind, and ideas and memories and notions sunk in there would float to the surface of his mind as if it were black water. "It's not as if I recovered a repressed memory, like, oh yes, Father put on the Satan horns and oh my, yes, Mother was there too, I remember it, yes." But things, things were haunting him, things he doesn't fully understand.

Perhaps the Man was part of the flotsam that metaphorically floated to the top of his mind from that black water in his memory one day. "Hell, I don't know, for all I know making the Man was…this huge midlife crisis, and I was obsessed, I knew it." He's sort of rambling and not making any obvious sense. "The more you think, the more vast your ignorance seems." But he holds fast to the notion that everything he was and knew and felt has nourished his ability to hold this curious job he now inhabits, "a job for which there was no applying and no standardized curriculum to prepare for."

Chapter Two

"YOU MAY ALREADY BE A MEMBER!"

The ritual was nameless the first couple of times. The name "Burning Man" came to Larry while he was obsessively watching a grainy video of an early beach burn. One detail on the soundtrack bothered him. A voice could be heard shouting "Wicker Man!" Larry has always bridled at the notion that his ritual was inspired by that movie, which he swears he didn't even see until well into the history of Burning Man.

"I thought, if you're gonna call it something, call it Lumber Man, for Christ's sake, or Wood Man," says Larry. "I figured we needed a name if people were going to call it that crap. Wood Man? Burning Man? OK, Burning Man. It felt right. Then it was Burning Man. Oddly enough, no one ever asks me why you call it Burning Man. It just seems so obvious. But it wasn't obvious before it was named. It-could have been Fire Man, could have been all sorts of things. It didn't even have to be *man*. It could have been…Floyd. It could have been anything.

"But because some idiot was yelling Wicker Man, it got a name. It was very much a carpentry deal, a fellowship of carpenters. Like my father being a Mason. A Fellowship of the Work. A man built like a house. That's why Wicker Man bugged me. But let's face it, Lumber Man sucks. 'Burning Man' is a great multivalent name because it's an action and an object and a shared experience all at once. During my worst obsession, everything I heard I would turn into Burning Man. I would hear it in fragments of conversations everywhere I went. 'Did you just say Burning Man?' They were probably saying Burger King. I finally got over it."

Neither Larry nor Jerry remembers precisely when they made the commitment to burn a Man again. Jerry supposes they must have occasionally mentioned to each other how much fun or how interesting it was in the year after the first burn, and that the decision to do it again had to have been made at least weeks in advance, because by 1987 the Man was nearly fifteen feet tall and took a couple of weekends of work to make. He recalls their girlfriends and possibly even his roommate lending a hand or a hammer swing here and there. It was still small enough to build and transport on his truck. "The first one was like a family picnic," Jerry remembers. "And the second one was like a bigger family picnic."

As Jerry recalls, "Larry had started to ponder what it meant and why we were doing it, what the available metaphors or implications might be. He was thinking about it and writing about it. Why did he do that? It seems to be his nature, I suppose. To me it was just a big adventure, just an exciting, curious thing to do. I wasn't as puzzled or intrigued as Larry as to why we were doing it. I just did it, consistent with our roles. I was a trained builder; he wasn't. While it was his concept and idea to do this thing, I was really the one who built it. He helped. The design motif was really his, but when it came to creating a figure out of lumber, I was the person who could bring that off in practical terms."

By 1988 they were committing to it fully—building a Man nearly as tall as he is now, around forty feet, and striving to attract an audience beyond their immediate friends. They began making posters and flyers and even T-shirts. Building and promoting the Man was taking Jerry many weekends, all through the spring, and he enlisted the help of some of his coworkers and others.

A later associate of Larry's thinks it is obvious why they kept doing it. Larry and Jerry were both insular, somewhat alienated men. "An adopted child of Dust Bowl immigrants and his buddy did something on the beach that made people come around and want to talk to them? Of course they'd do it again."

They got the new, taller Man up on Baker Beach in '88, precariously and barely. As Jerry remembers it, the pulley they used to elevate the statue popped out of the sand, and the Man, still mostly horizontal but a little more than human height off the ground, came crashing down. Human bodies scattered out of the way of his wooden one. They tried again, just human muscle pulling ropes, and got him up.

The Man was presoaked with kerosene, his legs and body stuffed with newspaper and wrapped with burlap skin, also all soaked with kerosene. It was another blustery cold evening, and he was on fire and the burlap and newspapers blew away in ashes, but the Man, though charred, was still standing.

That's when the Man had his first encounter with the Man, Jerry recalls. Some cops sauntered up, and "Larry and I ran back like a couple of cowards and hid in the crowd, hoping it would blow over." A gentleman with a large gong was part of the crowd. Surely, the cops figured, he was the ringleader of this vaguely disturbing little circus.

"They did the good cop / bad cop thing," Jerry says, "shaking him down like this was a real crime against humanity—'You wanna talk to me about this, tell me about this?'—like he'd murdered somebody, expecting him to say something like, 'Well, I killed my brother last year, and I'm really trying to work it out here.' Sure, he *just happened* to be down here with a gong while this giant statue is on fire. Larry and I then decided to talk to the cops, and after a short negotiation, they agreed to allow us to knock down the Man and finish burning it. We sawed him in half in a few places, threw him in a pile, and finished burning it.

"It was obviously an extraordinary thing for the cops. They sure don't come across that every day. They probably feared we'd start slaughtering goats there on Baker Beach. It presented a pagan profile. I presume someone in the nice homes on the sea cliff told them they saw a fire on the beach, a bit taller than the usual three-foot bonfire you'd see."

Despite the Man's inauspicious end, and the ominous signs that their spontaneous expression was bothering the authorities in San Francisco, 1988 was a pivotal year in the life of Burning Man. It was the year that the Cacophony Society discovered the Man, and liked what it saw.

The Cacophony Society was a curious outgrowth of mideighties San Francisco culture, born in 1986, almost certainly not coincidentally the same year as the Burning Man. As Larry put it, he and people like him felt like "remainders on the shelf in Reagan's America." San Francisco then didn't provide a ready-made radical identity recognized by the dominant culture, but Ronald Reagan's very existence seemed to vex and weary those who thought of themselves as artists and rebels. Punk rock had already petered out, and the hippies, well, they were so old they were starting to stink.

The Cacophony Society was a direct lineal descendent of the Suicide Club, which existed from 1977 to 1982, the brainchild of Gary Warne, one of those curious freelance intellectual troublemakers San Francisco nurtures. The Suicide Club began as a course Warne taught at the Communiversity, San Francisco State University's contribution to the Free School Movement. It quickly became its own separate secret society. It attracted a gang of 'twixt-hippie-and-punk intellectuals and edge-seekers—not the cool kids but the weird ones. It didn't seek publicity, though people did manage to find out about it through friends and friends of friends.

Chris DeMonterey remembers his initiation into the club. He's a self-employed building contractor in his fifties, soft-spoken and dry, with a thick dark beard and receding hairline. He has a love for solitude and the kind of unself-conscious strangeness that has a hard time explaining itself, having no idea how strange it is. He helped his father build a bomb shelter in the early sixties, and spent a lot of time there as a kid.

Lots of people have Chris DeMonterey stories. Larry Harvey's favorite is the time DeMonterey surfed into an Internet sex chat room. In a room where all this wet, steamy, sweaty, sticky stuff was going on continuously, well, someone's going to have to help tidy up, right? DeMonterey invented an icon that looked like a bucket and mop, and declared himself the janitor. "He was dealing with people desperate for human contact," explains Larry. And he started inventing chores for them. "'I've got to open the window to ventilate things—could you hold the bucket?' He had everyone in the room helping him to clean it up. *That's* interactive." Another person tells me wonderingly of how DeMonterey once put his Chinese food into a take-out container one grain of rice at a time—and seemed bewildered when asked what the hell he was doing: He answered, "I wanted to take the food home."

DeMonterey recalls the Suicide Club initiation beginning at the bookstore Circus of the Soul on Judah Street, owned by Warne. They put bread dough on his eyes (Chris thought it was plastic explosive) and a tight blindfold on, and led him and around fifty others to a van. They were then driven by a circuitous route out to Fort Funston. They were led holding hands down a path and were told they had to stay balanced or they'd fall forty feet.

DeMonterey put one foot off to the side of the narrow path and could feel something down there. He didn't know if maybe the forty-foot drop was six feet away or if they were just being lied to. "To trust your life to someone else when you weren't really sure who they were—well, you knew you were being very foolish," says Chris. "These Suicide Club types didn't seem dangerous, just interesting and playful, but we didn't have any guarantee of that. When you're blindfolded, your imagination takes over and makes everything wild, strange, exciting."

DeMonterey leaves the narrative hanging mysteriously. I press him: What happened at the end of the walk?

"I don't remember," Chris answers. "No one can say. It was too long ago. I think we had coffee or something." (Other accounts have it that they were given a single match to illuminate the dark bunkers beneath the fort and had to collaborate with strangers in the dark to escape, and then enjoyed wine and reverie.) The Suicide Club became a clearinghouse for urban adventure ideas, street theater, and the drive to experience life as if every day were the last, as per the characters in the Robert Louis Stevenson short story from which the club derived its name. Says Chris, "I remember one member once proposed we rob a bank. That didn't get very far. I thought it was an interesting idea."

The Suicide Club sputtered out by 1982, and then Warne died, but the spirit didn't die. A handful of former Suicide Club members launched the Cacophony Society, and the tradition continued. Cacophony was, according to its boilerplate on its newsletters, "a randomly gathered network of free spirits united in the pursuit of experiences beyond the pale of mainstream society. We are that fringe element which is always near the edge of reason. You may already be a member!"

That last part was key. Cacophony, unlike the Suicide Club, reached out in fellowship to the rest of the world, assuming that we could all create our own interesting good times together. By the time Cacophony stumbled upon Larry and Jerry's burning ritual, John Law and Michael Michael were two of its central organizers.

Law was a Suicide Club alumnus who avoided Cacophony for the first few months because an angry ex-girlfriend among the founders didn't want him around. Those wounds healed, and he quickly slipped into his role as a chief facilitator, discoverer of strange places to explore, and master climber. Law was a neon sign installer, inveterate bridge trespasser, and maven of secret niches in urban environments. A lover of strange and eldritch literature, he came to San Francisco from rural Michigan (running from a juvenile probation-violation rap), and in the estimation of one man who has worked with him—and sometimes clashed with him—for years, he is "a natural-born leader of men." He has a quiet and chameleon-like handsomeness, with the ability to blend into whatever role circumstances require, his facial hair and hair length changing constantly. He was the prime Suicide and Cacophony liaison with cops when such liaising became unfortunately necessary.

Michael Michael was a former computer industry entrepreneur, old enough to have been part of the drugs/sex ferment that made the sixties *the sixties.* He has a long history of being involved, as an old friend of his tells me, in adventures designed to turn on the world.

Michael once told me, as we sat in a wrecked '82 Honda sitting on top of another crushed car in San Francisco's Ace Auto Yard, a long and gripping story about being pulled over and charged with possession by Texas cops many years ago. It turned into a comic-adventure chase scene, in which he's taking out fences and KEEP RIGHT signs are peeling over his hood like strands of overcooked spaghetti and he's throwing himself in ditches and spending three days running through fields for his freedom. He knew they'd have killed him if they caught him. He hired a good lawyer later and it all got straightened out well enough.

The Suicide Club, Michael remembers, was so far underground he couldn't find it, though he'd heard whispered rumors of initiates doing the "most incredible, outrageous, and amazing things."

Cacophony, though, had a public newsletter dubbed *Rough Draft,* which Michael found one day in a Rainbow Grocery. He leaped in and eventually took over and formalized the newsletter. He decided that the Suicide Club's fading away was a result of their insularity and secrecy. He vowed to make Cacophony more wide open and tried to cross-fertilize its audience with other groups, tendencies, and events in the area and even around the nation. Michael led the attempt to franchise Cacophony, creating minigangs of mischievous gremlins in any American city where he could find someone to lead them.

The Cacophonist spirit was playful and subversive and, within the limits of flawed humanity, welcoming. It was not a haven for the cool but for childishly minded misfits. If any principle united them, it was simply that they wanted to make their own fun, no matter how amateurish, absurd, or sometimes illegal. Michael Michael spells it out: "Most people in our culture get entertainment and experience spoon-fed to them through established, programmed channels. There's no creativity and very little participation in most Americans' entertainment. TV, you sit and watch. Sports are giant orchestrated games in which the people involved are not participating. We have developed a society of mindless consumers who pretty much live for being a mindless consumer.

"Cacophony was about doing things, having direct experiences. We were not just sitting in a room with a bunch of people glued to a TV and not talking. Experience was important in Cacophony. Part of that involved trying to change the status quo of the culture through public outrageousness, street theater, bizarre costuming, and public acts of revolution. More so than Suicide Club, which was more private and underground. They were challenging and growth-producing for the individual, certainly, but I took Cacophony where it was very public and open, inviting people to experience that change. And Burning Man fit into that."

Cacophony staged public protests against the movie *Fantasia,* representing an absurd conclave of interest groups: parent activists upset with how frightening the movie was; environmentalists outraged that it encouraged water wastage; obesity activists peeved with the mocking of dancing hippos. They seeded the crowd with compatriots to get in yelling matches with the protestors, and got covered in *Time,* and then later made the *Wall Street Journal* for fooling *Time* into taking them seriously. They broke into empty gunnery emplacements in the Golden Gate headlands and commandeered them for more than a year, building an elaborate series of trip wires and counterweighted doors to hide their lair from strangers and creating a performance space and a place for formal dinner parties. They took over a BART (Bay Area Rapid Transit) subway car with a series of lounge acts, pretending to be a new service paid for by MUNI (Municipal Railway). They traipsed through the Haight giving away pennies to bewildered passersby. They set themselves up in clown uniforms at bus stops down an entire route, slowly filling the bus with seemingly unrelated clowns (a stunt originated by Suicide Club).

Less publicly, they were regular explorers of San Francisco's stranger and more out-of-the-way abandoned buildings, stores, and bridges, and provided a ready support group of friends and helpers for any artistic endeavors any one of them might be planning. Colorful costuming and absurdist theme parties built around such favored cultural icons as *Alice's Adventures in Wonderland* or *Twin Peaks,* late-night meetings at old-fashioned diners, public treasure hunts following clues throughout Chinatown, celebrations of lost American junk culture, and Marcel Proust reading support groups were all part of their repertoire of exotic amusements.

A group home presided over by Cacophonist and Proust-loving zinester P. Segal on Golden Gate near Baker became a clubhouse of sorts for them, a place where pranksters and art students sword fought from roof to roof, painters painted, and Segal had a ready squad of quirky aestheticians to help out with her artistic catering service. While the career-minded gravitated to New York or Los Angeles, San Francisco remained a haven for the more quixotic creative types whose only place in the world was going to be one they and their friends created through their own will and joy. Pre-Internet, word of such subcultural rumblings spread clandestinely, secretively, mouth to ear. Right after the '89 earthquake, the Mission was empty at night, with rooms available for $250 a month. Earthquakes and gang wars led to an exodus, widening the niche for the more daring or reckless to move in, giving them spaces to work, build, and play in.

Cacophony gave its collection of curiosities a sense of—you will get tired of this word, I know, but it is important—community to people who had generally been made to feel, or chose to feel, separated from most of the people and culture around them. "You always felt safe," remembers Cacophonist Nancy Phelps about the early days of Cacophony. "Everyone was friends. If you went through the sewers, you knew the person at your back was really at your back. It was a wonderful time. I guess we were all pretty innocent. I had had a hip replacement, and I couldn't walk very well. And if Cacophony was doing something that would be hard for me to do, someone—usually John [Law]—would figure out a way to make it safe for me, even if it involved pushing me around in a shopping cart."

Talking to Cacophonists about those days, the late eighties and early nineties, you detect a powerful wistfulness over salad days gone by. Cacophony colonized the souls of those who found in it a zest for life and a fellowship they never imagined could exist. As Phelps says, the Cacophonists are "the people I really care about—I love their intellect, I love their humor. In an ideal world, they'd be the only people in my world."

John Law and Michael Michael became expert at using Cacophony as a technology of brain-change. Michael lays out the technique: "A big part of it was separating people from their safe environment—going to a place where people are separated from their lifeline, that isn't easy to get out of. Whether it be an abandoned building, or anyplace where we'd provided the transportation. We'd separate them from their cars, load everybody into a rental truck, drive around the block a bunch of times, and take them somewhere where they didn't know where they were. Encouraging people to wear outrageous costumes that would be difficult to change out of was part of it." Encouraging people to drive two hours past Reno to the Black Rock Desert is an example of this strategy writ large.

☼

Cacophony began to spread, thanks to conscious effort on the part of Michael Michael. I spent a little bit of time with Timothy Leary—fairly or unfairly the archetype of the loopy sixties wizard—just before he died, and there is no other man I've met who reminds me more of Leary in appearance, twinkle, speech patterns, and style than Michael Michael, and vice versa—silvery, lean, with eyes of pure charm and mischief.

Science-fiction writer Bruce Sterling swung his hammer close to the nail head with his description from his cover story on Burning Man for *Wired* in 1996. He was merely referring generically to Larry's "running buddies," but I can't help thinking he meant Michael. Sterling wrote of "tribal elder hippie-guru characters. Time has given them the faces they deserve. They all end up with this spacey Crowleyan smirk…not *seamy* exactly, but some kind of terrible wisdom, like a cross between Gandalf and Nietzsche…When you're in their company you feel a distinct witch-doctor vibe." Michael—in his Burning Man identity of "Danger Ranger"—has a saying: "I've seen things you wouldn't believe, and I believe in things you can't see." Sometimes he adds, "And I know things, perhaps things that shouldn't be knowed." I've heard him drop this epigram a lot. Sometimes it seems as if he's kidding; and then sometimes it doesn't.

A lonely computer animator named Alan Ridenour, who had recently lost his wife to his best friend, found a stack of Cacophony fliers in a Los Angeles coffeehouse in the early nineties. He didn't realize that the group only existed in San Francisco. He imagined an International Cabal of Cacophony and assumed, of course, that they'd have a thriving lodge in Los Angeles. After sending a string of letters with ideas for Cacophony pranks and events to the PO box listed on the flier—a box manned by Michael Michael—and getting no response for months, he began to doubt the organization's existence. Then the mysterious Max—the identity Michael adopted in his first approach to this new acolyte—approached Al, impressed with some of the event ideas he'd mailed into the void.

Thus, the first escapade of the Los Angeles Cacophony Society was planned and executed by Ridenour—who adopted the Cacophony alias of "Rev. Al"—with help from "Max." They flyered a local UFO devotees' convention, claiming to be the "Brotherhood of Magnetic Light" and promising a Space Brother landing at Dockweiler Beach. The flyers promised some vague hoodoo about superscientific mystical space healing. Al felt a twinge of concern—just a twinge—that they might be doing the wrong thing when he saw someone on crutches waiting at the designated spot before he even arrived.

They concocted "a really sad little pathetic hot-air balloon—*balloon* is too good a word, it wasn't even that flight worthy," Al recalls. "More like a laundry bag with candles hung under it. From far away, people saw this wobbly orb of light leaking hot air. As it got closer and closer, it looked more like a laundry bag. As it got over the Pacific Coast Highway, it got caught in an updraft, twirled around, and sputtered out.

"But that was all secondary to what I was doing on the ground. I rolled out a two-hundred-foot aluminum-foil cross on the hillside and piled on flowers and burned incense. We created a magical Christ icon—a plaster Tijuana Jesus with a walkie-talkie shoved up his ass. When an acolyte would approach it with his walkie-talkie on, it would produce this interference squelching sound from Jesus. I began speaking in tongues. Rich Polysorbate [an L.A. noise musician who became a Cacophony mainstay, known mostly for adding inappropriate bursts of fire to any performance or event] of course starts shooting firework rockets into the air for no reason. Then Michael Michael came running up the hill in a silver suit babbling about how his spacecraft crashed."

Childish, absurd, it set the standard for L.A. Cacophony in the future. Michael was in L.A. doing consulting work for Caltrans, the state transportation authority, and the fact that the state helped fund the launch of L.A. Cacophony by paying for his presence in L.A. amused him. Al quickly realized that he had not found a secret ticket to a preexisting, fascinating, artistic, clever clique of bohemians in L.A. who would embrace him and offer him all their drugs and girls.

Says Al, "At some point I had the rude awakening that this was all Michael Michael in San Francisco designing flyers on a Mac and that I'd have to create that community down here. And I succeeded.

Had I not been coming out of a failed marriage and had no friends, I would not have had the time—or the need—to make this thing that I wanted to believe was true and was suckered into believing was true, true. To say, 'Fuck it, I'm not gonna let it not be true.' I did it by brute force and managed to pull together something that was of consolation and amusement to some people."

Al isn't sure to this day exactly what Michael thought he was trying to accomplish, or why, by deputizing him as leader of the L.A. branch of Cacophony. "It is not my role to question the mysteries of Michael Michael, or Max, or Danger Ranger," explains Al. "He told me to call him Max to be safe. This was in the beginning, when we communicated through the original L.A. Cacophony post office box, which was destroyed by the Northridge earthquake. It was under a freeway overpass—the only freeway overpass that collapsed on the 405. I flatter myself [by believing] that it was divine providence."

Ridenour and I are discussing the old days of Cacophony and Burning Man from the comfortable hardwood-floored library of the minimansion in Glendale he shares with his wife, comedian Margaret Cho. The shelves are filled with a wide selection of quirky curiosa of the depraved intellectual.

Ridenour decided he'd take Cacophony in his own direction—a direction that various San Francisco Cacophonists describe, with an almost awed respect, as "edgier" than the original—when he wearied of the "info packs Michael would send me about how to run things, as if I'd become an Amway salesman. I did try to adhere to some of the principles and thoughts from the official propaganda. I did use some of their catchphrases as I saw fit. Some of it struck me as too fey, too much of a dancing-on-the-rooftops flavor. But he was very particular about how the mailings were done.

"And the bookkeeping! We'd collect money for subscriptions to the newsletter, which I never really expected to work. I never imagined Cacophony as any kind of business venture. I saw it more as this absurd money pit that once in a while, unpredictably, would cough money back in your face. I never saw it as something to put on paper or to try to balance out, but that was Michael's profession, I think, among other things—wild-animal trainer, or something, I don't know what else he did. Another control element from the home office: For a long time I was sending him all the checks, which he deposited in a bank account—this utterly unnecessary money laundering. But he enjoyed being cloak-and-dagger about things, and I appreciated that. The account was in the name 'Children of Light,' and I enjoyed getting money-laundered checks coming back to me from the Children of Light. There was talk of a national Cacophony magazine and the like.

"There was a very courtly way to Michael. He liked ritual and formality and protocol. At an early Burning Man, he arranged a ceremony in which he gave me a vial of Gary Warne's cremains on a chain as a token of Cacophony's approval of me—the equivalent of Jesus being baptized in the Jordan, I suppose. Michael is timeless, like a desert rock, and I was just in my late twenties and I felt it was utterly absurd in a way since I didn't know Gary. But looking back, it was cool that he did it, with his manner so stilted, doing that ceremony in that messy, wild setting. But I still have the ashes, and I'm happy to have them. I'd like to think there was a legacy that I helped continue. I just called Michael a 'timeless desert rock,' so his spirit is obviously strong here."

Larry began to see Burning Man as not just a continuing ritual but an ever-growing one. He recalls an argument with Jerry James and Janet Lohr over why the Man had to be taller than his original eight feet or even the second fifteen feet: "I remember feeling very much put-upon, feeling so disappointed and kind of lonely that they couldn't see that it *had* to be. It just had to be." It seemed as if the Man had gotten too big too fast in 1989. His support beams were not thick enough for his weight and he cracked, contorted, crumbled to his knees, head lolling down. They had to burn him in a sitting-kneeling posture.

After discovering the Man in 1988, Michael Michael told his friends and associates in Cacophony about it and publicized the 1989 Burn in their newsletter, which was read and seen by hundreds around San Francisco. Burning a giant statue on Baker Beach for no stated reason was the Cacophonists' kind of absurd fun. So the crowd was again bigger that year than the year before. Feeling like the ritual had failed because of the Man's collapse, Larry was surprised when the local TV news station sent to cover the Burn—already, mysteriously, the Burn's hold on the media was beginning—continued on cheerily as if nothing was going wrong. Says Larry, "As far as thousands of imaginary viewers in TV land were concerned, we had burned the Colossus of Rhodes. From the ashes of defeat, the phoenix arose, because we had been on TV. We were big-time. It encouraged us, you know."

Larry knew that he had found His Thing, in a way that no one else involved could quite feel. He became obsessed in a manner that could, he recognizes, be judged insane. In the early nineties, he was doing tree pruning and grounds work for an orphanage, and on long lunch hours he'd climb up on a huge pine he had been lopping down. There was still a thick trunk with a fourteen-inch platform of sorts on the top.

Larry would climb the remains of the sliced limbs like a ladder and stand on top of the tree with a chainsaw in one hand, in the pose of the Man with his arms raised. He began to feel as if he were the tree, elevated on the platform like that, in a universal gesture of exaltation, like athletes after they'd won the cup. He recalled moments when he was a child and a primitive animism moved him, and he felt it again, this time through the power of the ritual he was shepherding and sustaining. Standing like that, imagining himself as his Man, was like something he'd done as a child—he'd swim to the center of the lake and spin himself around and around as if circling some imagined axis of the world that was connected, in his mind, to the vault of heaven.

Thanks to word of mouth and the promotional efforts of Cacophony, by 1990 the crowd had gotten so huge, crammed there into the edge of the Baker Beach crescent nearest the Golden Gate Bridge, that many attendees took to crawling along the bluff overlooking the shore in order to see the spectacle. The bluff was not so much treacherous as honestly and openly hazardous. The burst of camera flashes from the hills, Larry remembers, looked like fans taking photos in the tiers at the Super Bowl.

Cops had become expected at the ritual; they had shown up while the Man was lit in '89 but just milled around and left. This time, Cacophonists with radios patrolled the paths down to the beach as the pieces of the Man were hauled down. They were trying to keep the cops from figuring out what was going on until the Man was up and lit. One Cacophonist had a police scanner, and when he heard a cop was being sent in response to a call about a girl stuck on the bluff, John Law quickly rescued her himself, headed off the cop, and told him the problem was solved. The cop was standing only yards from the Man's legs.

They got the Man raised. The crowd was somewhere between five hundred and eight hundred strong; estimates by those there vary. Everyone was a bit rowdy and very eager to see a fire, the biggest one in town. They wanted the ignited arms of this Man blessing the San Francisco night. Then the cops came back and wanted everyone to leave. This thing was getting too big and too ridiculous. You can't gather hundreds of people to burn a huge statue on a public beach. For goodness' sake.

The nature of Burning Man's relationship with authorities was sealed in one of the event's most storied legends: The beach burn that didn't happen. Larry and his roommate Dan Miller, who had become one of the Man's builders, decided to negotiate a deal with the police: to raise the Man but not burn him. The cops said OK and then left it up to Larry's own radical and individual judgment by skedaddling so they didn't have to deal with whatever ended up happening. Larry remembers this as the first time he really made John Law's acquaintance: "He'd been around and doing stuff, but it was all so loose and I'm shy anyway, so I never know who everybody is."

Law became spokesman for the faction that advocated burning the Man anyway. He was experienced in dealing with cops from Suicide Club and Cacophony stunts that placed members in public places where it wasn't legal for them to be or where their activities were unnerving police whether they were technically illegal or not. He was confident the cops were merely making a required show of authority and would not be back and that there would be no consequences if they just burned the fucker, as the agitated crowd was demanding.

"That would have been a real underground move," Larry says. "Burn it and get away with it." Still, Larry insists, he gave his word, and his father's ghost would smite him if he went back on it.

The Man, then, was raised and not burned. Drunk and dejected, the organizers dismantled him and trudged back up the steep paths and took his body parts to a lot on Eleventh Street, near Folsom, whose owner had been allowing them to store the Man's bigger pieces.

By a strange confluence of circumstances, various people in the Burning Man's immediate family had become familiar with a very unfamiliar place: Nevada's Black Rock Desert, an enormous dry lake bed around one hundred miles northeast of Reno, a vast, lifeless, cracked void. John Law had been taken out there in 1987 and 1988 by a monster-truck enthusiast he worked with; Jerry James and a handful of Cacophonists, including P. Segal and Kevin Evans, had been there last Labor Day for a gathering of windsailing sculptures coordinated by artist Mel Lyons (known as Mel Function) in collaboration with a pottery maker named John Bogard who lived out there in Gerlach, the unincorporated village nearest the Black Rock's beautifully severe playa. Lyons and Bogard had already been using that flat desert canvas for weird art events, including a giant croquet game using trucks as mallets that had made the pages of *Sports Illustrated*.

Law and Kevin Evans, a painter and art student, had already been desultorily planning a Cacophony excursion to this bizarre landscape—they hoped to live out some desert fantasies, to build things and destroy them at will. "It seemed like a good idea," Evans remembers, "because you could do it out there and no one would get hurt. And it would be a neat spectacle. Sit around and blow stuff up. That idea rattled around for a few months, and then John told me about this thing on Baker Beach."

When the thing on Baker Beach fizzled, it made sense to think about dragging Larry Harvey's Man along on this planned trip to Black Rock to burn him too.

But while the statue's pieces were sitting in the empty lot to which it wasn't expected to return, the Man was "murdered," as Jerry remembers. The lot was converted to a parking lot, blacktopped unbeknownst to the Burning Man crowd, and the Man's body disappeared—in all likelihood, it was chopped up and taken to the dump. By then, it barely mattered to Jerry. He and Larry no longer wanted to work together on the project, for reasons neither man will discuss, and Jerry did not plan at that point to have anything further to do with Burning Man.

John Law, then, supervised the frantic rebuilding of the Man after hours in the sign shop he worked in, the American Neon Sign Company. When his boss discovered him there, Law pacified him by showing him Burning Man's first news clip, to convince his boss there was a sensible, media-approved reason for what he was doing. "It was a very Cacophony-like ironic twist," Larry notes, "that we were rushing to rebuild this thing just to take it to the desert and destroy it. If you like quixotic romance, that's as good as it gets."

Rather than wait for another solstice—after all, Law notes, they weren't Druids—they just decided to schedule that brooded-upon trip to Black Rock for Labor Day weekend.

Thus it was that *Rough Draft* No. 48, the September 1990 edition of the "Official Organ of the SF Cacophony Society," contained this listing:

Bad Day at Black Rock (Zone Trip #4)
When: Labor Day weekend, September 1–3.
Where: Black Rock Desert, Nevada
An established Cacophony tradition, the Zone Trip is an extended event that takes us outside of our local area of time and place. On this particular expedition, we shall travel to a vast, desolate, white expanse stretching onward to the horizon in all directions...A place where you could gain nothing or lose everything and no one would ever know. A place well-beyond that which you think you understand. We will be accompanied by the Burning Man, a 40 foot tall wooden icon which will travel with us into the Zone and there meet with destiny. This excursion is an opportunity to leave your old self and be reborn through the cleansing fires of the trackless, pure desert.

Activities include:
- The en-route ceremony of the caravan crossing into the Zone boundary. Bring with you something of symbolic value.
- Campsite erection in the tradition of modern dadaistic nomadic Gypsies.
- The construction of a brick oven for the baking of bread.
- A group ritual requiring your participation to raise and immolate the Burning Man.
- Night-time viewing of relevant desert videos on a big screen.
- Semi-formal evening cocktail party with music. Bring your favorite CDs.
- Visit to a natural local hot springs.
- Other activities as we make them up.

This event is co-hosted by the Cacophony Society, Burning Man Committee, and the Black Rock Desert Rangers.

The notion of the "Cacophony Zone Trip" was derived from Andrei Tarkovsky's *Stalker,* a beloved art-school film that features a mysterious Zone that looks like the rest of the world but in which bizarre, inexplicable things occur. A caravan of Cacophonists, about eighty people strong, drove east from San Francisco over the sheer but gorgeous Sierra Nevadas, through Reno, and arrived in the tiny village of Gerlach around daybreak. They enjoyed breakfast, and the stares of the locals, at Bruno's restaurant, then went about twelve miles past town to an accessible turnoff onto the Black Rock Playa. John Law drove the Man in a rented Ryder truck.

They all got out of their cars. Michael Michael drew a line in the playa surface, and the Cacophonists walked over it. They were in a different place now. Reality had mutated because they willed it thus. They had crossed into the Zone.

Chapter Three

"IT FELT LIKE GLORY"

It's a long, maddening, crazy-gorgeous drive out to the Black Rock Playa—a liminal experience, a funnel that deposits you in a new, seemingly magic realm.

From Reno, the nearest major city to the playa, you head northeast. You can either take the I-80 freeway or the 445 surface road, each of which deposit you on the 447 surface road, at least seventy miles of two-lane highway stretching toward Gerlach.

The hills and mountains hold more colors than you can name, but the primary notes are faded browns and a dusty, withered, dry yellow, dotted with small clumps of gray scrub. Some of the gently striated hills, though, are a warm flesh tone or a deep bone white. Some mountains glide smoothly from the ground; some bulge like goiters. They don't loom, don't overwhelm, give no dizzying titanic perspective, merely cradle.

Once the 447 goes past Nixon, located on the Pyramid Lake Indian Reservation, the road rolls ninety degrees to the right in a crazy roller-coaster rise. The valleys that once held ancient Lake Lahontan then spread out around you, and at this point you wouldn't be surprised in the slightest to hear the lonesome croak of a pterodactyl gliding overhead. Absurdly and arbitrarily, a sign from the state of Nevada tells you that the scenic route ends just at the beginning of one of the most picturesque stretches, the mountains an almost obscene profusion of colors and waves, like frozen poured motion, stretching forever around the pale and mysterious valley.

The drive is long, and there are few clues as to how far you've gone or if you'll ever end up anywhere but gliding on through the endless valley. Hardly anyone will pass you in the other direction, and those few who do will wave at you, and you ought to wave back. After dozens of gentle up-and-down sweeps of the road, most radio signals gone, you're conditioned for something new, the stresses and pressures and even the sights of human modernity having had a chance to-slowly ooze out of you. Then you'll pass the first (and last) store for-many dozens of miles, a small convenience store in the gypsum-company enclave of Empire. By then you see Gerlach in the distance, looking like a carelessly scrawled line of houses and trees at the foot of a pale, low mountain range. You slow down to twenty-five miles per hour for the twist to the left that takes you down Gerlach's three-block main street and then a twist to the right and then the fork in the road—you take the right fork, to the 34, and drive until you reach one of the playa's navigable entrances, named after the approximate number of miles they are past Gerlach, the Three-mile, the Twelve-mile.

The playa itself is big and long and wide and flat and talcum-white, with an eternally twisting, changing pattern of cracks. It's featureless on the large scale but mutates every foot if you keep your eye close to its spiderwebbed surface ridges and valleys. When it's slightly damp, it's like thick flaking tempera paints; when it's dry, it resembles plateaus and valleys in microminiature (with the valleys essentially underground) spreading in every direction, more ocean than earth.

The playa's ostensible owners, the U.S. Department of the Interior's Bureau of Land Management (BLM), have this to say about it, in language taken from an Environmental Assessment done for a later Burning Man: "The environment...contains no true soils; surface or ground water; vegetation; wildlife; threatened or endangered species; wild horses; paleontology; solid or hazardous waste material; wilderness; or cultural resources...In addition, the following critical resources are not present: Areas of Critical Environmental Concern, prime or unique farmland, floodplain, wetlands, or noxious weeds." Nothing, glorious nothing, plenty of nothing, and nothing's plenty for Burning Man.

If you traveled to Burning Man in the early to midnineties, you had only treasure-map clues as to where you were going—a turnoff and then this many miles and then turn so many degrees at this flag marker and head toward that peak. If you were off by less than a mile, you could go vectoring forever away from your destination, never seeing it, sailing off toward some muddy bog at the edges of the playa. If you approached in midday, waves of heat would make the encampment look like an island rising from a glimmering sea of pure light.

Once you settle in on the Black Rock Playa—get out of your vehicle, start pitching your tent or geodesic dome or whatever shelter you've chosen—the playa abruptly changes you. The place, to someone from normal human civilization, a civilization that typically situates itself near other life and then fills the space around it with its own inventions, is both awesome and ridiculous, an insane miracle that you can somehow, at least for a while, if you are crafty and careful and have help from your friends, live in.

But you will live on its terms, according to its nature. Because of the intrusive omnipresence of the finely powdered dust created once the playa crust is broken, you become within minutes a creature no longer simply human, but a playa-human chimera, a new skin of pale chalky white settling and attaching and growing over you. And it doesn't just take over your surface; your every breath takes in an endlessly refilled air-and-playa dust cocktail that invades your lungs and nasal passages.

And as the playa gifts you with dust, it takes water away. On a typical midday, the sun is like a thumb pressing down on your eyes with an insistent reminder that the heat and dryness are wicking water out of you almost as fast as you can drink it. You need to drink out there, always; if you aren't talking, you should be drinking.

During those first few years in the Black Rock Desert, Burning Man was not yet a constantly raging party or a marvelously fecund arts festival filled with thousands of friendly strangers. There were not hundreds of things to do and see and experience twenty-four hours a day. So in those early years, the limited circles of friends out there would talk and read and, if the heat allowed it, sleep. They built shade structures, which would often fall down in the unpredictable and strong winds. They enjoyed—for the first time in their lives, probably—utter silence. If you walked fifty yards away from everyone else, you would hear nothing, nothing at all. If you wandered one hundred yards from the encampment at night, you might never find humans again.

Stranded by themselves beyond civilization, the citizens of what would soon be known as Black Rock City began to re-create some of civilization's earliest gestures of comity: wandering around the campsite, offering small gifts to one another, and granting decadent hospitality to those that stopped by. Pickled fiddleheads, freshly made mint juleps, home brew, and barbecued ribs would be brought, made, and shared.

The action was low-key, unfrantic, and friendly, and included a fair amount of beer drinking, chemical indulgence, and fondly remembered daily (and nightly) trips to the plethora of nearby hot springs.

Burning Man was not yet exploding with art or public tomfoolery—the idea that it was an arts festival did not arise until 1992 and did not become a serious reality until a few years after that. Thus, early attendees felt as if they had fallen from the bare sky into this alien environment, charged with the thrilling task of figuring out exactly how they would survive. Humans being social animals, and first-timers being invincibly ignorant as to what they would need and want, the first priority became getting to know, trust, and in some ways depend on your neighbors. Conversations would begin spontaneously, based on this bare need to connect and survive, and lacking the usual inhibitions of the outside civilization.

"The whole experience became a living, breathing art form," P.-Segal remembers. A decade and more after that first desert Burn, she is still sitting in the living room where so many stunts, schemes, and unforgettable moments were planned, in the house where she lived with her Cacophony family when they were young and they glowed with the knowledge that something grand and important was happening, and that they were making it happen. "We had our own conception of what community was about. It involved not being spectators but being participants in forming our own world. We evolved the perfect urban experience for each other. We took with us to the desert all the things we loved about the city. The grand cocktail parties, the fantastic dressing up in finery, beautiful and eccentric—not necessarily what you'd wear to an opera in the city."

While listening to people reminisce about this time I missed, I find that the strangest thing is how…how *uncompelling* it all sounds. I mean, a camping trip to this strangely lovely (but often brutal and punishing) site was probably worth doing, even worth remembering. But what exactly was it that made it worth doing again and again, ritually, without fail, and worth telling everyone else you knew they should come too?

Fed up past the brim of his trademark Stetson with people whining that the old days were better/cooler/purer/more fun, Larry Harvey has taken to denigrating the "good old days" of early Burning Man on the Black Rock, in terms that are only barely endearing. "Sure, it was a blast," he'll deadpan. "If you were lucky, you could get someone to drag you around on a tarp behind their car." And, of course, go soak your privates in the hot springs.

So why did they keep doing it? The hot springs of the Black Rock area were a big draw, with the rich, vivid, phantasmagoric Fly Hot Springs most prominent in sweet nostalgia, the geyser a frighteningly awesome fleshy protuberance all the colors of the solar system, its spillage forming various pools, the faraway ones gloriously comfortable and the nearer ones fatally hot. (In a perfect example of the irony of how success bears within it the poison to kill the very thing that reared it, all area hot springs are now verboten to attendees during Burning Man because of BLM fears of the damage from so many people using them at once.)

The nothingness of Black Rock, Larry relates, makes anything that *is* seem more intensely real. This became true of the Man, another reason people kept coming back. "Something so very large and so startlingly like ourselves just seemed numinous," he explains. "It was a breathtaking thing. And who is not affected by oceanic space? Only someone with an imaginative disability."

And there was the Cacophony spirit, the Zone Trip spirit, which delighted in doing what seemed inexplicable, what no one else would do, venturing where no one else would go. "This was literally true,"

Larry remembers, "in the case of erecting this giant Man out there. Who would do this? We could let our imaginations run wild—who had ever done it in the history of mankind? It felt like glory. It felt like glory. That sense of special election we all shared—as time went on in the next few years, some attached more value to it than others. We were all close, but inherent differences started to show, things started to diverge. What I didn't see was that to some people this sense of special election depended on the exclusion of others. The dark side of it became that as more people showed up, there was more resentment of those people. To me the playa seemed so big it could accommodate a nation."

During the first Burn, a few women tried to conjure some goddess energy to counter the male Erector-set mentality of the Man by building a clay oven and baking Venus of Willendorf–style figurines representing hearth and earth and domesticity and the harvest and all that wonderful Hestia-Demeter stuff. The wiseacres of Cacophony were, at best, indulgently amused (at worst aggravated) by this hippie Earth Mother vibe. Kevin Evans and his pal Sebastian Hyde (who made the first T-shirts commemorating the desert Burning Man) formed clay penises that were, grudgingly, also baked in the goddess's oven.

Meanwhile, others were discovering the alchemy of mixing water with playa, making a deliciously gooey and comforting slick mud that dried and flaked and transformed you into a bizarre, primitive creature of the earth, a Mud Person, when applied to the skin. "The first year it was an aberration," Evans remembers. "By the second year it had become fashion."

No one involved with Burning Man told the BLM, the owners and managers of this excessively useless land, that they were coming that first time. But people back in Gerlach caught wind of *something* they didn't like and called in complaints hinting that Satanists were cavorting 'neath the playa moon. John Law saw the BLM agent driving into camp and intercepted him. First impressions were crucial, and he always liked to be the first one to talk to the cops.

"I said, 'You're probably wondering what's going on,' and he was tense until he saw that it was just a bunch of freaks. He's used to major cattle rustling and real criminals, so we just invited him back for the big bonfire and he left. Two Washoe County sheriffs also came out, and I walked over to lighten them up. I explained how we had anchors and cables on the Man; I climbed halfway up and shook it to show them how sturdy it was. They said OK and left."

John Law had deliberately placed the encampment as far away from the road and as deep into Pershing County as possible, for reasons both practical and fanciful. The practical one was that he hoped the location would guarantee minimal concern or interference from police. Gerlach was in Washoe County, a large, heavily populated county that also contained Reno. But the deep playa, and the Burning Man encampment, was in Pershing, whose county seat of Lovelock was more than 130 highway miles away. Pershing had fewer than seven thousand citizens and, thus, very few police officers.

Law also hoped to "make a fantasy place in the middle of nowhere, to make it so you couldn't orient it to anything, displaced, floating in a void. To me that was integral. It made it a different place. It's why people didn't act like dicks." It helped people realize that just themselves, just their community, was all they really had, and should be treasured. It also allowed for a more primitive justice to reign. "[When we had] our first incident with an asshole guy from town, we [just] took his keys away."

The first time the Man burned in Black Rock, his burner was also burned. Dave Warren, a founder of the Suicide Club, spewed flames from his mouth to ignite the figure, and the wind blew the fire back into his face. Warren had told a friend that after performing with fire so many times with no damage, he had come to believe that fire could not hurt him. He then learned that it could. No permanent damage was done to the flesh man. The wooden one collapsed and burned away to ashes. Flares glowed green and red in the Man, and fireworks in his head shot up as the fire claimed him. Steve Mobia, a Suicide Club alumnus having his first experience with the Man, saw those fireworks and thought they were the final thoughts in the Man's head, winging heavenward.

Mobia noted that the Man inspired an awe that approached religion. Someone confessed to him an almost irresistible urge to fall on his knees before its apparent immensity. If the Burning Man is an object of veneration, Mobia noted, it is healthy that he's burned. With the ritual annihilation of the sacred object, the worshipper is freed.

Freed to return and worship again. As early as 1991, smaller hand-built versions of the Man began appearing among devotees. (This is an object I've seen in many Burners' homes. Some are as tall as a regular human. While that word, *Burners,* may be pejorative to some, it is a fair moniker for someone who would actually treasure such an icon.)

The population doubled the following year, to around two hundred. Most people's memories of dates and at precisely which Burn certain things happened in those early days are hazy. The only detailed contemporaneous source accessible to me was the collection of audio diaries made by Steve Mobia upon returning from Black Rock every year from 1990 to 1999.

Mobia arrived in San Francisco in the late seventies after being thrown out of college in Long Beach for a bit of performance art that accompanied a poem he read to a class. He urinated into a bucket, filled a squirt gun with the effluent, and began firing off over his fellow students' heads. Then he crushed three mice on a table. Maybe San Francisco was a better fit for him anyway. He went there to pursue his interest in experimental film. He spent his first night in the city sleeping next to an orgone box on the floor of a Reichian therapy center. Ah, San Francisco!

Mobia became one of Burning Man's first civic functionaries: the lamplighter, the one who lit the kerosene lamps that hung from posts on a path toward the Man. Larry began to imagine an organization to the city, some civic architecture that, as the anarchistic and iconoclastic John Law noted with some dismay, seemed to glorify and focus attention on the Man.

As the encampment/city grew and the need to demarcate roads grew with it, Mobia soon became chief of a band of lamplighters. He's retired now, but the tradition he launched continues. Clad in flowing robes with flames that rise from the hem, hundreds of monastic volunteers selflessly and silently trudge through Black Rock City at dusk every evening, bearing over their hunched shoulders the poles from which hang the lanterns that they hoist to the lamp spires.

The lamps don't provide much illumination to the city (you couldn't even read from the lanterns' light if you were directly underneath one), but they do create its shape. The vague dreamy lights floating in the air show you the curve of the city's frontal road (called the Esplanade) and define the path out to the Man. Mobia composed an invocation for the lamplighters: "We bring light to unite the boulevards of Black Rock City: the light of civilization, navigation, and celebration. In honor of the immensity of the desert and the immensity of our dreams and visions, we hang our lamps high." The whole ceremony was meant to resemble the motion of phantoms, or the progress of time. Civilization is symbolized by the controlled flame of the lamps, in contrast to the untamed fires that otherwise raged over the playa by the midnineties, when most of the art in the city burned and anything else people had an urge to see aflame burned as well.

The notion that what they were doing had as much to do with civilization as it did with unbridled freedom to do whatever-the-hell in this magically unsupervised land came upon them early in the nascent Black Rock City. Many in the Burning Man community could not help thinking of what they were doing—building a minicity for themselves that was completely isolated from the forces of control and repression (as well as from those of comfort and technology and markets)—in terms of underground cultural theorist Hakim Bey. Bey wrote that the best a cultural rebel can expect in our modern world of institutions of total control is to create limited liberated areas. He called them Temporary Autonomous Zones, or TAZ. (Larry himself was never much of a Bey enthusiast.)

But to be a responsible TAZer, a freebooting corsair with love for your brothers, you had to take on certain civic responsibilities yourself. By accident and uncoordinated individual choice, that civic structure began to develop around Burning Man. The idea of the camp as a city started as a bit of a joke, but Cacophonists, when they got their claws on a joke, played with it pretty rough. The people who populated the young Black Rock City were wired urbanites and people of letters and media, and thus pirate radio stations and a newspaper, the *Black Rock Gazette,* were among the first civic innovations.

During those early years, attendees began to take care of one another out there, to build the structures of civilization, because they wanted to, because they could, because no one else was going to. When people were suffering minor health problems—cuts, burns, dehydration—community member Michael Lyons became a camp medic. Chris DeMonterey thought the city needed a central shade structure/hangout that would be communal rather than personal, where people could meet without any lingering feeling that they might be encroaching on someone else's territory. So he built one. They'd all help one another out, informally, both in the planning to get out to the playa and in actually living there, with money, supplies, and labor for whatever needs arose. The needs were more limited at Burning Man then than they are today. The encampments didn't tend to be as elaborately and madly decked out; the event was still only three days long rather than the week it now lasts.

Thanks to Michael Michael, perhaps the most significant civic innovation came along in 1992—officers of the peace. He and Rob-Schmidt began acting as a committee of civic heroes, the Black Rock Rangers, emulating the legendary Texas Rangers. They mostly patrolled the wild borders surrounding their fragile civilization and rescued people who had fallen victim to the real hazards of the playa, particularly getting lost in its trackless vastness or mired in the often mucky and impassible edges. If you were out on the open playa on your own and your car stopped working, or got stuck, or you got lost, you were very probably dead unless someone like a Black Rock Ranger found you.

Michael adopted the identity of Danger Ranger—"legendary protector of our desert society," in later Burning Man literature. As a character, that Danger is quite a character. He often intimates that he can see the future; sometimes that he is *from* the future. He claims he can bilocate and that he does his best work at 3:00 AM. It may well all be true. People were growing to realize that the flat expanse of Black

Rock made for a grand and wide stage for playing out chosen identities rather than just assigned ones. Nothing can be more liberating to a human being, trapped in old skin.

Early excursions to the Black Rock were intimate rituals for the tight circle of friends who made Burning Man. Many of them would meet near the baseball diamond in Golden Gate Park and caravan out to the desert, links in a chain stretching nearly four hundred miles from San Francisco to the Black Rock Playa. The early pioneers would plant little flags to guide those coming later, indicating where to make the turns and reset their odometers.

Upon arrival, most people would camp in a large circle, unplanned and unmapped. "Except," remembers Cacophonist Peter Doty, "those who deliberately wanted to be alone out in the open playa. Even at that time, I thought that was a bad idea because there were yahoos driving around drunk at night, and being in a tent, well, you could easily get slammed into."

Going out there to do art was not necessarily the understood purpose at the beginning, Doty recalls: "It always surprised me that people were doing art out there. I didn't think of it as something people would necessarily do. I thought of it as more of a camping trip/party type of thing. So anytime anybody did anything, it was like, 'Oh, wow, someone did something!' And back then, people actually *slept* at night. There weren't a lot of generators. In 1991, I'm not sure there were *any* generators."

Doty, who grew up in Maine, was attracted to San Francisco for its classic bohemian allure, but his ocean-born heart felt no pull toward the distant desert. He knew about the first desert Burning Man and deliberately declined to go. But he heard the reports of glory from his Cacophony comrades after 1990 and decided he had to go the next time.

Doty is pale with an airy beard, projecting an aura of Shakespearean insouciant theatricality. He's fond of lush, colorful costumery, and so it is appropriate that he entered Burning Man lore as the executor of what is recognized as the first of one of Burning Man's unique and curious contributions to modern art and community: the theme camp.

The theme camp is devoted to creating—often with fanatical dedication—a sustained and planned environment to entertain, enchant, and interact with the other citizens of Black Rock City. These days, if you let Burning Man's organizers know about your theme camp plans in advance, you can earn assigned real estate within Black Rock City, including coveted Esplanade space—frontage on the road that faces out to the Man himself and also looks out on most of the large art installations.

Some Burners debate whether Doty's Christmas Camp truly deserves the title of First Theme Camp. Certainly, there were already people trying to act out and present a unified, created experience, including the Bolt Action Rifle Club in 1990, pith-helmeted adventurers portraying the spirit of soldiers of the Raj with tea and authentic weaponry.

Doty himself bows down before the efforts of Vivian Perry. She pulled off something he remembers as "Elegant Camp"—"though it wasn't really a theme camp like we know it now. There wasn't any open house or hospitality or people stopping by. But she was going all out for elegance, and it blew everybody's mind. She had a champagne bucket and fresh-cut flowers. She was eating oysters and caviar off china and silver, and it was all over-the-top extraneous and superfluous and completely inappropriate, and that was what was so wonderful about it.

"Vivian was the talk of the playa. She managed to stay pristine the entire weekend. The rest of us were covered with dust and grungy within minutes of arriving, and she remained daisy fresh and clean, with fluffy hair. Her white silk blouse was completely spotless, and her black velvet riding pants looked like they'd just come out of her drawer. Not even any dirt on her boots. People were talking about it—how is Vivian doing this? Turned out she was taking four showers a day and had multiple pieces of the same outfit; [she also] had a little damp rag she was carrying around, wiping off her boots constantly. We hadn't seen anybody do anything so conceptually obsessive out there yet."

Doty, with ideas supplied by two friends, Lisa Archer and Amanda Marshall, decided to do Vivian one better—and to be more social about it to boot—with Christmas Camp in 1993. He dressed as Santa, of course, constantly blasted tapes of Christmas carols (some nearby campers got so aggravated that they moved), festooned the camp with Christmas decorations, placed a freshly chopped pine in the center of camp, and supplied thick, boozy eggnog in the desert heat—forcing would-be Christmas drunkards to eat a slab of fruitcake before they could enjoy the drink. The playa dust gave an appropriate "white Christmas" look to September in the desert.

"I even staged a dysfunctional family freak-out because, after all, that's what Christmas is really all about. I started screaming, 'Why can't we for once just go out to the desert and have a perfect Christmas? Is that really asking too much? I hate all of you; I wish you all were dead!' Then I'd run sobbing into my tent, which gave me cover to change into the Santa outfit." Santa Doty grabbed a loaded shotgun in one hand and a bottle of bourbon in another and posed for pictures with topless girls sitting on his lap. "That became my Christmas card that year."

The endless space and solitude on the Black Rock Playa, John Law explains, supplied a particularly weightless and surreal sort of freedom. In this alien environment, you could almost imagine yourself born afresh into another *planet,* released from any old boundaries of behavior or thought.

He fondly recalls what it was like, a couple of years into Burning Man's residency on Black Rock, when his then-girlfriend, Vanessa Kuemmerle, and he would go out to the playa ahead of the event to meet with the BLM people to show them the planned site for that year's gathering. (By that time, they were going through an easy permitting process with the BLM. Law had gotten his first call from a BLM recreation planner the same day he was ready to drive out the truck for the 1991 event, and talked him into faxing him a simple one-page permit. Getting a permit is a lot more complicated now.)

"Black Rock was almost always completely empty," Law recalls, "except for a wind sailor or two. You could go up on the peaks by the northern end, especially at night, and see if there was anyone out on the playa. Usually there wasn't.

"Whenever I could afford it, we'd get a really good rental car, maybe a Lincoln Town Car, and make sure it was *fully insured*. That was the important part.

"I consider this the ultimate metaphor for the nature of the early days of Burning Man: We'd go to the middle of the playa after we knew no one was out there and just *drive*. As fast as we could. Flying on mushrooms. Drinking wine out of a bottle. With the lights out, only the moon and Milky Way lighting the way. And Vanessa and I would be fucking and shooting guns out the window at the same time, Jane's Addiction blasting from the stereo. I consider that my peak *American* experience.

"We weren't trying to destroy any of the vehicles, just ride them hard. And when we returned them, I'd send in Vanessa in a little-girl costume, pigtails and a little dress. We'd try to get the dust out, but things like bullet holes and smashed windshields would be pretty apparent. The functionaries of the huge car rental companies didn't care much. They'd just look at the car, look at the paperwork, look at Vanessa, and say, 'We see you have *full insurance*.' If they'd ask what happened, she'd say something like, 'I'm not really sure, but you should have seen the other cars!'"

Law's happy reminiscences are outrageous, perhaps, but not unique. Within the Burning Man community, the early days (especially to those who never experienced them) are legends of liberty, license, a lost golden age of limitless tomfoolery. No rules—almost no cops—unbridled freedom to drive—access to all the area hot springs all day and night—and Guns! Guns! Guns!

The legendary glory of those days was the Drive-by Shooting Range. It was set up not in the central Burning Man encampment but-miles across the playa by the side of the dirt road leading toward Frog Hot Spring, a small, warm, sulphurous pond beneath a shade tree. Michael Michael puckishly convinced his fellow Cacophonists—

and eventually even some locals—that Frog had once been the site of a whorehouse, and that traditionally it had been known as Bordello Hot Springs. He made up both the history and the name. Both names are still in active use today. Michael now says there was something mystical, not just silly, about this reality hack, an attempt to summon female energies to the area.

The first Drive-by Shooting Range was managed by Joe Fenton. Fenton was a former army man who fell in with Cacophony, went out to the desert with them, and loved, among other things, the freedom to shoot his guns. By the late nineties, he was a higher-up in the Black Rock Rangers, using the playa name Boggman. (He has since left the organization after a public altercation with another Burning Man worker.) When he first tried to become a Black Rock Ranger, though, Michael Michael refused his services.

"They wouldn't let me be a Ranger until the Burn in '94, I don't think," says Fenton. "Michael said I was too aggressive. And he was right, I was. I didn't take shit, always packed guns. Even if I was wearing a suit, I'd have a shoulder holster. Hey, I'm in the middle of nowhere with a bunch of acidheads—I'm going home alive. Fuck you, I don't care what your voices tell you to do. You're not doing it to me."

At the Shooting Range, you could set up whatever you wanted off to the side of the road—stuffed animals (and particularly Barney the dinosaur) were favorites—and go cruising by on car or bike and unload any number of pistols and automatic weapons on your chosen target or just the ground. Michael Michael's prize chariot, the 5:04 Special, was a favorite out at the range. It was an Olds Cutlass Supreme that had been crushed by a brick wall from about the passenger seat back in the 1989 earthquake in San Francisco (which occurred at 5:04 PM). Michael rescued it from the scrapyard, someone at Earl Scheib gave it a fresh paint job just for the silliness of it all, and it became a Cacophony joy—from the front it looked cherry, but the back looked like the thing should not, could not, be in motion. Kevin Evans, whom Michael often let drive the car, recalls sending families of strangers into tearful panics when he'd innocently pull over on long road trips to picnic in the grass. They were certain they had stumbled upon a horrific accident scene. The car was perfect for the Shooting Range because the crushed back end made a perfect depression for a couple of human bodies cradling rifles to nest in and fire from at will.

Also involved with wrangling the Shooting Range was Kimric Smythe, a former air force man and an explosives expert from Survival Research Laboratories (SRL). Kimric was responsible throughout the nineties for the pyrotechnics on the Man, along with his father, Bill, a former United Nations functionary. SRL was San Francisco's most notorious art-machine-destruction gang in the eighties and nineties. While SRL-style shenanigans—building absurdly destructive machinery and destroying things—became a characteristic part of Burning Man in the mid- to late nineties, SRL itself never had a presence there, despite some erroneous press reports and the careless conflation of San Francisco art-weirdness collectives in some people's minds.

One year, an Australian TV crew came out to the Drive-by Shooting Range. Bill Smythe straight-facedly explained their seemingly mad and reckless games by telling the Aussie reporters that in many American neighborhoods, the ability to shoot accurately out of a moving car with your muzzle-loading .44 revolver was a necessary survival skill. An Australian friend later wrote Bill a Christmas card asking him what the *hell* he was talking about on TV.

Over the course of the first three years in the desert, gradually and with no one giving official permission, people began to realize that lots of fun things could be pulled off out there, things that would be impossible or illegal or just way too unsafe in everyday civilization. It could all seem spectacularly grand. Even minor gestures became magnificent and transfixing. In a place with nothing, anything seemed like everything. Kimric Smythe built a wall of fire with a long line of sawdust and kerosene, a flat plane of flames bursting abruptly from the ground, violently silhouetting everyone lined up in front of it. He, and later his wife, would festoon themselves with as many projecting and bursting fireworks as they could fit on their bodies (while wearing a helmet and protective suit) and dance and cavort around: the

Exploding Man and the Exploding Couple. Casual Cacophonist silliness abounded, and today, more than a decade later, people remember it vividly and fondly—for example, Peter Doty leading marchers in chants such as "You can't make me chant! You can't make me chant!"

During a sunset procession out to the Man, surrounded by torches and dressed in richly imagined finery, Steve Mobia realized that these people were not just wonderfully ridiculous but "extremely profound on a transcendent archetypal level as well as a comic level—the epitome of jollity and abandon and whimsy as well as mystery, and it transported me completely. At Burning Man, the sublime and the ridiculous get pushed close together—almost fused."

The first wedding on the playa took place in 1992, and the first artist not part of the San Francisco Cacophony community to discover and work at Burning Man arrived that year. Serena de la Hay came from England and made human-size wicker effigies on-site. They stood up, looking from a distance like dashing, dancing humans who happened to be fraying at their edges. She spent much of the summer living in Cacophonist Nancy Phelps's house, working on them there as well. The first rave camp attached itself to Burning Man that year, a mile or so from the main encampment, glomming parasitically onto Porta-Johns that Burning Man organizers had begun renting.

That year also marked the first plane crash in Black Rock City. A four-seater's wheels dug too deep into the playa upon landing, and the plane flipped over. No one died, but the pilot earned the first Donner Award. This was a Michael Michael invention, intended to honor the person who made the most outrageous and impressive move toward endangering his own life on the playa for the year. Various Cacophonists posed with their foot on the plane's nose, rifle held triumphantly in the air.

By 1992, Burning Man had also become a ticketed event, with admission costing around twenty-five dollars. Early tickets, following the Cacophony spirit of playful fakery and reality hacking, were larded with bogus counterfeit security measures, such as fake colored dots and perforations. Now such measures are real, and a Burning Man ticket would be almost as tricky to counterfeit as U.S. currency, although people still occasionally try.

But it was easy not to pay in the early nineties. The gate was an abstraction, at best a trailer off the Twelve-mile exit to the playa with a bit of picket fence around it, generally manned by a surly-jocular fellow or gal with heavy weaponry. Thus, the organizers couldn't necessarily count on ticket sales to pay for all Burning Man's needs. John Law still helped finance transportation on his credit cards; Dan Miller and Chris Campbell, a new member of the carpentry team, spent most of their summer building the Man for free. (Jerry James came back in 1991 but never reclaimed much of a role in executing the event.) The ticket money was used to pay for Porta-Johns, stamps, recordkeeping, Larry's rent, and the many small incidentals that arose from organizing, even as loosely as early Burning Man was organized, a big party.

Burning Man has always depended on fanatical devotions of time with no recompense and, in later days, large interest-free loans from more well-off enthusiasts. In the beginning, like everything about the event, such loans were small and personal. "I loaned some money for Burning Man early on, and they weren't able to pay me back for quite a while," Doty recalls. "I was very pushy about it too. I was insistent that as interest Nancy [Phelps] had to pay me tapioca pudding. And Larry had to feed me. I said I'd come over for dinner every night until they'd paid me back. Larry was a very good sport about it, and he's actually a good cook too. I remember once I insisted he make me a cake since I'd heard he was a good baker. I went to pick up the cake, and he answered the door covered in flour—as if he'd been beaten up by the Pillsbury Doughboy."

Larry Harvey believed that Burning Man would become more than they saw, would mean more than they could guess, pretty much from the beginning. In his contemporaneous diaries, Steve Mobia remembered talking with Larry about community and Burning Man's significance as early as 1991. Larry already believed the experience had long-lasting effects and would have a profound influence on society outside the desert and their circle of friends.

Because Mobia had had lots of experience with the profound, yet ultimately transient, effects created by the combination of psychedelics and powerful works of art, he doubted that Burning Man would necessarily have such a long-lasting impact. The human soul, like statistical series, has a powerful tendency to return to the mean. But Larry truly believed, and when you talk to him, it's hard not to believe too. "We know this" is one of Larry's favorite conversational tropes. He throws it in frequently after he's made some sweeping pronouncement. He's saying that you and he see things the same way. Here we are, humans united in space and time, talking, coming to a sweet commonality of understanding, eye to eye, soul to soul, mind to mind. *We know this.* It's powerful juju. Larry Harvey can come across as a fragile, shaking, distracted man, but he has a strength even he might not recognize. As one old Burning Man hand who goes by the name of Flash once told me, shaking his head at the naïveté of one of his oldest friends: "And he doesn't even know it's a cult. Can you believe that?"

Larry was not only sure that Burning Man was rewarding, worth the trouble for him and his friends, but also certain that many thousands of others would find it rewarding as well, if only they knew about it.

"I think it was between the '91 and '92 events that people started really talking about how this was going to take off and be a big thing," Doty recalls. "Which I thought was nuts. I mean, how many of us *are* there? There aren't that many weird people wanting to do something kooky like this to begin with. And way the hell out there? It took several years in Black Rock to even get the same crowd you'd had on Baker Beach in 1990. Nancy Phelps was telling me there were going to be thousands of people and all this artwork and all this media coverage, and I thought she was completely deluded." Nancy had become Larry's assistant in the early nineties, helping handle the small but growing business end of the event. She shared and fed Larry's faith.

"I thought it would get big," Larry admits. "I had grandiose ideas—often not realistic. But I was thinking in the right direction. But what you never imagine when you dream grandiosely is the responsibility that comes with it. Burning Man will keep growing! It'll be great! I'll get to go to meetings every day! Didn't have a clue about that part. The Man looked so powerful that even from the beginning I imagined thousands of people coming. It was quite irrational. But that was faith. And they did come. And it wouldn't have happened if I hadn't had that irrational faith. That's the funny thing about faith. What really produced the result? I don't know. It was a blooming miracle, and I only say that half ironically."

By 1993, the world had definitely crashed the Cacophonists' formerly private party. Enough documentarians' cameras showed up that year—from HBO, Brazilian TV, PBS, and local Reno TV—that people were already starting to grumble about media overkill on the playa. Attendance continued doubling every year up until 1996, with people learning about Burning Man from that TV coverage, from zines, and from often computer-based word of mouth. The San Francisco community from which it arose was the incubator of the nineties computer revolution, after all.

Burning Man was being fed from outside its San Francisco birthplace and nexus by the lengthening threads of the Cacophony Society as well. Cacophonists from Portland started showing up, as did Rev. Al's crew from Los Angeles. The first year he brought a contingent of L.A. Cacophonists and hangers-on up to Burning Man, one of them, confused about the premise and expecting more of a spiritual retreat than a chaotic protocity, became alarmed by all the drugged gunplay.

"He was talking a lot about shamanic experience, which should have been my first tip-off that I shouldn't have had anything to do with him being there," Al recalls. "He totally flipped out and began stealing everybody's guns and stockpiling them, in his mind to ensure that nobody got hurt. I got a letter from him months later about how he thought he was getting into a transformative experience and instead it was just a bunch of drunks with guns. I, of course, sided with the drunks with guns. It's always been weird to me, the diversity of people attracted to the event for their own curious and inexplicable reasons."

His first year at Burning Man, Rev. Al strolled around covered in mud with a tire hanging around his neck from chains, lit sterno cans adorning the tire. He became an impromptu whirling dervish, spilling lit sterno out onto anyone near him. Rich Polysorbate followed behind, spritzing aerosol into the flames. "I was asked by Michael to desist," Al recalls. "He gave me this long 'are you sure this is safe?' lecture, which he did a lot of with me."

In 1993, L.A. Cacophony brought their Burning Baby, a grotesque papier-mâché-and-chicken-wire infant with obligatory fireworks installed. It was intended to be destroyed in a pointless ritual involving people shuffling around the baby shaking rattles. After that year's storm, it became just a structure for people to huddle under. Its skin was torn off by the wind, lost across the playa. The night before the storm, Al decided to do a bit of pre-event promotion for the Burning Baby and interrupted "some spiritual awakening thing in front of the Man by rolling this baby pram piled with fireworks, which I lit and pushed through the crowd until I realized I didn't really know how to handle the stroller with burning magnesium in it. I'm trying to steer and trying to act like it's all funny while wondering how much of my wardrobe was really flammable. I know it sounds simple, but those were simpler times."

Because Burning Man brought them out there, other artists began to recognize the magic and possibilities of the playa and its environs. From 1993 to 1995, early Burner William Binzen, a photographer, organized events that were more like what Burning Man later became.

He called them Desert Siteworks, and with the help of John Law, Michael Michael, and other artists, he set up multiweek encampments at area hot springs—each year a different one, Black Rock Hot Springs, then Trego, then Frog (aka Bordello). The crew installed sculptures, lined ponds with underwater neon, performed as long as anyone was awake, all the while living together in long-term (a couple

of weeks or more, though some came and went) isolation, with passing trains sometimes throwing newspapers at them. This was something more than just the long weekend that Burning Man was in the
early nineties—it was, as Burning Man later became, a true experiment in intentional creative community.

Here's how Binzen remembers his intentions in a written reminis-
cence:

> Desert Siteworks was an event comprised of site-specific instal-
> lations and improvisational performances based on ritual themes.
> The project is always held at a hot springs, following the Islamic
> sense that the village spring is the center of desert life. Our vil-
> lage is laid out in a way that harmonizes with the terrain features,
> spring, dunes, and sere scrub brush. Artists collaborate on sculp-
> ture and earth projects and collectively we engage in ritual per-
> formance actions, loosely based on scripts adapted from sources
> such as the Qabbala and Tarot, and on contemplations of issues
> we all face in contemporary life. During performance, we use a
> ceremonial witness, sitting in the witness chair, whose presence
> defines and holds the space.

The first two years he held it earlier in the summer than Burning-Man; the last time, he held it simultaneously with the event.
Although Binzen still considers it an ongoing project, he hasn't done
it since 1995.

The rules and mores of Black Rock City evolved slowly. One of its
central defining characteristics since around '95 or so is that no commerce (with one exception) is expected or permitted in the borders of
the city. But that idea came later. There wasn't much selling to begin
with, and it was mostly among friends, so no one saw a need to make
a fuss. As late as 1993, Larry's old buddy Flash was selling tacos, ham-
burgers, and beer. Sebastian Hyde and Joe Fenton sold T-shirts; Fenton
also sold a handmade tarot deck with Burning Man–related symbols.

Chris DeMonterey sold official Burning Man Blast Shields, transparent Plexiglas sheets through which to look at explosions and fires. A professional espresso truck was also around. By '95, most of this had been shut down or just went away. P. Segal was granted the right (or responsibility) to continue running a central café, with money going back to the organization. To this day, that café (no longer run by Segal) is the only aboveground commerce at Burning Man. Burners often engage in fervent debate over whether it provides a necessary social center for the otherwise chaotic Black Rock City or is a regrettable exception to a rule that would be better enforced with stern purity.

There were no rules, no expectations, no theorizing about or definition of what these desert seekers were up to at all, at first. They were going to an interesting place to enjoy its possibilities, to enjoy one another's extended company with no distractions. By 1993, the first explicit sloganeering defining the Burning Man experience appeared on the playa. Someone had hung a banner demanding NO SPECTATORS on the side of a bus. Certain people at Burning Man were connected with a still-active shadowy guerrilla army known as the Billboard Liberation Front. The sign was "liberated"—altered—to read NO S E TATORS quickly enough.

Through obscure quirks of fate, Burning Man began to attract those who needed to be there. Chris Radcliffe was fleeing a lurid life in Los Angeles in the late eighties and eventually ended up in San Francisco and talked his way into a sales job with the neon sign company that also employed John Law. "He had a cheap suit and a cheap attitude," Law recalls, "but there was something about him."

Radcliffe first entered the world of Burning Man and Cacophony at the Fort Mason barge event in 1991. The Burning Man crew had talked a local arts group into donating the use of a barge on which to raise the Man and display him once again in his hometown. Law was sitting up on the Man's shoulders; he stationed his new buddy Radcliffe at his feet to make sure everything was tight and battened down.

The barge floated between two docks that jutted parallel to it and perpendicular to the shore. For a good video opportunity, they let the barge, with the Man standing in glory, drift back down between the two docks. Cacophonists stationed on the docks were supposed to tug back on the ropes, keeping the barge berthed so it could return after it floated away from shore a bit.

"The barge started moving down the dock, and I started noticing people on the docks who were supposed to be watching our ropes wandering off to get a new beer," Radcliffe remembers. "We ended up with only two people holding the rope on one side, three on the other. And we're picking up speed.

"I shouted up to John, 'What do we do now? Go to Tahiti?' 'Cause we're about to launch this enormous barge into the bay without any hope of getting it back. I grabbed a couple of hammers and began pounding a cadence on the deck of the barge to get people's attention. By the time people ran back to the dock to grab the ropes, we had about ten feet of hawser line left."

Radcliffe quickly apotheosized himself in the Burning Man community. There's no way all the stories about him are true—though I'm very fond of the one that has him building a mock wedding cake for a playa wedding out of stacked propane canisters and shooting them up for an awesome explosion to launch the new couple's adventure—but he inspires an almost inexplicable affection on the part of his old buddies for someone who, to an objective outside observer, might seem a very difficult man. He has a way, P. Segal tells me, of making you do things that you never dreamed you were capable of.

I later learned how this worked firsthand. At a clandestine event on a playa near the Black Rock in 2003 (one of a handful of gatherings that have arisen to re-create the now-dissipated outlaw air of early Burning Man among people in the Burner community), Radcliffe managed to masterfully manipulate me into "borrowing" a huge, block-long, and difficult-to-drive art car early one morning. This is the last thing in the world I would ever normally do, out of both respect for other people's property and my own paralyzing anxieties about fucking up when dealing with huge machines that could easily crush other people's tents, cars, spines. But I did it, it was enormously fun, no one got hurt, and I think, despite the means (which I could never countenance or approve of, even though I did it), that my life has been better for having done it. I learned that there was less reason to let fear prevent me from living my life than I suspected. Radcliffe's sly smile and cocky bouncing stance seem to promise that if you play along, *maybe* he'll teach you to have as much outrageous fun as he's having.

His recklessness also makes people nervous to be around him. I am told a Cacophony newsletter once, for the first and only time, announced that a specific person—Radcliffe—would *not* be present at a certain event, to make sure others wouldn't be afraid to come.

Fascinated by the barge event and this curious, adventurous bunch he'd fallen in with, Radcliffe drove out to Burning Man with a couple of friends in 1991. On the last stretch, he started collecting the corpses of the suicidal jackrabbits that haunt the 34 after dark. He wanted to feed them to his dog. He cut off one jackrabbit's head with metal shears.

Shortly after he arrived at Burning Man, the 5:04 earthquake car cruised up. Radcliffe and Sebastian Hyde leaped to the hood while Kevin Evans drove, faster, faster, spinning, spinning, and Radcliffe and Hyde tried to balance themselves by each grabbing a rabbit ear. They stood precariously, a rabbit head floating between them. Radcliffe ordered Kevin, "Head whichever way the rabbit points," and they surfed the hood of the 5:04, swaying and rushing through the void.

"I realized I'd done the most dangerous thing I'd done in years," Radcliffe recalls. "And that gave me an incredible sense of freedom. I also sensed I was with a group that, even if I fucked up badly, my life wouldn't come to an end. Short of actually dying, I'd be OK. On the drive out there, I was sure I was getting lost, and this place seemed impossible to navigate and I felt responsible for my passengers, and I was confronted with a deep sense of my own inadequacies. But by the time I stepped off the fender of the 5:04, my life had changed. I started living again instead of living in fear."

It's no mystery to Radcliffe why this group felt dedicated to doing Burning Man again and again. "There was this group awe of what we'd done. The synergy of the place, the statue, and our isolation taken as a whole made us realize we were doing something new. There was no imposed ritual or meaning. We had backed into a new version of an induction ritual. By having this shared experience, in this amazing place, it created a unity among us that nothing else possibly could. We had this continuous group 'wow.' The words we used to describe it were all monosyllabic—*wow, cool.*"

On Sunday mornings, as the sun rose on the last day of the Man's corporeal life, a ritual developed. Kimric Smythe, Burning Man's pyro and demolitions expert, would appear at the feet of the Man wearing a cow's-skull helmet, pushing himself on a little hand truck with a horse's head on it. He was the Java Cow. He would distribute coffee to all supplicants who held forward their mugs. The Cow would ask if you wanted cream or sugar. The proper response was to shout back, en masse, "No! We like it black!" and down the brew.

Upon finishing their coffee, Radcliffe recalls, everyone would dash to his or her car, shining in the warm rising sun. Then a high-speed race, fifteen or twenty cars in a ragged row, would commence, heading for the edge of the playa and the Black Rock Hot Springs. There, they could see the sun rise a second time that day, over the mountain that gives the playa its name.

"We had the clarion call of sunrise, then this massive, chaotic race, not trying to kill each other but burning off all this octane and testosterone just so we could squeeze two sunrises out of one day. We used to indoctrinate people into that, the coolest thing we could share. A glorious cavalry charge."

Everyone who was there seems compelled to share tales of one particular night during the early desert years of Burning Man: the lightning storm of 1993, which descended on them as the Man burned.

The storm had been brewing for hours. Lightning was flashing horizontally across an ominous wall of dark clouds, thunderheads closing in from three directions, over the Black Rock and over the Granite and Jackson ranges on either side of the playa. The Man was down, and people closed in and danced and cavorted and hooted around his pile of burning remains. A woman was leaping across a section of the fire. A man jumping from a different direction clipped her, and she fell into the burning pile of charred wood and hot nails.

"For me it was like the old Nancy Drew cliché," Peter Doty remembers. "My heart leaped into my throat. I saw someone falling into a fire, probably the most horrific thing I'd ever seen in person. People dove in and pulled her out, and at that very moment the storm hit. It was like the gods wanted a human sacrifice, and they were denied that sacrifice and now they were unleashing their fury on everyone."

The burned woman was placed on the back of a huge horse-shaped sail cart. Doty, as Santa, took the reins of the horse; three men pushed it against the whipping wind and dust. "Someone showed me a picture later. It was a very Christmassy image of a Santa on horseback going through what looks like a blizzard."

In the chaos of the punishing wind and swirling mud-dust, no one could see more than inches ahead, and it was impossible to find where you were supposed to be or wanted to be, so any shelter would do. Doty made his way back to his tent and found six people already hiding out there, all strangers. One of them was a reporter for the *San-Francisco Bay Guardian*. In a year-in-review essay discussing all his experiences in the year 1993, the writer declared that moment—being caught in a dust- and rain- and windstorm at Burning Man and finding shelter in Santa Claus's tent—as the high point of his year. "He dedicated the entire year [of 1993] to me," Doty recalls.

The winds were god-mighty; one woman was actually blown out of camp and tumbled down the playa while still in her tent. The HBO documentarians, on-site for the first time, panicked and did the worst possible thing you can do when the very air is becoming a thick, swirling wall of opaque water and sand: They got in their RV and tried to drive to safety, inspiring others to panic and make the same mistake. Weird ghost lights from cars circled and disappeared and reappeared in the murk.

As the storm battered the camp, Chris Campbell dashed for shelter into the truck belonging to the lone BLM representative out there, who was wearing a three-piece suit spattered with rain spots along the collar. The BLM guy asks him how's it going. Campbell says pretty good, and the BLM guy asks, "Who's in charge here?"

"Looks like God," Campbell says. If the rain keeps up for long, the BLM guy tells him, the playa will turn to glue, and no one will be able to go anywhere.

Well, sure. I better go find my tent, Campbell says, and he runs into his buddy there, but because his buddy is coated with thick layers of dark, wet dust, Campbell doesn't recognize him. In his confusion and mania and under the effects of the acid he took before drumming wildly on a trap set before the Burn and the storm, he refuses to *believe* it's his friend.

"I've never felt more like the hand of God was just gonna sweep us off the face of the earth," Campbell remembers. "I figured, if I die today, there won't even be a print. It'll all be gone; wind and dust and rain would have just washed it all away." He confessed all this to his friend, not even knowing it was his friend, who replied, "Mm, interesting. Are you coming next year?"

"Well, fuck yeah, man. Damn right."

By morning, stunned, staggering citizens were asking one another, 'Anyone got a Dustbuster I can borrow?' The civic order of Black Rock City was dusted and soaked and battered but unbowed, and maybe the media had left but the people—the people!—endured and continued to endure.

Burning Man became the tail wagging the Cacophony dog as the nineties danced along. Peter Doty would find that for months before the event, everyone's attention was so dominated by thoughts and preparation for Burning Man that other Cacophony activities suffered, that everyone's energy was pouring into Burning Man to the exclusion of everything else. "This bugged me big-time," Doty says, "because I always thought there was something much more subversive about having events in downtown San Francisco in the financial district in the middle of the week than out in the desert, where *everybody* is trying to-do weird, crazy stuff. Out there, everyone is trying to outweird the Joneses, and everyone is succeeding in outweirding the Joneses.

"And that's cool. But there are fifty-one other weeks in the year, and if we are living in an urban center, I think sabotaging the mundane is a wonderful subversive civic duty that we have as weird bohemians."

By the midnineties Burning Man was no longer just Burning Man, an event held one weekend a year. It was "The Burning Man Project," and thinking, preparing, and promoting it were beginning to take a dozen or so people's time for months, often many months. Stuart Mangrum, a former air force man, zinester, and computer industry worker who became Burning Man's press liaison and propagandist in '93 (and left that post after 1996), loved the term *The Burning Man Project*. "It sounded a little bit scientific, a little bit social-controlish, and a little bit Alan Parsons. Perfect."

Indeed, the term summoned around the event a Freemasonic aura of mystery, redolent of secret societies plotting to warp our world into something more to their liking. As Michael Michael slyly said to me one night while discussing my book in the middle of a loud Burning Man party, "Everything you do is your contribution to the Project." You could hear the capital letter in his voice.

By 1995, the civic form of Black Rock City was almost filled in. This wasn't because a genius city planner came along and saw how this encampment of friends could become a convincing instant city. Every new development was just something someone thought would be fun, or useful, or amusingly absurd, to do. They had a big WELCOME TO BLACK ROCK CITY sign up near the gate, complete with absurd insignia of made-up fraternal and civic organizations. The daily paper, the *Black Rock Gazette,* had been in business since 1992 and was getting more elaborate and professional each year.

More out of hope and imagination than reality, Larry had dubbed the event the "Black Rock Arts Festival" in 1992. (It has continued being plain old Burning Man ever since.) But big, ambitious art did start to show up. Pepe Ozan, a sculptor, filmmaker, and theatrician from San Francisco's Project Artaud, came out after attending Desert Siteworks in '93 and became one of the art kings of early Burning Man. Every year, he built new and more elaborate variations on his fire lingam, which eventually evolved into creepily alive-looking clusters and castles made of rebar, mesh, and playa mud and filled with wood that would eventually burn. The bases had vaginal openings; the towers were always tall, sinuous, sexually suggestive. Pepe staged "operas" around them—mixtures of drumming and dancing and chanting and singing with lovely-scary costumes and dark-sexy bodies that became a central attraction through the rest of the nineties, the other big ritual besides the Man himself.

In 1993, Chris DeMonterey started building his annual (with some years off) series of increasingly large camera obscuras, usually in pyramid constructions that people could crawl inside, navigating a dark, turning passageway and then, in the central chamber, contemplating a projected 360-degree image of Black Rock City outside.

Art cars were appearing in increasing numbers at Burning Man as well, merging two of humanity's deepest needs: transportation and art. John Law had invited his buddy Harrod Blank, an art-car maker and booster who was working on both a book and a film documentary on the phenomenon of motorized vehicles altered and tricked out to be mobile works of art. Harrod thus knew almost every art-car driver in the country and spread the word, and Burning Man, despite being hell on motor vehicles, thus became one of the biggest destinations for art-car drivers in the country. (At least they didn't have to worry about being street legal out on the playa. Nowadays, Burning Man attracts more than five hundred art cars a year.) The space and freedom of Black Rock were being used in increasingly thrilling and silly and foolish ways. Destructive robotic devices were there, frightening and delighting the citizenry. "There wasn't a lot of regulation," Mangrum remembers. "If you wanted to drop acid and speed your car across the desert, no one gave a shit, but no one did *incredibly* stupid things."

Four thousand people were on the playa by '95, and media from *Spin* to HBO to the *New York Times* to *Outside* magazine had noted the curious goings-on out on the Black Rock. In one film documentary, shot around then, probably 1994 or 1995, Larry Harvey is seen lounging against a tree. He's talking about negativity and evil forces, and he says the devil isn't welcome in Black Rock City.

But then he pauses and thinks about it. Well, maybe they *could* invite the devil out. "Maybe we'd learn something about ourselves."

They did. And they did.

Part Two
RADICAL SELF-RELIANCE

Chapter Four

"IT AIN'T EVER HAPPENING AGAIN"

In Steve Mobia's audio diaries of Burning Man in the desert, he mentions every year the amazement he and others felt that, despite all the heroically fearless recklessness and exploding mortars and raging fires, no one ever got seriously injured or killed.

After 1996, he didn't say that anymore. Before that year's event even began, Michael Furey was dead, his head nearly sliced off by the mirror of John Law's truck.

The truck, hauling a trailerload of stuff for Burning Man, was being driven by a fellow known as SteveCo, with his buddy Mark Perez riding shotgun. They were running an encampment called Plundertown at Burning Man that year. Its centerpiece was a city-block-long replica of the children's game Mousetrap, with a bowling ball playing the role of the small marble used in the actual game. It was, at that time, the most mechanically elaborate and ridiculous undertaking anyone had tried out there. People's ambitions and achievements were starting to get as big as the Black Rock Playa. The Mousetrap never really fully worked, though they could—and did—just drop a piano from a crane as a finale and make the crowd happy. (Perez is striving to perfect the Mousetrap and take it on the road to this day.)

I've talked to almost everyone who was on the scene the night Furey died. Some little details are remembered differently, but by most accounts, it seems to have gone down like this: Furey and a buddy known as Pogo (later Burning Man's intrepid and beloved crane operator, who would help set up the projects too tall and heavy for human hands) were drinking at Bruno's bar in Gerlach. Drinking *a lot*. A female friend offered to load up the two men's motorbikes on her trailer and head out to the site. (By 1996, Burning Man was taking a good week to set up before the event officially began.) Pogo judged his own drunkenness accurately and agreed. Furey insisted on riding his own motorcycle alongside the trailer.

As the group traveled out on the playa, their path crossed SteveCo and Perez's, and Furey began zooming around them and zooming toward them and only swerving out of the way at the last moment. SteveCo cursed the reckless Furey—a well-known hellion in the community, a funny-dangerous firebrand who hung out with the punk-polka act Polkacide. SteveCo decided he should just keep driving his regular speed—around forty miles per hour, heavily loaded— straight forward and let Furey take care of himself.

It worked for a little while, and then it didn't. Furey was coming at him, and he wasn't going to stop. SteveCo tried to turn out of the way, but the best he managed was preventing the truck from colliding with Furey head-on. Instead, he died hitting the side mirror.

Oh, it was ugly, and SteveCo was kicking the truck and cursing Furey for a motherfucker when Vanessa Kuemmerle came along. She was then chief of the Black Rock Rangers; a short, serious slip of a girl, she was legendary for her ability to manage the wraths and conflicts of men quite literally twice her size. She got all the other cars she was caravanning with to head out to the Burning Man site without noticing the carnage. Mark Perez was sent back to the camp in one of the cars; John Law was summoned to the accident scene, and Vanessa headed back to Gerlach to call the coroner. Despite her telling them Furey was quite and completely dead, they sent a Life Flight helicopter anyway. Joe Fenton and a couple of other people were also at the death scene by then.

Then Larry Harvey arrived. Accounts vary, but the common denominator is that an unsettled Larry announced to the grieving assembled—possibly three times in a row—"There's no blood on our hands."

"This got turned into a big story about 'all Larry cares about is insurance,'" Larry says. "But that missed the point. All the way out there, I kept seeing blood on my hands, and I was just relieved to discover there was nothing we could have done to stop it."

Vanessa and Fenton, and especially John Law, indeed took Larry's comment as an indication that he was more concerned about insurance and covering Burning Man's ass legally than about the fact that their compatriot was dead. At that moment, Law felt something break in his head, and he knew that his relationship with Larry and with Burning Man was wounded, possibly mortally.

While performing during Burning Man, Polkacide made some futile attempts to get the Devil's Night–wild crowd to show a moment of silent respect for their fallen hellion. When the band members realized the futility—and really the inappropriateness—of this, they instead requested a moment of the most passionate and raucous cacophony the crowd could muster.

Things had begun to get a little dark at Burning Man even before 1996, before Furey's death. As the crowds grew, the transgressions—even if they were never *intended* to hurt anyone—were multiplying and getting more daring, to the point that the more sober and decent could easily worry that things were getting out of control. By '95—my first Burning Man—things had started to get very Walpurgisnacht after the big fire. The Man burned, and then everything else did. This was part of the glory and the danger of the cusp years of Burning Man, when it was well past a gathering of friends and friends of friends but not yet heavily policed and regulated.

Burn Night in 1995 was somewhat of a preview of the even more intense hellishness of '96, thanks to Chicken John's discovery of Burning Man that year. Chicken John was a punk-rock circus impresario, a quick-talking New York con man, and a former member of GG Allin's band the Murder Junkies. Allin was the most repulsive-man in punk rock, assaulting and throwing feces at his audience and vowing to kill himself on stage. (An ill-timed heroin overdose ruined this fine plan.) Then based in L.A., Chicken had taken his first-circus on the road that summer, a rolling catastrophe of poorly planned, poorly executed bad-gag mock-vaudeville—Speed Metal Tap Dancing! The Man-eating Chicken! The Reverse Stripper! The Vegan Geek!—documented in painful detail in the underground hit documentary *Circus Redickuless*. They exhibited "Olympian ineptitude," one newspaper critic wrote, and Chicken was always kind of proud of that one. He dragged the tattered remnants of the circus with him to Burning Man after their summer tour had sputtered out. Where else?

Chicken was a sometime rock 'n' roll roadie as well, and he once worked for legendary heavy metal punch line Ronnie James Dio, the dwarfish also-ran who sang for a while with Ritchie Blackmore's Rainbow and briefly replaced Ozzy in Black Sabbath. Dio, being a heavily mystical dude, relied on such fantasy stage props as a rickety plastic sphinx (maybe three times the size of a Saint Bernard) and a Great Pyramid that was in fact painted fabric.

Dio was going through a brief retirement from touring and was happy to let his erstwhile roadie make off with some of the detritus of his pomp-metal past. Chicken brought both dumb props on tour with him and hoped to use the pyramid as his tent at Burning Man. But the tent poles were bent, having flown off the van when Chicken slammed on the brakes to better scope out a pair of sunbathing ladies. Without its support poles, instead of rising majestically in its fresh desert home in the new world, the mediocre pyramid flopped limply, one end pinned up to the side of the van, the rest dragging in the crushed-chalk dust.

Frustrated with his inability to re-create the glories of the pharaohs in Black Rock, Chicken took the legacy of the sainted Ronnie James Dio, Master of Metal, and condemned it to a particularly unhealthy immolation after the Man had burned in '95. This act of bad judgment emboldened others, including me. Although I was camped hundreds of yards away, it was the biggest fire I'd spotted besides the-Man himself. I dragged over the wrecked remnants of a filthy two-man fiberglass boat I had found abandoned in an alley in Los-Angeles, brought to add some minor atmosphere to "Shangri-La Di-Da," a water-themed oasis I camped with that year. Thick black clouds, doubtless filled with many substances with dire and frightening names ending in *zene*, billowed forth and shadowed the entire encampment.

"It was fucking toxic," Justin Atwood, then Chicken's right-hand man in the circus, recalls. "People were running from the other side of the city, complaining we were smoking them out." Then Howard Hallis—an L.A. animator, showman, and former assistant to both Timothy Leary and Perry Farrell who entered Burning Man iconography as the red, grinning fellow in the two-page spread in Bruce Sterling's 1996 *Wired* cover story declaring Burning Man "the New American Holiday"—was overcome by the moment and tossed his own store-bought plastic tent into the inferno. "All these angry enviro-hippies saw this and assumed Howard was the one responsible for the whole thing and began screaming at him about how uncool and unsafe this all was," says Atwood. "He was naked and painted red. It's like they were screaming at the fucking Noid from those Domino's commercials."

When you are surrounded by so much fire, so much behavior that's exciting and compelling even as it's ill advised and objectionable, well, politeness and restraint and good sense just burn away. After the toxic fire had died down, Chicken and a ragtag gang, including myself, fueled with a gallon jug of warm supermarket gin, wandered from encampment to encampment joshing and yelling and engaging in the kind of inspired badinage that is the funniest thing you have ever heard while it's happening, but whose specific memory tends to fade with the hungover morning mist. A hunter by the name of Bob had driven in from the hills surrounding the playa, attracted by the fires. Chicken unnerved him greatly by weaving weird head games and implying that we were either worshipping or preparing to sacrifice him.

The long night ended after dawn as the ten or so of us left ended up at the camp bulletin board, where, then as now, people left notes telling friends where to find them or trying to find someone heading to Portland, or Seattle, or L.A. to give them a lift home. I think my friend Summer started the final act of our long, wrong night. She was past speech then, and began slamming both fists into the board with the slow deliberation of a cranking gear. The wood began to splinter. That was it. Once something showed weakness in front of a crowd in our mood—and it wasn't an evil mood, no, just one where any impulse that was unusual, unexpected, and *wrong* would be rapidly seized upon by the whole gang—well, it was all over for that board. Others joined in kicking it and cracking its legs, and then suddenly Chicken knew why he'd been carrying around that jerrican half filled with gasoline. Soon the board, the pieces on the ground and the pieces still standing, was on fire. A reporter from *Spin* magazine was there, and she got a quote from someone that I guess explained it: "We wanted to do the only thing you could do out here that would be a really fucked-up thing to do."

Well, that wasn't the *most* fucked-up thing you could have done. Pepe Ozan's opera had a goat in its cast that year, kept penned in with straw bales at his camp. A different band of roving jackanapes had torched the bales. (The goat was rescued.)

L.A. Cacophony kept coming back, and they contributed manfully to the more dark and destructive side of Burning Man's liberatory ethos. Every year, they'd construct a tableau, each one progressively more complex and labor intensive, then burn it and blow it up with escalating recklessness.

Their installation in '95, Burning Toyland, relied on the endless supply of stuffed animals they got from Al Ridenour's second wife, Veerle, who worked for a company that imported knockoff toys from China. They were all staked out on display, a forest of delightful little plush friends. The planned climax involved some Rube Goldbergish shenanigans that ended with a burning teddy bear splashing into a wading pool filled with gasoline that was set on a large plastic tarp. The ignited gas was supposed to melt the pool and spill over the tarp in an impressive gush of fire.

The mechanism didn't work—failure rates are high on the playa, with people trying unprecedented stunts two hours from the nearest hardware store and usually while impaired to boot—so everything just got blazed manually and willy-nilly. Still, most of the audience probably got the point, such as it was. Through the entire show, speakers blasted a disturbing multilayered sound collage made by Rich Polysorbate, a hideous mix of old commercials for beloved childhood toys, songs from kiddie LPs, and screams from slaughterhouses.

"I imagined hearing that tape would be like having your mental epidermis peeled off with a knife, causing intense pain," Al recalls. "I thought people would be really bummed out by seeing childhood toys destroyed, and I know people brought children by because during the day it just looked like all these wonderful, colorful toys out on the playa. Then everyone hears it's Toyland time! I don't know what they expected: some kind of magical Geppetto's shop where all the toys come alive? Or obnoxious loud people throwing gasoline on things hoping they will burn faster?

"That was the first year we used oxyacetylene bombs, which I guess everyone was using for a while after we did." The ridiculousness of staking out claims in this nutty world strikes him. "'Well, the Shriners used them, but I'd say the Elks were using them much earlier. And the Knights of Columbus used more oxygen in the mix...' Those were really deafening, very percussive. When I set off a test one in my backyard in Hollywood, friends reported hearing it from miles away. I knew they'd be effective in harshing people's mellow on the playa."

Having reduced a fantasyland of beloved stuffed animals to ashes, L.A. Cacophony decided to do the same thing in '96 to a scale model of the Hollywood Hills, with life-sized figures of iconic Hollywood actors and symbols standing throughout like cenotaphs. Burning Tinseltown, they called it. The whole tableau was wired with loads of-firecrackers, gas bombs, and anything else that would burn and preferably explode. The fusing was slapdash, done by hungover non-professionals in shadeless 100-degree-plus heat. Thus, all the carefully calculated explosions didn't go off in the planned order.

To achieve the more wildly raging inferno and explosions he envisioned, Al had to run through the living fire spastically shaking a can of gasoline, stoking his conflagration. Flames licked up to the spout of his canister. There's something exhilarating about seeing someone dashing full-tilt-boogie through and between walls of roaring flame with a gasoline can in his hand, a tight, demented grin alight on his face. There just is.

Al's L.A. Cacophony crew had rigged three huge gasoline bombs—bags of gasoline sitting over lines of black powder that were supposed to have gone off in series during the burn, but some connection must have gotten severed, or wasn't done right in the first place. The delighted, fire-stoked crowd had rushed into the guttering blaze after the obvious danger seemed to have passed. A smiling Al assured them, Willie Wonka style, that no, really, they ought not to be here. There are still large gasoline bombs among the wreckage, as yet undetonated. Then one of them exploded. "I talked to people later who told me they got some melted plastic on them as the burning bag rained down, but they still loved the show. So that's what I choose to remember," says Al.

Al doted on the little details the punters probably missed—like how one day when he was at home making the giant photocopied blow-ups of famous actors that dotted the display, feeling overwhelmed, Cacophonist Chuckles the Clown "came over and rejuvenated my spirits by cutting her arms open and smearing blood all over the lips of Doris Day and John Wayne. People probably couldn't see the brown stains, but it added to the authenticity."

Al was running into a fire with a gasoline can to burn representations of the Hollywood Hills, iconic actors, and an Oscar "out of misanthropic glee and disgust with society at large. There was never in my mind any kind of redeeming moral slapped on. There was no ardent protest against corporate America or the entertainment industry per se. That always bothered me, to lace things with hidden messages about conserving Mother Earth's resources or whatever. I never wanted things to get tilted [toward spreading messages] for Cacophony. It might happen that way [in San Francisco], but it didn't happen down here. Because I squelched it, crushed it under my jackboot!"

Though retired from Cacophony and four years gone from Burning Man at the time we're talking, the hesitant, nervous Al Ridenour appears to find some satisfaction, perhaps even pleasure, in remembering when. Prior to 1999, Al fondly recalls, "there was no fire marshal and there was some potential for vast personal injury and destructiveness. There was this wonderful atmosphere, for a few years there, this teetering feeling that there was a good chance lots of people would be killed in the most colorful possible way.

"Raging fires everywhere, an apocalyptic feel, which to me was really invigorating. I always had this attraction to fire, and the only chance I really had to set fire to things in an unsafe way was at Burning Man. It was great having that sort of license. And if you are going to burn something, you might as well make it worth burning. And if you are going to put a lot of effort into building something worth burning, it's nice to have a big crowd to tell you how wonderful you are and applaud and give you beers.

"In the end, no matter how studied and structured you made your piece or what kind of performance you surrounded it with, things would always dissolve into people running into the fire and kicking-stuff over. That was always the best part, when people would break the safety lines out of sheer self-destructive exuberance, get in there with the stuff and confront it at close range. Just a riotously good time."

The level of irresponsible destructiveness was rising at Burning Man, to be sure, but that wasn't the only thing growing. The visions of what could be accomplished in artistic terms were getting bigger, grander, wilder, and stranger as well. Meet Steve Heck.

Heck is a thick Grendel of a man, massive and boyishly energetic, with clear, deep-set eyes and a long beard that he hacks with a knife and ties off at the bottom. He can move a piano more than a foot merely by smacking it with one hand. He lives in a warehouse in Oakland. Plato would be amazed at how the perfect idea of clutter has somehow entered the phenomenal world down this dismal Oakland side street. Heck inhabits two stories and a huge yard, and the warehouse takes up an entire block. Every inch of space except for a narrow walkway, is not only filled but piled, cluttered, overflowing with everything—vehicles and woodpiles and clothes and furniture and boats and carts and engine parts and sculptures and appliances and racks and magazines and presses and lathes, everything Heck ever got his hands on, except the things that burned when his old house caught fire many years go.

That fire, that crisis, imbued him with a calling—perhaps a mania. Heck had been a piano mover. His house was filled with so many pianos you had to walk over them to get through the living room. Suddenly he had hundreds of burned pianos. He was seized by a compulsion to make something of his tragedy.

That compulsion, the notion that nothing can leave his care until he has transformed it into a work of art, imprisons him, really, behind walls of endless junk. He makes versions of famous images—ones that he hopes everyone will instantly recognize—out of any material at home, including cracked porcelain, burned wood scraps, chunks of old books and magazines. He proudly shows me examples of his Marilyn Monroes, and one piece re-creating that famous picture from the Vietnam War of the prisoner being shot in the head. Wheeled clothing racks form impromptu doorways in the middle of the one narrow path that goes through the second floor, a floor thick with shifting torn pages from old magazines, knobs from drawers, and bits of jewelry settings and guitar strings—listing specifics is wearying and pointless; it's all there, in wild profusion.

He's been fighting for years with city officials and landlords over his junk-besotten lifestyle. He feigns complete irrationality so cops and code officials will throw up their hands and give up. He tells me, over and over, that if his life has any message, it is: "Don't be me."

He can't halt his pursuit of the alchemical transformation of every object, every reminder of his past of loss, into art, and he looks forward, as if to his arrival in Zion, to the moment when the last piano or found photograph or broken chair in his possession has been thus transmuted and he will be free of the burden of the physical world. Not a bag of garbage ever leaves his house; he mixes food wrappings and typical household trash with cement to make sculptures. You'd call him insane, with no compunction, if not for the intelligent lucidity with which he details his own obsessions.

Late in the summer of 1996, Heck had a vision of his burned pianos in the desert. He had never been to Burning Man, but he knew

John Law and Vanessa Kuemmerle through work they had all done together at Survival Research Laboratories shows. He called them and asked if he could bring his pianos and was told sure, bring 'em out, set 'em up here just past Plundertown.

So he brought them, and he dumped them out on the desert floor, and he contemplated them. John Law drove by in a truck with some of the guys and asked Heck if he wanted to come with them for a hot spring soak. Sounded good enough. He went, and then afterward they stopped in Gerlach for dinner at Bruno's. Then they wanted to reload the truck, and Heck, who was desperate to tend to his pianos, to realize his vision, rebelled. He stalked angrily away from Bruno's, no warning, no good-byes.

Heck had paid no attention to how far they had driven, to how far from Gerlach the encampment was. So he walked. And walked. He hadn't drunk anything but rum since hitting the desert. As he arrived at the Twelve-mile playa entrance, he flagged down a pickup truck. "I am sitting in the back of this pickup truck," he remembers, "and it starts to rain, and it feels like people are shooting me with .22 shells and I am so pissed at them and at everything else and I am thinking this is the worst experience I have ever had in my life."

Tired of dealing with the high-speed battering from the rain, he jumped ship. "Fuck it, I'm walking again. And I can see lights, and all of a sudden the lights disappear. And it's still raining. And I am wearing a wife-beater T-shirt and a pair of shorts. No socks and these shoes I never, ever wear. I have three hundred dollars cash and a knife in my pocket. And the winds come in, and through the dust and the rain I can see a car and I start running after it, waving the knife and the money. And this is what I learned about perspective out there—it can be five miles away or five hundred feet away and it looks the same. But I'm chasing that car and chasing that car, and I see a train and run toward the train and I am way, way, way fucking lost. I have no idea where I am, and I'm seeing these lights and they are like ghosts, so I can see through them and my feet are killing me. I take my shoes off, and my feet are swollen and I can't get my shoes back on and my feet are bleeding.

"It was eight o'clock at night when I had started, and I wander and I wander and then I had cramps so I get on my hands and knees so the body warmth doesn't go into the earth. And I get up again, and I walk and when I look up there are these two things the size of basketballs. Eyes…like eyes…like…they are so intimidating and making this noise, like, *EEIEEKK!* And I get up, and they pass me and I am chasing them and then they are following me and every time I collapse they get closer. I am playing a game with these two giant floating heads, and there must be some alien ship or something and they are watching me and they would get really close and at a certain point they would stop, like there was an invisible line they couldn't cross."

Deluded, dehydrated, mad, Heck wandered toward a tree he spotted at the edge of the playa, across the railroad tracks, and approached Trego Hot Springs. And he walked over a section of earth that was in fact a thin crust over bubbling hot spring water, and his feet broke through the crust, which ripped back his toes and scraped blood from his shins. "And there is no one who can find me, and there is no one who knows where I am. And there are eighty-eight pianos dropped off in the desert, and there are a bunch of hippies who will beat them with sticks. I didn't think about my mom or my grandmother, just these eighty-eight pianos that will be left and no one will ever see me again. Or know why, or what.

"Finally the sun is coming out. I'm on knees and elbows, and the sun is hitting my ass, so I can figure out which direction I was going. At night, I had never seen so many stars. Everyone talks about tracking by the North Star, the landmark, right? Yeah, *right*. Well, the sun is coming up, and in a couple of hours I'll be fucking dead. And I see an RV. It might be a hundred miles away, but I'm gonna find it and drink the damn toilet if that's all there is, so I get off my knees and elbows. This is gonna be the death march, and God help them on that RV if they try to run away.

"My mouth feels like a leather bag full of sand, my lips are bleeding, and suddenly, before I reach the RV, this little car is crossing my path and I'm waving my T-shirt, my city skin is being baked, and the car pulls up. The kids in there look at me. I'm making noises like,

Araogaghrghrh. I've got a knife in one hand and three hundred bucks in the other, and I'm prepared to kill them if they try to drive away. They hand me water, and I can't even feel it as I'm drinking it, and all I can say to these kids is 'Don't be me, don't be me.'

"They give me this tiny Asian pear with a little leaf, and I'll never forget how good that tasted. I even ate the leaf. They were these nice hippie kids, and they took me back to my truck and I slid under it and ate five pounds of grapes and drank fifteen bottles of water." For the rest of the week, his feet were so swollen and ruined they wouldn't fit into any of his shoes. John Law was so angry with Heck for disappearing that he screamed and cursed at him when he came upon him the next morning, with his grotesque feet hanging out of his truck. "I can't believe I was yelling at Steve Heck. The guy could completely crush me with one hand."

With only two assistants and stacked boxes to slide the pianos up on, Heck built a structure, three pianos high (stacked not bottom of one to top of one beneath, but side on top of side) and double thick, a sort of open cathedral of pianos (it is often difficult to describe art objects at Burning Man; they are so sui generis there's often no way, other than offering tedious and never-ending descriptions of every element of their shape, to really explain what they look like or what they are) called the Piano Bell.

Most of the pianos were already in various stages of collapse, burned, their inner workings exposed. For days, Heck's piece became a giant metapercussion instrument, with everyone plucking and banging strings and the pianos' bodies. It generated a constant resonant smack-boom-hum, and it was so much like nothing you had ever seen or heard before that it became an instant Burning Man legend. At the end, yes, it burned.

Robot artist Christian Ristow recalls, "How could you possibly rationalize bringing ten tons of half-burned pianos out there? It was the apex of that illogical, dangerous frontier mentality. And such a phenomenal personal vision. One of the most amazing things I've seen."

Flash has the final word on Steve Heck: "He's a beauty, that kid. Did you see his Piano Bell? Unbelievable, really. That's what people came to Burning Man to see and still come to see but will never see again. We all try to do our best when we're out there. But he…it was something far beyond what anyone could imagine."

As excessively good a time as Burning Man was for the artists and the crowds, things were getting less purely fun for the organizers as the event grew—grew out of control, some thought—and by '96 they were feeling anxious, even before Furey's death and the rest of that year's developments strained the old model of Burning Man to the breaking point.

That old model had already changed from those innocent first few years in the desert. At night, you can still hear snarky comments around fire barrels, where high-level Burning Man gossip is bandied about, some saying that the only reason Larry Harvey became the official leader of Burning Man after it got big is that he had the least to lose if someone decided to sue all their asses.

Joe Fenton remembers them joking about selling a Burning Man calendar, in which January's photo would be Larry sitting on the sidewalk with his hat pulled down and a cup of pencils in front of him. "He never had any fucking money at all," says Fenton. Larry had injured his back, gone through vocational rehab for a while, and was mostly just unemployed. John Law and Michael Michael were managing Burning Man's money. They made sure Larry's rent was paid and his needs were taken care of.

Larry did have the least to lose. But that was not the *only* reason he was the official director of the Burning Man Project. He had earned respect as one of the men who launched the ritual, and as its chief theoretician. Cacophonists could have justly noted, though, that the first desert Burn was far more a Cacophony event than it was Burning Man No. 5, Act Two. It was just Cacophony Zone Trip #4 to them. One Burning Man artist noted that "Larry was just burning a scarecrow on the beach before he met John Law and Michael Michael."

By 1996, Burning Man had owners and an organizational chart. The art party had morphed into a business.

They had an insurance policy even before then, purchased through the neon company that Law and Michael, with Chris Radcliffe, had started in 1992. As a neon company, they were insured for a million dollars of damage they might cause by, say, accidentally shorting out a neon sign and burning down a building. They used it to insure an event that deliberately burned down a neon-lit sculpture. Radcliffe is still amused by the irony.

Liability was still a worry for anyone who could reasonably be considered responsible for the event. A company was formed to function as Burning Man's legal face to the world. It was arranged as the three men soaked together in a hot spring—in 1994, they seem to remember—when Law and Michael made a pitch to Larry suggesting they form a tripartite partnership to legally own and operate the event. While they would continue to have group meetings at which all Cacophony members would assemble, along with any other hangers-on who felt they had a stake in Burning Man, they thought they needed a more streamlined and decisive organizational structure. Those three had, in their minds, claimed ownership by their labor (and I've heard no real objections from others involved back then). John was handling logistics, transportation, and camp setup; Michael handled the books and was the first organizer of the Rangers; and Larry was general planner, conceptualizer, and art manager.

Memories of the early days of the partnership are undoubtedly colored by the way it eventually splintered. But Larry says today that he felt uneasy about limiting the ownership of the operating structure to just the three of them, given how many people were helping out in some capacity. Simultaneously, he also didn't like the idea of ceding any control of the trademark to the others. They had not, after all, been around when the idea was first hatched and executed. Law and Michael's preexisting partnership in Cacophony and in the neon company made him fear he might be outnumbered.

"I began to mock the whole thing," Larry remembers, "referring to us as the Temple of the Three Guys. I said, OK, we've made it into property, haven't we? But how are we going to get people to help us if it's *our* property now? Before, it was just an immediate thing that we all did, but now it's ours and we need people to help us and how can we do that if we don't take them into our trust and create a larger, more inclusive organization? Instead of telling them, yeah, we're all in this together, and then the three boys go off."

That sounds sensible, but the more inclusive committee of ownership for Burning Man created after the Temple of the Three Guys crumbled is now only twice as large. Despite this, it has managed for years to attract—in a system Larry seems satisfied with—thousands of volunteers and helpers who can feel they own a piece of Burning Man emotionally but have no actual equity.

Law, for his part, was increasingly disturbed by Larry's devotion to the central symbol of the event, his Man. Law advocated burning a different big thing every year—pigs, dogs, *whatever,* and detonating them with, say, flying balloons of flammable gas. Change it up, make it new. But Larry would brook no interference with the continuity of the ritual of the burning of his Man.

Law wanted to just let different camp centers organically form on the playa; Larry desired a more centrally organized city built around the Man. Law wasn't sure population growth could continue and still sustain the unique magic of the experience; Larry wanted the whole world to see the Man burn. Things had begun to fray between the two men even before the 1996 event. On the very day that Furey died, a friend who spent part of the day with both Larry and Law separately remembers that they were already deeply unhappy with each other.

Larry had ended up among Cacophony but was never quite of it. He appreciated their identification with the Dadaists and Surrealists, and made friends among their ranks, but after all, they came to his ritual, not he to them.

Through the rave community that had latched onto Burning Man as a particularly fascinating setting for huge all-night dance parties; through word of mouth in San Francisco and the surrounding Silicon Valley, where most of the digerati lived; and through some hip media coverage, Burning Man, by 1996, had become the playground of choice for the then-rising digerati and the computer industry's temporary nouveaux riche, who seemed to own the business and cultural future of the West.

An article in *Forbes* declared that Burning Man was "the cyberculture's de rigueur power-networking retreat." *Wired,* that world's flagship magazine, shaper of its thoughts and plotter of its destiny, sent science-fiction writer Bruce Sterling to Burning Man in 1996, and he wrote a cover story that declared it "the New American Holiday." *Time* ran an article in '97 referring to the event as the "bonfire of the techies." That same year, *Wired*'s short-lived book publishing imprint issued the first book about Burning Man, a coffee-table picture book, because of what one of the book's editors, Brad Wieners, calls the "fairly organic" connection between the world of *Wired*'s staffers and audience and that of people likely to love Burning Man.

Burning Man, the meme spread, was a physical analog of the Internet, a place where every tendency, every subculture, and every idea in the world were all instantly, dazzlingly accessible. Mark Pesce, a virtual reality programming pioneer, saw the playa as the only real-world physical analog to virtual space. "I get to the playa in 1995, and I see an endless plain with pointy mountains impossibly far off—that's a virtual world. If you'd been to a computer role-playing game environment, that's what you'd see, everything built on it a human construction. It's cyberspace." If you worked or thought in computer culture, business, or new media and went to Burning Man in the midnineties, you'd run into a lot of friends. Pesce thinks '95 was "a tipping-point year, when people who were supposed to be there, were. In the core nucleus of the San Francisco rave/technology community, everyone went that year."

Erik Davis, an enthusiastic Burner and author of *TechGnosis,* a book on the links between cutting-edge computer technology and spirituality, notes that as *Mondo 2000* (a hipper-than-*Wired* magazine that defined the intersection between technofreaks and underground cultural weirdness) types got rich in the midnineties, "the cool, freaky hacker now making one hundred thousand dollars a year or more needed a place to still be a cool freak. Burning Man became a place for people to burn away the ungodly excess in a potlatch gift economy." Davis points to more and more elaborate theme camps and displays coming into Burning Man from Microsoft workers and dot-com millionaires in the mid- to late nineties.

Howard Rheingold, author of *Smart Mobs,* theorist of the influence of new computer technologies on community, and Burner, thinks the connection was simple and obvious: The computer industry tended to attract young, adventurous people into machinery, people with a yen for unusual events, art, and blowing shit up and in command of history's best means to tell their friends about cool things they had discovered.

John Law thinks that the whole Burning Man-is-like-the-Internet idea was basically a sales pitch to get more people in San Francisco—where the Internet and its possibilities ruled and every hipster in the-world was within reach of some life-changing stock-option jackpot—to buy tickets and show up. Burning Man, that brainchild of two lonely men, had in a decade achieved local celebrity in San Francisco.

By the midnineties, Chris Radcliffe recalls, "back in San Francisco if you dropped the hint you worked with Burning Man, Christ, you couldn't buy a beer. All of a sudden we had notoriety, and we weren't necessarily the kind of crew looking for notoriety. Lots of the things we did were only quasi legal, at best—crawling around on bridges and through sewers."

As a practical matter, Burning Man, lacking much of an ad budget, depended on viral marketing and word of mouth if they wanted more people to come. And Larry most definitely wanted people to come; he was thrilled to see that his early predictions that the Burning Man would serve as a beacon attracting people from all over were coming true. E-mail—still not a daily part of everyone's life in the midnineties—spread word of mouth more efficiently than any other human invention. Combined with Listservs, it made the creation of widespread intentional communities easy in an unprecedented way, and Burning Man's organizers began to understand and play to this.

Stuart Mangrum helped revise and fancy up the Burning Man Web site. In 1996, Burning Man organizers pulled off the first live Webcast from Black Rock City, after Andy Pector, an old friend of Michael Michael's now working for the event, talked Nevada Bell into running an ISDN line all the way to Bruno's hotel in Gerlach. "We sent a microwave signal to a tower at Bruno's, and from there through the ISDN line," Mangrum remembers. Who, really, would get much out of a choppy single-camera view of the Man burning—an event whose impact depends very much on direct experience? "We did it because it had to be done," Mangrum says. "Once you have a daily newspaper, where do you go after that? Webcasting was a big deal then, and it seemed huge and stupid and had a high *Fitzcarraldo* factor. Even if it didn't work, it was a heroic struggle, and if we failed, at least we could say we failed big."

The Internet/digerati angle guaranteed a more desirable class of attendees. Mangrum remembers that they started referring to the kind of press they hated as the "orgy in the gunsights" story, the kind emphasizing only freewheeling nudity and sex and gunplay. He and Larry became concerned with managing the message that the press presented to the world about Burning Man. "Yes, we are radical, but in a somewhat structured way," was the message Mangrum tried to convey. "Burning Man is not a complete meltdown. It's not a place to go shoot up the world and shoot out the lights. Beyond that, be free to draw your own conclusions."

Thus, their attitude toward the press became reactive—more concerned with what Burning Man did not want to be perceived as than what it really was, especially since what it "really was" was marvelously undefined. Burning Man wanted to control image then not so much for political reasons—their main concern today—but for recruitment considerations: What sort of people did they want showing up, and for what reasons? "People who just want to see naked women with mud smeared on their breasts, or people interested in building something, participating, being part of a social experiment?"

☼

Every year more people were bringing more art, more performance, more absurdity to the playa. Larry, not untypically in Burning Man's history, ran to the front of the parade to start leading. (For example, John Law strongly suspects that many of Larry's ideas about art and community and their place at Burning Man arose from William Binzen and his Desert Siteworks experience, and Binzen insists that's so. Larry denies this. Michael thinks both events cross-pollinated ideas in the early nineties. The historian can only throw up his hands.)

Larry realized that if different art pieces or performances at Burning Man were arranged spatially—say, in a line—and certain things were planned to happen in temporal succession, you could imagine them as linked in a narrative chain. The combination of those individual works of art would make for one big meta-artwork.

By 1996, this idea evolved into the official Burning Man "art theme." There is a fresh one every year, and it remains Larry's most visible contribution to the event. Not everything that goes on at the event is part of the theme, of course—that level of planning of thirty thousand people's expressions would be impossible. But nowadays Burning Man funds art as well as hosts it, and that funded art has to fit, in some way, with Larry's theme. (At least you need to write a proposal document that can convince Larry and LadyBee, Burning Man's art curator since 1999, that it fits into the theme.)

The theme in 1996 was the *Inferno*. The pressures of the event's growth, the growing tensions among the organizers, and the increasing rowdiness of the citizens were such that "I knew we were in for hell," Larry says now. "At some point we just decided, well, let's do it! Let's sublimate some and not deny it."

The big idea, the metaconcept that bound together the various little shows and displays and sculptures and fake news items in the *Black Rock Gazette,* was that Satan, through his ravenous megacorporation Helco, was out to buy Burning Man. A little blasphemy, some anticorporate comedy—it was a perfect mix for their audience, and the playing out and combustive fruition of the routine is still spoken of with awe by those who saw it.

Most people involved in Burning Man then consciously operated on an underground impulse that opposed "successful" mainstream culture; they were passionately devoted to loose coordination, no bureaucracy, the whole TAZ model. That all changed irreversibly with the growing population and growing attention from the media, the police, and the BLM. There were cops at Burning Man all the time now, though still not many, and they mostly wandered around bewildered and made almost no arrests.

The Helco pageant touched on anxieties that were real for those who made Burning Man happen, both in the organization and in the crowd: the corruption and selling out of their experience, their community, their reality, to large, sinister forces.

Given the demographics—it still took a fair amount of nerve and insider knowledge to hit the playa—mockery and derision and fear of corporate forces were both obvious and effective. Flash played Papa Satan, in hideously smooth and darkly gorgeous red face paint, horns, and a dapper red suit. He laid the hard sell on Larry. Think of what Burning Man could accomplish with some serious corporate money behind it! Why, we could have tram rides taking everyone from theme camp to theme camp! The Man could fall and be raised again every hour on the hour! It could be the greatest show on Earth, Heaven, or Hell.

Larry was hesitant, doubtful. Burning Man was supposed to belong to everyone who inhabited it. In itself it was nothing but a statue and a fire. The city, its growing wonders—why, they couldn't be bought, couldn't be designed—imprisoned—in any corporate ledger. The crowds watching the Last Temptation of Larry Harvey shouted encouragement toward his best nature, his most independent, most fuck-the-corporations-and-their-commodification-of-culture side. Don't do it, Larry!

Oh, in the end he couldn't. He just couldn't. "I—Burning Man is *you,* it is not for sale. I cannot sell it." Depart, ye cursed! Papa Satan is-denied, defeated, dragged back to his hellish corporate tower. The-Helco Tower stood all weekend anchoring the Helco Mall, an elaborate construction of mock corporate signage and structures—

predictable comedy, perhaps, but elaborately and ferociously executed. "Caca Bell," "Submit," "Starfucks." A preacher harangued from a storefront church: Some of you out there are sinners against the gods of Burning Man. Some of you are *not creative*. Some of you are *not spontaneous*. Sexy dominatrices dragged unwitting passersby through the Satanic strip mall.

Kal Spelletich of the Seemen—a machine-art troupe, a spin-off of sorts from SRL—had supervised the building of the mall. He and his crew, including fellow roboticist Christian Ristow, who later ran RoboChrist Industries in Los Angeles, managed its methodical, loud, and messy destruction in the pageant Saturday night, bringing the drama of Helco to one maelstrom of a denouement. Ristow's pet machine, the Subjugator, which he operated via a remote control panel, all crushing treads and man-sized extending clamping metal jaws and fire-spit, led the orgy of crushing, rending, wrecking, and arson that sent the Helco Mall back to the lake of fire from which it arose.

Burning Man had rejected Satan's blandishments, run riot through his shopping center, but still his corporate HQ stood impassively, untroubled by the annihilation of its subsidiaries. Mere write-offs, nothing to unduly affect the balance sheet or the stock price. Its core position was solid there at the heart of Black Rock City, as tall as the Burning Man himself.

Ah, but not for long. John Law, Western hero in the long white coat, put out his cheroot and leaped to duty, fires vibrating all around him. He clambered up the side of Helco Tower, all the way to the top, more than forty feet up. With a lit road flare in his free hand, he detonated a giant powder bomb Kimric Smythe had wired at the top, pulled a cord that dumped a bucket full of gasoline placed halfway down, then knocked over another gas bucket up there on the top.

The tower was fat with wood scraps and plastic jugs of gasoline. It instantly roared into a forty-foot flare of orange-white flame. One second passed—the crowds' eyes couldn't have been shoved back in their heads with a hammer, Jesus, that guy was *still up there*—maybe a little more than one second (a true showman knows how to hold the spot-

light exactly long enough), then John Law threw his body back and off
the tower and into the atmosphere almost solid with ashes and heat and
grabbed a handle attached to a zip line and slid at a harrowing angle
down and away and crashed through a neon sign ordering everyone
to CONSUME and hit the ground. Vanessa was waiting with a fire extinguisher, in case he was ablaze, but John Law knew how to do all the
things you should never try at home without killing himself or others.

The people of Black Rock City were gasping and shouting and
jumping, and until dawn it was all mad release and sudden love and
destroying and reinventing human civilization from scratch with
nothing but wood scrap and fire. Hell was burning all around them.
Satan was told to fuck off with radical bravado.

Events on the ground in 1996 were ugly for those who had to feel
responsible for everyone's health and safety. I can assure you that those
of us who merely attended and had the luxury of not having to care
about the hows and whys had what could fairly be called the most
amazing time of our life. One Burning Man artist wonders if you could
even say you had ever experienced *Burning Man* if you weren't there in
1996. The sense that *everything is permitted* and *we are immortal* has never
pulsed through these veins more purely, more madly. I miss it still.

One Burning Man artist remembers that 1996 "was clearly not a
sustainable event. That was an apocalyptic event. Things were going
wrong. It felt like we were at war. But there was still this curious sense
that there was something very important going on—that it was *imper-
ative* that we, together, create this thing. Something was at stake. A lot
of people had come to that collective decision and were self-organizing around an unstable common goal. The public was beginning to
notice. The forces of chaos had also noticed, and those forces collided
in a very compelling and scary way."

On the inside, oh, it was ugly. Larry recalls hearing rumors of a
brewing Ranger revolt, and being warned that for his own safety he
might want to just leave the playa. John Law says Larry tried to rush
the execution of the Helco show to satisfy the waiting crowd before

the crew had fully worked out all their safety plans. (Larry recalls his intent as just trying to find out what was going on, not encouraging reckless speed.) Chris Radcliffe remembers choking Larry when he tried to suggest John Law bore responsibility for Michael Furey's death, forcing Larry to drink absinthe with him, and then choking him again. (Not everyone involved in these stories remembers them the same way, or at all.)

Larry recalls the moment when he realized how the fault lines in the Temple of the Three Guys would likely resettle their relationship. After Furey's death and people's reaction to it, after all the fights over issues big and small he and John Law had that week, he knew the Temple could not stand in its current shape. In the midst of Larry's confusion and despair, Michael Michael visited him in his trailer.

"Are you with me, Michael?" Larry asked.

"I'm with you," Michael said. After he left, Larry cried.

Despite the internal drama, life went on as abnormal in Black Rock City, most citizens blissfully oblivious to the many medevacs, freakouts, and injuries.

It's shortly after sunset, and I'm hanging out in Plundertown, home of the block-long Mousetrap and other amusements, watching the flaming bowling alley. Nude body-painted ladies glowing, men on stilts with five-foot-tall hats, and unidentifiable figures wearing giant animal masks all mill about the lane, some waiting their turn to bowl, others just surveying the scene.

We're bowling on the moon, I think to myself, the flat plane of cracked alkali bordered only by black night and the unsullied glitter of the Milky Way staring indulgently from above. The ball is coated in alcohol and ignited, and the bowler sets it spinning pretty quickly down the makeshift lane. The ball spits green, white, and red flame as it rolls, scatters the pins, and hits the backdrop, where the fire burns itself out. Stray flaming puddles trail behind it down the lane. The crowd laughs, hoots, cheers at each roll of the torched ball. A throbbing techno beat in the far distance makes feet tap involuntarily.

A shirtless young man swaggers forward for his turn at the ball. The lane attendant grabs the can of alcohol that gets poured on the ball, providing the fuel for its fiery sheath. But what comes out is fire itself, already alive in the can, probably from a spark that danced unnoticed up the spout of liquid last time it was poured. The blaze spills and spreads over the young man.

Fire rushing down his right arm, across his torso, he drops the ball, dashes back five quick feet, and tosses himself to the dusty ground, rolling frantically. Right then—but with no apparent connection other than the synchronicity of doom—a transformer sparks with a crack like a gun's report nearby, and someone standing near it falls backward, startled. An acrid ozone scent cuts through the smoky pungency of dozens of distant fires. A thin, pale young woman in a cat-ear cap sways momentarily, shocked by the noise, by the man on fire. She collapses. Her friends pounce, drag her away for resuscitation. The crowd is tense, abuzz with panicky whispers. *Is he...? Is she...? What happened...?* But only for a moment. A line of bowlers still await their turn.

In the background, a car—fully on fire—is rolling slowly along, being towed away somewhere where it might pose less danger to the rest of the community. Or not.

John Law and Chris Campbell were a little worried about the effect the Helco/*Inferno* theme might have on people's moods. So, in order to diffuse some of that dark energy and turn it to whimsy, they installed amid the Man's neon a smiley face, and didn't tell anyone else. They set it up on a timer to flash on occasion, late at night.

Most of the seeming chaos, the aggro roving mobs whooping and setting fires, was not, really, dangerous or mean-spirited. It was a release of energy, a dropping of inhibitions, a short vacation to an experiential edge by people who really did not want to hurt themselves or others and, accordingly, mostly, did not.

But things turned genuinely, not just playfully, horrific late Sunday night—early Monday morning really—when a seemingly drugged-out man driving recklessly cruised out near the rave camp and drove over a tent—a tent with two sleeping people in it. He then crashed the car into another vehicle, spilling scalding radiator fluid all over a woman in another tent.

Joe Fenton, called to the scene as a Ranger, remembers that the sheriffs held off on calling a medevac until they'd seen the injuries. "Their brains were in the dust," Fenton recalls. "The burned woman was screaming at the top of her lungs the whole time" waiting for the medevac to arrive. The first chopper only had room for the two head injuries, so she continued screaming, waiting for another one. "Some of her raver friends sat fifteen feet away from her and played drums" in an impromptu healing ritual, Fenton says. "It didn't help."

All three of the wounded lived, although one man had permanent injuries. He received a payment through Burning Man's insurance. The driver was arrested.

It's smoky dawn after the Man was gone in '96, and my night is still kicking. Someone's sound system is blasting Seal's "Crazy" louder than nature—who the hell knew why, but after the tenth repetition it turned from maddening to funny. We're stealing other people's camp-fires by gingerly sliding whatever's burning onto a slab of plywood and dashing off, dodging the car lights arcing in every direction. Pairs of lovers stand around the fire, propping each other up. Like most times you push on through straight to a new day, it was worth every nerve-stretched moment.

John Law staggers to the heaps of stolen fire we are laughing around to talk to some of his old friends. It's the first time I'm ever in his presence. His hair is a mat of playa dust, his eyes deep and haunted, and his hands are quivering near the radio on his belt. "I hope you enjoyed this," John Law tells us, "'cause it ain't ever happening again."

Chapter Five

THE FALL OF THE TEMPLE
OF THE THREE GUYS

The Man burned again. He always does. He did it, though, without John Law's help.

Money was short after 1996, and no one quite knew why. Burning Man had slowly become a large-cash-flow organization. With at least eight thousand people on-site in '96 and a ticket price of $40, theoretically the organizers should have been sitting on around $300,000.

But there was no official budgeting process, no central comptroller. A gate-worker in those days remembers that Michael Michael would just drive by sometimes, count the money, and take whatever pile he thought needed to be squirreled away someplace safer than the lone trailer off the Twelve-mile playa entrance, or had to be spent on gas or food or whatever need came up. Then, an hour later, John Law would come by and do the same thing. If there was money and something the Burning Man organization needed to spend it on, one of them would usually take care of it, without necessarily asking, or even telling, anyone else.

Stories about how Burning Man handled money up until '96 are delightful in their way, myths of lost innocence and the strange mystery of how you can become rich without even trying, when other people love your dream so much they are willing to pay for it: the magic of a pure, free capitalism. We're talking about the gross, not the net, of course. With Burning Man, somehow, there is almost never a net. All through Burning Man's history its leaders have managed, I am told, to spend almost everything they get, no matter how much that-is. Michael Michael once described Burning Man to me, with a balance of good humor and irritation, as "a machine for burning money."

The cash they were accumulating seemed like a comic fantasy to them at first. Larry remembers Vanessa writhing around nude like a playful little girl in a huge pile of bills in John Law's tent. *Look, look at this ridiculous shit we have!* Some people could, with no cognitive dissonance and quiet pride, see the money as a sign that they have Done Good. People loved what they were doing, and the people were rewarding them. There wasn't really anyone in the burgeoning Burning Man organization who could openly embrace the notion that it was OK to accumulate lucre. From the beginning, the event was rooted in the ideology and practice of volunteerism and community. It was not intended to be about piling up cash, and the underground impulse from which it arose has always been uncomfortable with money, a fact that has made the Burning Man organization seem a little defensive about the reality that they are selling a service, regardless of their motives and their lofty goals regarding community.

They began to worry about the treasures they were collecting onsite for practical as well as ideological reasons. (To be fair, ideological worries about the money gathering in the Burning Man organization were far more common among the citizens than among the organizers themselves.) Thefts, mostly by locals, had begun to plague Black Rock City. Larcenous folk began to notice that many thousands of people, some of them with very nice bicycles and generators, were gathering on the playa right before Labor Day every year, and these people were so naive and in love with their little intentional community that none of them ever locked anything up.

Sure, whoever was at the trailer where they collected money and tickets had weapons. One early video documentarian captured William Abernathy out there with his rifle and asked an obvious question: "Is that loaded?" With strained patience, as if talking to a slow child, Abernathy replied, "Of course. If it weren't loaded it would just be a *stick.*" John Law instructed the gatekeepers to keep their eyes peeled for glints on the surrounding mountains—telltale signs they were in someone's scope sights.

They knew the money had to go somewhere more secure. In '96, they dug a hole in the playa with a backhoe and submerged an old water heater. They thrust a pipe into the water heater, left the other end of the pipe flush with the playa surface, and erected John Law's tent over it, with a hole cut in the bottom over the pipe. Daily, bagged wads of cash were shoved down the pipe.

Andy Pector was in charge of the gate. He was told to put the currency, in set bundles, into little plastic food Baggies. He was not told it was being placed beneath the water table. More concerned with compact stacking than waterproofing, he cut the corners off the bags to squeeze out air pockets.

As a result, once unearthed, the tens of thousands of dollars in currency were soaked. Vanessa had to deposit soggy mounds of mushy paper into a safe-deposit box in Reno. The cash had to be literally laundered—or dried at least—at John Law's house, Michael remembers.

Black Rock City 1996 had disappeared—mostly. The staff had retreated back to San Francisco, except for John Law and a small skeleton crew—he credits Chicken John, Chris DeMonterey, Vanessa, and one or two other hardy souls—who spent weeks bent-backed, picking up debris over the city's multimile footprint, tidying in the aftermath of the world's wildest party. When his crew members needed food, or rent money for their apartments back in the city, or another Dumpster, Law would pay for it with Burning Man money.

Back in the city, dark imprecations flowed about John Law's management style, and what's he doing out there, and why are we in debt? Many of the rumblings came from Flash, one of Larry's oldest friends and the former Black Rock City taco and burger hawker, the only man in the Burning Man community born to play the role of Papa Satan, the evil charmer.

Flash, born Michael Hopkins, is an intense, wiry man, with a body that's lived-in but still vital. He is usually slightly hunched and grinning, his beard usually long and wild and mostly gray, and he seems to glide through life with an air of this-is-all-so-much-fun-it's-making-me-tired, but-what-the-hell? When he focuses his attention, he's a million percent there, more with you, more amused by you, than any indulgent parent or adoring lover could ever be, his mouth wide open in anticipation of your next word. He punctuates his own comic tales—he's a raconteur of startling energy and imagination—with a wheezing, crying laughter that quickly ratchets beyond the range of human hearing.

Flash met Larry long before Burning Man. He came from the world of old New England money and had dated Ellen Into's daughter—Whittaker Chambers's granddaughter—for many years. On a mother-daughter double date on one of his first visits to San Francisco, where Ellen had already been living, he met Larry Harvey. "He looked like the character from the Dutch Boy Paint label," Flash remembers. A strange friendship was born. "Instantly, I knew, I like this kid! I liked him better than the ladies!" Flash's voice is a ham actor's, but still marvelously convincing—he *sells* every sentence, pushing whatever emotion he thinks is appropriate, from exuberance to amazement to weariness.

Flash ended up moving to San Francisco, and he started watching out for his new buddy. Flash skated for around a decade in state-sponsored vocational rehab, making sure that he never quite managed to land a job in any of the many areas they tried to rehabilitate him for. He informally launched what he calls "the Flash School of Economics," dedicated to encouraging his friends to similarly try to squeeze as much cash and training from the state as possible without actually falling into the trap of employment.

Larry was doing landscaping work for an orphanage in the late eighties. "He'd call me up with a blow by blow," Flash remembers. "'They're gonna make me use a chain saw.' *Chain saw?* 'They're gonna make me climb a tree.' Climb a *tree* with a *chain saw?* Do you know how fucking dangerous that could be? You could ruin your back! One day he came home cheering: 'I ruined it! I ruined it!' Great, great!"

In the end, his pupil disappointed him, refusing to milk rehab for long. Larry did get some training on the state's dime in video camera operation at the beginning of the desert-era Burning Man, in order to document his own ritual. He told his caseworker about how he and his friends would take this wooden giant to the desert, the remotest place you could possibly imagine, and burn it. And *that* was what he intended to do with his life. "She really felt sorry for me," Larry remembers. "It was her job to help people along in life, and after all this effort she'd expended, this poor fool, me, used their resources to do this insane thing. I always wanted to run into her so she'd know… not to prove anything but to say, 'See, it wasn't in vain; you did a good job with me.'"

Flash made sure he stuck around for his old pal's party, and started selling beer, tacos, and hot dogs. Whatever problems the organization-had with money or its disappearance, Flash could afford not to care—"I had my concessions. I was the only one who made money every single time."

Their characters could not be more different, but there's clearly a strange, almost brotherly link between the shy, stammering intellectual and the vivacious, wild adventurer. To this day, Flash gets away with things at Burning Man no one else could—including reviving an on-the-sly burrito concession, dragging in for free everyone who caravans with him, even picking fights with workers in the Burning Man staff commissary. And Flash cannot say enough good things about Larry. They are both surviving in weird little niches. Like all people who don't want to work for others, Flash says, he finds himself working twenty-four hours a day. He hustles, builds giant installation art all over the globe, and bartends freelance, usually with a crew of gorgeous, cruel Amazonian sidekicks.

He owns some nice properties and tells me I should never believe you need a lot of money to buy real estate. You just have to eschew the obvious things like, say, using a *real estate agent* (a phrase he utters with contempt). He lives part-time on hundreds of acres in rural Placerville, out east of Sacramento. On the long dirt road past the gate to his house, there's a giant mermaid statue standing sentry beside a lake. He originally bought this parcel hoping to store horses, but instead, he mock-complains, it has become a giant parking lot for all his friends' aging, tricked-out, and troubled vehicles. He is host to a constantly shifting bunch of friends on hard times, friends who just want to hang out, and, all summer long, big Burning Man art projects that need a lot of space to construct. This all makes his spread look (and feel) more like Black Rock City than anywhere else I've been.

It's summer 2003, and we're sitting in a lovely cove under some shade trees in front of the house he built himself, a water mister keeping us cool in the summer dusk. The inner altars and decorations for the giant temple on which the Man will stand this year are under construction nearby, as is the giant white-whale art bus and the Eyes of Gawd—giant electroluminescent-wire eyes floating in the air on a delicate metal frame. Flash's property is littered with trailers, always ready to extend overnight hospitality to any member of the extended family, most of them linked, somehow, to Burning Man.

Flash and I are talking about what happened after Burning Man '96. Larry hurt when he saw his Burning Man team falling apart back in '96, and Flash didn't like to see his buddy hurting. "You ever see Larry when he's really, really mad? It's funny. He just doesn't know what to do. He gets so frustrated, he wants to kill. But, ah, he's opposed to killing. Whereas for me, when I want to kill, a little blood will do." Larry believes in forgiveness, Flash tells me, and tolerates lowlifes that Flash just will not abide. "I don't understand that kind of thing. I understand vengeance and disdain."

Flash had developed a well-earned reputation as Larry's bulldog. If Larry had a problem, Flash would take care of it—by any means necessary. When he caught wind that John Law had become a problem for Larry, Flash, by most accounts, began spreading accusations that Law had misappropriated Burning Man funds, that he had used them to supply wicked and destructive drugs to his crew, and was himself a dangerous and out-of-control drug user. (These rumors, Law says, were not true.)

While John Law knows Flash was leading the attack publicly, he still blamed Larry. Law is convinced that Larry operated like an underground Machiavelli, telling Flash bad things about him in an effort to deliberately enrage Flash enough to go into attack mode. Law believed that Larry wanted to drive him out of the community and destroy any influence he might have over Burning Man's future—or lack of future.

Because as far as John was concerned, their experiment in ordered anarchy was over. It had gotten too big, and they could no longer rely on the essential good sense of the participants to avoid deaths or hideous injuries. Law had no interest in helping impose the increasing controls and rules they'd need to safely manage an event of the size and nature Burning Man had grown to.

Larry knows what Law thought but insists that Flash was acting according to his own nature and on his own recognizance. "Ugly things were said, but I didn't say them," says Larry. He still criticizes what he saw as Law's easygoing and unmanaged spending of Burning Man money on his crew. But he paints it not as dishonesty but merely as lack of respect for protocol or the interests of the Burning Man organization as a whole. But the invective, the accusations, the phone calls threatening to burn down Law's house? "That was Flash. Watch him operate and see he doesn't need any encouragement. I will admit some responsibility. I was close to him, and I'd poured out my heart to him on what I'd been through. It was in many ways the worst thing I'd ever been through. But I'm not responsible for what he did with that [information], and I never told him to do it."

As people back in San Francisco were wondering why Burning Man didn't have as much money on hand as they'd hoped after 1996 (the project was, in fact, in debt), John Law was still in the desert, cleaning up after them. "For them to judge me on anything rankles me to this day," Law says. "Implications about the money being all gone—it was a setup. I'm sitting in a mud puddle for three weeks cleaning shit up and that's what I get when I get back."

Law's last appearance at anything related to Burning Man was at a group meeting of Burning Man workers after his return from the playa that year. Nearly everyone I spoke to who was there has a slightly different memory of what happened, but Larry remembers that Law was sitting at his immediate right and that Larry, chairing the meeting, began taking comments and assessments of the state of-the Man from his left and went around the table. This left Law to defend himself last. Imprecations on his judgment and handling of money abounded.

By the time it was Vanessa's turn, on John's right, she slammed a tambourine on the table and loudly excoriated everyone over how unfair and absurd it was that John Law's reputation was being traduced. Law, by most accounts, marched out, saying nothing, finished, not interested in defending himself, with Flash yelling angry accusations. "That was it," Larry remembers. "That's how he left—with curses at his back."

John Law would have liked Burning Man to lay itself to an earned and glory-ridden rest, but he did not, he says, want to be the man who killed it, not so as long as others whom he respected or cared about were dedicated to its continuing. While the breakup with Burning Man left deep wounds—and at least temporarily strained his friendships with many who chose to stay involved—Law did, and does, recognize the event's continued value to many people, although he no longer wishes to have anything to do with it. A new legal entity called Paper Man was created to hold the copyright of the name and image of Burning Man, still the property of the original three guys. The operational control, though, shifted to a new limited liability corporation (LLC) Larry put together.

Law is still leery about discussing Burning Man, and the old wounds clearly still smart. He perceives a cultish devotion to Burning Man on the part of thousands of acolytes and tells me you can expect proverbial snakes in the mail if you're publicly perceived as Objectively Anti–Burning Man.

When you talk about Burning Man's history with Larry Harvey or John Law, inevitably the subject of the other man comes up, and it's not pleasant when it does. John Law is willing to call Larry evil and imputes the most uncharitable possible motives to his actions, backed up with the observation that he *knows* the man and worked with him for so long that he saw Larry's true self. He claims that Larry's charm and apparent good intentions are merely camouflage.

Larry could afford to be generous to Law's memory, but he isn't really. He can't resist jabbing at Law, just like he jabbed back then. In

Larry's telling, the notion of an *arts festival* was anathema to tough-guy John Law. Larry says, "Whenever the word *art* came out of his mouth, it was appended to the word *fag*.

"In the clash of personalities, he would suspect me, and I would mock him. I have to stop myself from mocking paranoia, and when it comes to hipdom, I don't even stop myself. I just mock it. That made it worse, I'm sure, but I don't know what would have made it better."

Larry limns their conflict as one of his openness and inclusion versus Law's "hipdom." In Larry's eyes, Law wanted Burning Man to remain a little secret of the Cool Kids Club. For his own part, Larry says that he "from the beginning hated the hipster attitude of keeping out the uncool people. My obsession was inclusion. That was, for me, a redemption: to make a society that everyone could come into. It was an antidote to the alienation I grew up with."

I have spent some time with John Law in his post–Burning Man life, on various adventures, from running a haunted house in Los Angeles to dodging zipping and raining fireworks in Mexico, and I disagree with Larry's perception of John's motives (as I also disagree with Law's perception of Larry's). Law's position on Burning Man and his reasons for leaving—putting aside for a moment his bitter disillusionment with his old partner—is that he loved putting on Burning Man because it was a specific type of experience. And despite his love for the wild, reckless gesture, he wanted to pull off grand stunts like Burning Man in a way that no one got hurt. All his fellow Cacophonists have stories of John Law doing everything he could, within the context of the outré things they did, to ensure everyone got out unscathed. That was becoming impossible with Burning Man. He saw what would have to be done—things that in fact *have* been done— to ensure that a constantly growing Burning Man could survive, to adjust to the changes required when two hundred friends and comrades become eight thousand, and then many more, strangers. And he didn't want to have anything to do with such strictures. He thought encouraging more growth for Burning Man was irresponsible, both to what was valuable about the experience and to the desert.

And, not to put too fine a point on it, Law couldn't stand working with Larry any longer. Law was insulted and hurt when, during an argument at a coffeeshop among the Three Guys, Larry told the other two that Burning Man would have gotten where it was with or without them. Law once overheard Larry promising someone who needed work done on an event that Larry would have "some of our artists" take care of something. Law heard this and took it as a signal that Larry was beginning to see the entire movement arising around Burning Man as a property of *his*. "The event became a direct extension of Harvey's ego, and if you see it as anything different, you don't know him," Law says. "Taking all that energy, power, and art and funneling it through and aggrandizing an empty central symbol is monstrous. I started finding it disturbing around '94, when I realized how important the symbol was to Larry."

Still, it took the crises of '96 to finally impress upon him that he needed to just walk away. He was transfixed until then by "genuine interest in the bizarrity of what was happening. It was just astonishing. People were starting to do fascinating things in big ways." Steve Mobia remembers one night at Burning Man '94 when John Law beatifically laid his head on Mobia's shoulder, saying, as if confessing, how genuinely blissed out he was by the possibilities they were creating, how he was "transported by the vision of the thing actually beginning to happen."

Law, a serious and often worried man despite his seemingly devil-may-care adventures, felt weighted down with the burden of bringing other people into the Burning Man experience: "I felt like I couldn't leave because something bad would happen and I'd be responsible. And also because I'm human and people were kissing my ass a lot and treating me like some kind of rock star, and that, frankly, is a drug. A dangerous drug, but it has its appeal.

"We were totally into role-playing in Cacophony, making up characters," recalls Law. (He uses a variety of alter egos in his culture-hacking activities, but John Law, believe it or not, is his actual given name.) "Michael made up Danger Ranger, which he then became, I guess. Larry made up the character of the Man in the Hat. My character was running around covered in mud with a twelve-gauge. I could have made a life out of that. Making characters was part of the appeal, but then people we didn't know started taking it seriously."

In his zine, *Twisted Times,* Stuart Mangrum, Burning Man's press relations maven from 1993 to 1996, wrote a very perceptive analysis of the state of the Burning Man Project in the wake of 1996. He wrote this after deciding not to work for Burning Man any longer.

> Many of the misconceptions surrounding the event spring from Larry's own dueling views about what it really means. On the one hand, he can describe it in highly spiritual terms, likening it to the ancient mystery cults where sensory dislocation and communal exertion bred personal epiphanies and a direct experience of the divine. On the other hand, he takes great pains to point out that Burning Man is not a religion: that it has no priests and no dogma, and that each individual is free to interpret the experience as he or she sees fit. On a third track, he has been known to shelf the spiritual angle entirely and paint the event as strictly an arts festival and an experiment in temporary community…The conflict speaks of an internal struggle he has yet to resolve in his own mind. Larry wants history to remember him, and religions last longer than art festivals; but prophets tend to lead short, nasty lives. The empty-center position, the notion that Burning Man is only as spiritual as you make it, represents an uneasy compromise between the extremes of religion and art: more than a party, less than a faith. It suggests that the event's organizers are morally superior to showmen, but relieves them of the odious responsibilities of priesthood.

This tension that Mangrum noted in 1996 has never been resolved, and it gives a curious greased-pig quality to attempts to grasp the meaning of Burning Man.

He does roundly slap those who would call Burning Man a cult: "Though Burning Man has many of the trappings of pre-Christian religion—idolatry, flaming sacrifice, trance dancing—it is no more a system of faith than the Rose Parade."

Mangrum went on to blame his own PR apparatus, which was operating in a business-growth model, for bringing out too many people who were perhaps not up to the responsibilities of life in a mostly unpoliced community where all sorts of crazed behavior was implicitly encouraged.

Mangrum is also the only close working member of the inner circles of Burning Man who has publicly written his assessment of Larry Harvey:

> Larry is intelligent, quick-witted, and a near-total stranger to the work ethic; a charming man who has known the poverty of labor and aspires to never work another honest day in his life. In another era he might have sold patent medicine and done pretty well at it, only occasionally winding up in the tar and feathers…Drunk one New Year's Eve, sick of hearing about 'the desert' and 'out there,' I accused him of confusing obsession with genius. It was probably the cruelest thing I've ever said to him, but I'll stand by it. Larry really wants to be a genius, and maybe he deserves to be, but passion and rhetoric are no substitute for substance. He happened onto a Big Idea, and he's riding it for all he's worth, but he doesn't own the idea any more than a surfer owns a wave.

After the Temple of the Three Guys crumbled, Larry created a new, larger LLC to operate the event. Because so much money had been lost, the notion of starting over as a nonprofit made a certain sense. But the laws governing nonprofits demand a board of directors made up of people who are not involved in the day-to-day activities of running the company—disinterested overseers who can make sure the entity stays true to its mandate. For a group that saw themselves as hands-on activists with a deeply personal stake in both making Burning Man happen and experiencing it, that just wouldn't do. "Who were to be these disinterested benefactors who would make the final decisions but not do any work?" Larry wonders.

There were dozens of people doing important work to make Burning Man happen by then, but the first board consisted of Larry, Michael, Crimson Rose (a fire artist who first arrived in '91 and had been coordinating the actual burn of the Man and the invited stage entertainment), Will Roger (a former photography professor, Crimson's boyfriend and occasional fire performance partner, who took on John Law's responsibilities in transportation and site management), Joegh Bullock (a San Francisco event promoter), Harley Bierman (now Dubois, a Cacophonist attending since '91 who had begun coordinating theme camps), Andy Pector (an old friend of Michael's who had become a general business wrangler for the event), Carole Morrell (their lawyer), and Marian Goodell (then a Web designer, also then dating Larry—she took up media and government relations).

They launched this LLC with an idea they thought clever and in keeping with Burning Man philosophy: Just as Black Rock City was temporary, so would be their company; it would dissolve and re-form every year. This drove Andy Pector, who was handling their business negotiations, crazy. It made them seem flaky and unreliable. By 1999, he, Bullock, and Morrell had dropped out for various reasons, and a permanent six-person LLC was formed: Larry, Michael, Crimson Rose, Will Roger, Harley Dubois, and Marian Goodell.

Going into 1997, Larry knew the anarchistic "just come out here and do what thou wilt" model had to change if his ritual were to survive. Unbridled liberty and fire arts were no longer going to be the main selling points. "We believed it was a community. We knew people were feeling it to be such. But there wasn't a social framework" to fully shape Burning Man around that idea. "We decided to build a vessel to contain a community. We realized we had to create a real city. If you look at the [Burning Man] newsletter in '97, it's one big propaganda sheet for community. That's when the litany began—community, community, community. People grabbed onto it."

Because of the chaos, accidents, medevacs, and mess of '96 (Law and his tiny crew had done their best, but there are limits to what five or so people can do to clean up after eight thousand people spread over miles), they didn't even want to bother trying to work with the BLM and Pershing officials for permits on the Black Rock. They wanted private land. Andy Pector led them to it.

Pector is a squat, heavy, bearded, terribly friendly man who was running a successful industrial glass supplies business. He was old friends and occasional housemates with Michael Michael, and was the first person to bring a motor home to Burning Man, in 1991, inadvertently triggering an ongoing debate in Burner communities over what is or isn't proper Burning Man behavior. (Any shelter more solid and industrial than a tepee, a yurt, or a Bedouin tent can be derided as too bourgeois-yuppie-soft-spectatorish by the Burnier-than-thou mentality.)

Burning Man was a new world for Andy, and he loved it and treasured his part in it. He is the only person I've run into in the Burning Man saga who had good words to say for everyone else involved, even those with whom he'd been engaged in bitter conflicts in the past. Andy painted a huge Burning Man image on the back of his bus, which he used to make sales calls across the country.

Andy had already been in business with local landowner John Casey, owner of the Fly Ranch, home to Fly Hot Springs. The Burning Man crowds invading Fly had gotten so large by the midnineties that the sheriff began patrolling the private property. So in '95, Pector, playing on his own role as a fellow landowner (both men had some holdings in Montana) and not mentioning Burning Man, called Casey and rented use of Fly Ranch for the week of Burning Man for-$200.

Andy let his Burning Man friends cavort and soak freely in the springs, and Casey found out. Casey told Andy a rental for him *and his friends* for next year would run $7,500. Casey also owned some poorly tended property near a small playa in the Hualapai Valley, near the Black Rock Playa, land so obscure that it didn't even have a name on the map. That playa came to be known as "the Hualapai" in Burning

Man lore. Andy talked to Casey about Burning Man using that playa to build their city in '97.

Larry remembers Casey with a bemused almost-fondness. "He had vast holdings everywhere. He was land mad—Dickens could have written such a portrait of him. Dickens was fascinated by people absorbed, deformed by their passions, and Casey's passion was owning the land. He was famous for starving his cattle. And in one story, which I believe is substantially true, a group of half-frozen Laotians was found on one of his spreads. He treated them like he did cattle. He was in long-running feuds with the BLM over the way he treated his cattle." Rumor has it the BLM would sometimes have to airlift food to Casey's neglected cattle lest they die. "But Casey hated the federal government, hated bureaucracy, and the BLM had come to regard him as a thorn in their side because he ignored their rules. I believe John Casey fancied the idea of irritating the federal government by letting us use his land."

Casey left the negotiations up to his niece, Annie Westerbeke, and her husband, Van. The exact capacity in which Annie acted as agent to her uncle was never precisely defined, Larry recalls; John Casey was notorious for not signing documents unless leaned on by his lawyers. When negotiations with Washoe County, in which the land was located and which quickly became very interested in regulating Burning Man, became heated, the county officials wanted to know precisely who was in charge of what when it came to Hualapai. Casey proffered a gnomic note asserting only that his niece was free, white, and over twenty-one.

The Burning Man team first took Annie and Van to be simple country people. Annie would slobber over them—oh, she just *loved* artists—and she'd fantasize about year-round retreats on Hualapai and about really making herself and Van a permanent part of the Burning Man family. Waves of Burning Man volunteers hit the Casey property edging Hualapai all summer, and many of them stayed for the duration. They revitalized a well, installed solar generators, and, most ridiculously, had to drag out dozens of dead cows.

Casey's neglected cattle had roamed into a ranch house, the only shelter on the property, seeking shade, and died there, presumably from lack of water or food. "The house was filled with beasts that had gone to their reward," Larry remembers. "And John Casey wasn't used to giving man nor beast much of a reward."

Full corpses and bones littered the whole house, including the basement. They had been rotting for years. Tony Perez, aka Coyote, a San Francisco musician and bartender who later became supervisor of Burning Man's clean-up operation, was one of the volunteers spending his summer vacation hauling cow carcasses on the Casey spread. "We had the bright idea to turn the existing structures into housing for medical and cops during the event, so I grabbed a shovel," says Perez. "The house had no windows or doors, and the only thing in it for the last twenty years was the cows. Before they died, they were shitting all over the house, so there was three feet of cow shit everywhere, even squeezed into the closets.

"Every time you pulled a wall panel out, you'd find this whole ecosystem of snakes eating birds, rats' nests—we started worrying about hantavirus. One dead cow in the bedroom had shriveled to rawhide and bones and was light enough to carry, but when we used shovels to spatula it off the floor, floorboards came up with him. We moved him with bandannas over our mouths. We ended up renting trailers anyway. We never did get to use the house."

With some typical Burning Man magic, they transmuted the decay to art; sculptor Michael Christian used the cow bones to construct an arch that spanned the entrance to Burning Man that year. Then those bones were attached to the chassis of a moving sculpture in 1999 by Flash and his partner, Dana Albany, to make a roving Bone Tree. Reduce, reuse, recycle.

Van and Annie were freaking everyone out with erratic mood swings, and the Burning Man crew began to think that Annie might be screwing with them for her own benefit. She refused, for example, to ever settle on exactly what she expected from Burning Man as payment for using the land, even while the workers sweated and strained and dug through decades of cow shit and death to rehabilitate her uncle's property for free. Van—"a Haystack Calhoun–type wild mountain man" as Larry remembers—skeeved out Burning Man's female volunteers by approaching them every morning insisting that he "needed a hug to get his engine running!"

Annie put off on settling the deal for the land until just days before Burning Man was to start. Their climactic negotiating session, Andy Pector remembers, was in a Thai restaurant in Reno. Annie was pressuring Andy for a huge lump sum, more money than they had. Andy begged her to take a percentage based on tickets sold. She was obdurate.

Until Andy—a very friendly man, always ready to use Burning Man as a conversational gambit with any lovely young woman—asked a couple of high school girls who'd wandered into the restaurant if they were going to Burning Man. The girls lit up and went on about how, my God, of course they knew about Burning Man, and they wished they could go but they were only in high school and still didn't have their own cars but everyone they knew was going and it was going to be so cool and so huge, they heard hundreds of thousands of the crème de la cool were trekking across the wastes of Nevada…As they walked back out to the parking lot, Annie coolly floated the good news to Andy: On further thought, she could be a mensch and settle for a portion per ticket.

There were further gothic complications in the relationship with the Westerbekes. In order for Larry to exorcise them from his soul, he and Marian dressed like them—Larry as Annie, Marian as Van—for a Halloween party at P. Segal's: They had been instructed to come as their worst fears.

Larry remembers his last encounter with John Casey. He and Casey were talking in a room at the Fantasy Inn, a Reno sex hotel Casey owned. "He was sitting in bed scarfing a hoagie. He was a man in his eighties, biting off big chunks of sandwich, and talking all the while about acquiring more land. He was still dreaming of more land even as a year later he was interred in it. The land eluded his grasp at last, and *it* possessed *him*."

Using Hualapai for Burning Man launched a maddening series of crises barely averted that continued on through the event. Still, one thing about that playa thrilled Larry's heart: "The virtue of that site was an irrigation trench dug the length of it. This playa was inaccessible from any other point [but their gate]. For the first time in our history we had a barrier that would allow us to charge every person who came to the event a fee, which we styled a tax at that point. As citizens, you pay a tax to maintain our city. We had been limping forward with a third of our city not contributing. Our campaign that year was to create a sense of civic spirit, and the first step was to ensure a civic income."

In 1997, imagining the benefits of Hualapai over Black Rock, Larry wrote, "When I saw that trench, it seemed like Zion and the Grand Canyon combined. It will make a huge difference. Now everyone must pay."

The Westerbekes were only one front of Burning Man's war of 1997. Burners had been sliding through Washoe County for years, of course (Reno, Gerlach, and the long road between them were all in that county), but the event itself had transpired in Pershing. In the early days, Pershing's then-sheriff was perfectly happy to pay little mind to what the San Francisco freaks were doing so deep in the trackless wasteland.

Still, though they hadn't had to formally deal with Washoe officials prior to '97, "our reputation preceded us," Larry remembers. "And our reputation in those days in the media seemed unsavory, especially to them. By their reckoning we were hooligans, anarchists, and ne'er-do-wells, everything you would not want your daughter to associate with. This was a new kind of challenge, and we were utterly unprepared for it. We knew no one. We were lone citizens without resources fighting city hall."

So Washoe's regulatory apparatus cranked up, and mindful of the fact that these Burning Man types were by all accounts untamed pyromaniacal Satanists, Washoe imposed on them a long and complicated series of demands. "We were looking at a sheaf of requirements that was larger than the Gerlach and Empire and several other local towns' phone books combined."

But Larry was *going to burn his Man.* "If they ask us to eat an alligator, we'll provide them with a plan," Larry vowed. "We'll have some husky guys—no, let's specify it, let's make it five—five guys on his tail, and we'll have the biggest man we can find with a bib and a knife and fork and we will *eat that alligator.*" Burning Man supporters appeared before Washoe's county commissioners to stress Burning Man's civic virtue and artistic importance and generally assure them it would not result in a fiery holocaust of nipple-ringed marauders eating all the local cattle and fucking in the water tanks.

Washoe did criminal background checks on the LLC members. Burning Man was told whom they were going to hire for services like fire control, and how much they were going to pay. "There was no fire that got out of control, though I understand why they would be worried—*Burning Man,* right?" Larry says. "But the event happened to coincide with a budget shortfall for Truckee Meadows district, and we had to handsomely recompense them for having fire trucks out there.

"The only service we got from them, as it turned out, was when [someone] borrowed Marian's car and took it on a joyride and got a piece of turf wedged up near the catalytic converter. When he drove it back to the staging area, there was a small fire under the car. It didn't damage anything, but it set off the car fire alarm. A fireman came over and tore out the alarm and damaged the car. That was the extent of a couple of hundred thousand dollars' worth of services we paid for."

The news and rumor mills caught on to the tense and unresolved negotiations between Washoe and Burning Man, and "there were reports they might have to have road blocks, turn people away, search all cars coming in," Larry remembers. "Riot gear was brought forward. We estimate we lost a couple of thousand people who would have attended. Which of course meant the loss of tens of thousands in income."

Burning Man's fight with Washoe attracted the event's most extensive national press yet. ABC's *Nightline* aired a segment on the embattled artists trying to build a unique community while stymied by officious government interference and police harassment. *Nightline*'s reporter referred to "sheriff's helicopters hovering annoyingly overhead throughout the event."

"What all those cameras witnessed," Larry says, "is exactly what we claimed it was: a civil community. There was no need to arrest anybody. People behaved better than in a normal city, and it has been so ever since. It was our triumph. We worked so hard to build a sense of real community based on the faith that there was a community there. And it turned out that our faith proved true."

Washoe didn't officially grant the permit until the day before the event started. The permit was larded with requirements obviously pointless for Burning Man, which was occurring miles away from any other living humans, including the demand that no officially sanctioned event begin after midnight.

The county didn't trust Burning Man to pay the more than $300,000 in fees that Washoe insisted it was owed, so the Sheriff's Department partnered with Burning Man's gate staff. The cash box had two locks; one key was held by Andy Pector, the other by the sheriff's accountant. When Burning Man had just one volunteer at the gate and he needed a bathroom break, a uniformed cop would take and sell tickets—doubtless something of a shock to the road-weary persons arriving for their wild fun at Burning Man. And in the end, Washoe just walked away with every penny collected.

Christina Harbridge was a fresh volunteer for Burning Man in 1997, and in her professional life, she was an expert in negotiations with governments. What she saw between Washoe and Burning Man was not a repressive government trying to prevent Burners from enjoying their groovy freedom, but "wolves licking their chops. I told Marian and Larry that they [were] going about this the wrong way. Washoe is taking you for a ride. There are dollar signs in their eyes. Marian and

Larry just pooh-poohed me. I told them, you are not powerless. They want you."

Larry and Marian were convinced they were fighting for their very right to survive; Harbridge was convinced Washoe was just trying to squeeze out as much cash as it could and had no intention of actually stopping Burning Man. "When (Washoe County sheriffs) took the till that year, I told [Burning Man] that's patently illegal. They cannot do that. You have them by the balls. But everyone was so afraid," remembers Harbridge.

Washoe officials did, later, figure that they had taken more money than they needed to cover their expenses, and gave about $50,000 back. Burning Man got some permanent benefits from the forced partnership with Washoe, in Larry's estimation. "They imposed on us a city grid. And we needed it. In '96 we had let the city expand like a cancer. It wasn't safe, and we knew it. We intended to address it. We began to learn some things from the regulations [Washoe imposed]." Without a street grid, Washoe insisted, how can emergency vehicles reach people, or know where to find them? *The green tent near the shark car twenty yards north of the giant Doggie Diner heads* wasn't good enough.

Now Black Rock City had defined roads throughout. It was a grand step toward Larry's more civic, less chaotic, vision of what Burning Man should become. As far as he was concerned, the fact that Burning Man was *not* a TAZ was settled that summer solstice on Baker Beach in 1990 when he let the cops order him not to burn the Man. As Flash, in some ways Goofus to Larry's Gallant, told me, "If you kowtow to the police once, you'll be bending over for the rest of your life." Larry just calls it "cooperating with authorities," and says it's why Burning Man still exists. "TAZs burn the Man and run away," Larry says. And while it *felt* like a TAZ to most people up through '96, that TAZ proved, appropriately enough, temporary.

"I recall one night my heart nearly broke," Larry says. "I stepped out of my trailer and had a view of the traffic coming in. It was twilight, and I was acutely sensitive to the traffic because I knew every pair of headlights was someone who had bought a ticket and I could only hope we would eventually see that money. I remember looking at them like red corpuscles in a vein. It was our lifeblood I was looking at across the playa, and I knew the flow was insufficient. It finally dawned on me that that was our fate, and I went back to my trailer and spent an hour alone in the darkness and I despaired.

"The next day, I rallied and decided to make a speech and appeal to our people for help. They had been as good as gold, and we had worked hard to knit them together and they had been with us all the way. In the year before, people had begun to grumble that we were exploiting people, making so much money, and no one could say that now. They saw what we were going through, and they identified with us. There was a lot of love in the air, let us say.

"There is nothing like struggle to bring people together. So I improvised a speech that tried to condense everything I understood about the value of what we were doing. I delivered it while standing on a straw bale, smoking. Someone pointed out it might ignite the straw. I said, 'They'll never forget me if it does.'

"I asked them to do something that you would never reasonably expect any group of people to do: to give us more money. Having, as it were, already consumed the event, to pay us more. We knew the authorities would not confiscate that money—it would be too naked an act; there were too many cameras present. The police on the ground had begun to realize that this was not what they thought it was. It was not just frightening licentiousness. The police were actually starting to feel sympathetic. So we made the appeal, and a man wrote a check for some huge amount—a few thousand, I believe—and it was one of the most moving things I've ever experienced. It was the reward of faith in tangible form. I'll tell you this: Disneyland will never collect money from people as they leave. It gave us enough to limp on without immediately defaulting on some bills."

Thus, volunteers shimmied through the roistering crowds and smoky chaos on the final night of Burning Man '97, town-crier mendicants announcing that the cops had taken *all* the money. This whole mad experiment was doomed unless we opened our checkbooks generously, right away.

Chicken John had spent the past three weeks building a bike repair shop on the playa out of sheet metal, broken tools, and the sweat of the crew of trick-bike mechanics he had dragged across the country from Minneapolis in a bus that broke down all the way. In his three years at Burning Man, he had seen plenty of chaos, confusion, and precarious planning to pull off the impossible. How many times, he wondered, could you build a city, just to watch it burn?

"If it can't happen," Chicken told the begging Burning Man volunteer, "let it not happen. It won't be the end of the world. We'll all find something else to do on Labor Day weekend."

Chapter Six

"OF COURSE IT'S ALL RIGHT TO SHOOT PAPA SATAN!"

For the second year in a row, Larry realized they couldn't pull Burning Man off the same way again. Larry, Will Roger, and other Burning Man associates spent much of the fall and winter of '97 and on into '98 scouting for a new Zion. In the meantime, fingers crossed, they filed a permit request to return to the Black Rock, hoping that a ban on driving and their spiffy new city grid would show the BLM that they would be more responsible tenants. They also suggested that they encamp in the Washoe portion of the playa, right outside Gerlach, to avoid Pershing County's concerns.

The BLM did not *deny* the permit. Instead, they announced they wouldn't even consider it.

BLM claimed to have no prejudice against Burning Man; it was just that they really were awfully busy that year and did not have the manpower to process the permit. It was in the midst of developing a new Recreation Management Plan for the whole Black Rock Desert area, and was simply swamped. Larry was outraged; he thought this was analogous to the postman refusing to deliver your letter because he's too overwhelmed.

Burning Man's handling of Nevada politics became more active and sophisticated under Marian Goodell. The eldest daughter of an Ayn Rand–loving industrialist—he had his own silver '58 Pullman railroad car named the *Dagny Taggart*—Goodell had been raised to mistrust government interference in the productive lives of citizenry (though she was by no means a committed Randian). She realized that Burning Man had no presence, no face, with which to defend its interests with the BLM. She decided that face would be hers and began showing up at Nevada BLM offices and public meetings. She learned that a private wise-use group called Public Resource Associates was encouraging the BLM to keep Burning Man off the Black Rock.

Burning Man threatened to sue the BLM, and Marian ginned up a-letter-writing campaign over e-mail. She launched a periodic e-newsletter to bind and communicate with the Burner community, which was every year becoming farther flung, less strictly Bay Area. This campaign was the first show of the community's political strength, the first time it rallied publicly in defense of Burning Man. Marian reminded BLM—not threatened, just reminded—that word of mouth and the growing legend of Burning Man meant that thousands of people would show up in the area whether Burning Man was officially happening or not. BLM reconsidered and eventually granted the permit.

The Burning Man had returned to the Black Rock. But the encampment was no longer a far-off and mysterious Brigadoon; it was within sight of Gerlach, right there off the Three-mile playa entrance from the 34, and completely enclosed in a plastic hurricane trash fence.

In 1998, the people of Gerlach could actually see Black Rock City, hear its hippie drummers and rave thumping into the dawn. When Burning Man first breezed through Gerlach in 1990, the strangers disturbed many locals. The rumor spread through town that they were a band of big-city Satanists coming out for a sacrifice.

Slowly, over the course of the decade, what started as complete mistrust bordering on panic turned into détente, understanding, and even appreciation. Warming quickest to Burning Man were the two businesses that profited the most from the presence of hundreds, then thousands, of extra tourists: the Empire Store, in Empire, the last place to buy provisions before the playa, and Bruno Selmi's various operations in Gerlach: restaurant, bar, hotel, and gas station. Bruno recognized the benefits of these thousands of strangers, even if they might look disturbingly strange and sometimes grossly try to shower in his bar's bathroom sink. By the midnineties, he was graciously allowing Burning Man to lock some of its excess cash in his safe and store some of their infrastructure on his property.

Gerlach has no real city government and no mayor. But it does have something akin to a king, and that is Bruno Selmi. Bruno came to the United States from Italy when he was twenty-three years old, more than fifty years ago, but he still speaks in a thickly accented, highly lyrical voice of songbird pitch and inflection, an almost clichéd operatic Italian voice.

He is not to be trifled with. When the British knight Sir Richard Noble was bivouacked in Gerlach in 1997, planning his soon-to-be successful go at setting a land-speed record on the playa, one Burning-Man associate recalls witnessing some contretemps between Noble's crew and Bruno during which this knight of the British Empire was "genuflecting as if the bar were an altar," going through a litany of *yes, Brunos* and *no, Brunos,* nodding and shaking his head alternately. The exchange ended with him and his crew being dismissed airily from the barkeep's sovereign presence. "Had it been the queen herself, it wouldn't have made any difference," the observer concluded.

The Empire Store now has a banner proudly proclaiming a slogan Stuart Mangrum invented for Black Rock City: "WELCOME TO NOWHERE."

Contemplating Gerlach and its relationship with Burning Man, I found myself asking an undoubtedly insulting question to a few residents: Why does anyone live here? It delighted me to imagine pulp-noir tales of reaching the end of the line, fleeing the consequences of dark secrets, feeling complete disgust with civilization, and entering witness protection programs. The answers weren't so steeped in drama. Love for the solitude, the ability to, as Gerlach's justice of the peace, Phil Thomas, puts it, get an idea to go somewhere or do something and not have ten other people with the same idea beat you to

it,-to get gas and a money order without waiting in lines or at stop-
lights—these are the advantages to living in a remote, sparsely populated place like Gerlach.

The railroad depot is no longer big business, so Gerlach hosts a
bunch of retirees plus a fair number of gypsum workers and road
workers for the Nevada Department of Transportation. Despite the
isolation and the dust and the heat and the unsafe levels of uranium
in the drinking water and an anecdotal cancer rate that could be considered alarming, this being a nation of free migration and cheap bus
tickets, most people in Gerlach live there because they love it.

Judge Phil, as he is affectionately known in the Burning Man community, in some years was deputized by Pershing County (although
he is a Washoe judge) and actually served instant justice in Black
Rock City itself. Mostly, though, he just enjoys Burning Man as a
rowdy attendee. (The first time I met the judge, around a burn barrel
late one night at Burning Man in 2000, he told me he had arrived by
plowing his truck through the trash fence. He didn't notice it, he said,
until it was already behind him.)

Burning Man caused plenty of worries for Gerlach at the start,
Judge Phil admits. No one liked the heavily laden cars speeding down
Main Street, where the town's children often played, and hell, the
freakiness of them all. Certainly, he admits, the residents have their
own peculiarities in Gerlach, but they've all had time to get used to
one another. And then with the Burners returning year after year,
Gerlach got used to them as well.

"As time went on, we realized this girl with purple hair has a perfectly fine mind. She just has purple hair. We'd wonder about piercings and the like—why would you do that to yourself?" Judge Phil is
perfectly aware that incomprehension in the Gerlach/Burning Man
relationship can be mutual. "I'm sure they look at us and say, 'What
the fuck are you living out here for?' What brought me out here was
the desert. A lot of people look at the desert and don't see anything. I
look out on the desert and see everything."

John Law thinks a mutual love of guns helped thaw chilly relations
between Gerlach and Burning Man in the early years. As time went

on, Burning Man hired some locals to work for them, opened a permanent office on Main Street, gave free (later just highly discounted) tickets to locals, and even had some of their employees move into town. Sure, there are people in Gerlach who still give all the freaks going through the evil eye—a local two barstools down from me and some pals drinking at Bruno's on the Fourth of July in 2003 loudly asked the bartender if the circus had come to town early this year. Local matriarch Mama Lola assures me most of the locals who still swear opposition to Burning Man are hypocrites, bitching about it incessantly but still always eager to go soak in the strangeness. Burning Man's ability to weather the ill will from some in Gerlach could be the result of a real brotherhood of spirit between these two western towns, one permanent, one temporary.

America's West has always both attracted and inspired a freewheeling liberty combined with an uncoerced communalism that has people waving at each other as they pass on these lonely, glorious roads, all of them knowing that they will, almost certainly, need their fellow man out here sometime. You'd damn well better be ready to help, because someone will be ready to help you. Black Rock citizens, exiled by choice with nothing but what they've brought, dependent on their joint resources to deal with unpredictable natural dangers, need to live by the same code. And with the Empire Store the only shop within hours of driving, Gerlach is living a life nearly as-noncommercial as Black Rock City. This combination of self-reliance and community binds the two cities.

The most fervent opposition to Burning Man in Gerlach came not from any stone-faced desert hermit or uptight church ladies (there are no churches in Gerlach itself) but—exemplifying Freud's concept of the narcissism of small differences—from Gerlach's own local art freak, John Bogard, who operates the Planet X pottery store about ten miles down the road from Gerlach's Main Street, down the fork that heads away from the playa. He and his friend Mel Lyons, remember, were doing weird art events on the Black Rock before the Burning Man people—whom he memorably condemned as "Druid puke" in an early magazine feature on the event—showed up. Up until a couple of years ago, Bogard busily filed environmental complaints against the event with the BLM, striving to ban it from the playa. He thought Burning Man was permanently scarring the desert surface, leaving too much debris despite the clean-up crew's best efforts, and was in general a cancer on the playa's pristine white eternal blankness.

It's easy to scoff at such concerns. After all, the playa resembles—as one BLM official who understandably asked not to be named told me—nothing so much as an ashtray in its lifeless indestructibility. (An anti–Burning Man Web site points out that despite the apparent life-lessness, there may be hibernating shrimp living on the playa surface, perennials left over from the winter floods that mostly turn the playa into a shallow lake.) Just truck out the visible waste—which Burning Man does passingly well each year in pursuit of the grail of "Leave no trace"—and what's left to hurt? There are burn scars, of course—dis-colorations and hardening of the playa surface caused by fires—which Burning Man now mitigates by insisting on burn blankets under all planned art burns. But it is hard for most people to be too alarmed at the thought that a few yards of the playa's four hundred square miles of lake bed might, a few years down the line, be a slightly darker shade than all the powder white around it. To sincerely lament damage to the playa by Burning Man requires an almost mystical belief that there are certain surfaces mankind just *should not touch*. That same BLM official is impressed that Burning Man actually found a recreational use that delights tens of thousands for a place that had never been of much use to anyone except handfuls of land-speed record seekers, wind sailors, and rocket launchers.

As Larry remembers it, his team at first conflated Gerlach society with what went on in Gerlach's bars—the only public space they knew about. Eventually, he says, "we realized there was a civic entity, and we could deal with that. Society there didn't simply consist of intoxicated people in bars. Bars selected for a certain type. Things were witnessed in those bars at night that you wouldn't see in San Francisco. It's a great open land out there and a lonely place, and inhibitions break down. People *know* each other there.

"But if you judged only by the bars, you might have a dim view of Gerlach. You could satirize it, make the most of it as a seriocomic portrait of human frailty. But then we began to know people" and began donating money to the town, thousands every year, for local senior citizens' centers, schools, and water treatment. "We were genuinely giving to them. Of course it was an intelligent political thing to do, but also a decent thing to do."

After a few false starts with direct giving that didn't always end up where they thought it would, Burning Man discovered the Gerlach-Empire Citizen Advisory Board, which functions as a substitute for city government in dealing with the Washoe County Commission. Burning Man now both owns and rents ranchland about twenty miles on down past the Twelve-mile playa entrance, used as a storage and building area for the event and as a home to the crew who build and tear down the city—Black Rock City's Department of Public Works (DPW). The ranch was known for years as Eighty Acres and last year was renamed Black Rock Station (with the addition of a newly purchased parcel of land behind the original leased land). The freaks from San Francisco are now another local Gerlach business. Even if they aren't pumping all their money directly into the town, they are still almost certainly its highest-grossing concern.

Gerlach has many separate axes of power. After all, there can't be too much unity in a town that housed fewer than four hundred citizens and five bars when Burning Man people first started coming through. (There are only three bars left now.) Humans crave companionship and succor, yes. But it is equally true that people crave enemies and feuds, and secretly treasure the joy of griping about that bastard over there, that sonovabitch in the bar down the street. Those hanging out in *this* bar could entertain themselves and add some drama to their life by talking smack about those hanging out in the bar next door. That's another gift Burning Man gave Gerlach—something new to talk about and feud about.

Then, in 1997, Flash came to town to stay for a while. In his own memory, he was explicitly there as an ambassador for Burning Man, to help soften up the place. Larry is quick to stress—especially considering how Flash's adventure in Gerlach ended—that, as always, Flash acted on his own counsel.

When I asked Flash how he managed to insinuate himself so thoroughly into Gerlach society so quickly, he proudly shows me a snapshot of himself, in full wild-man mode, lanky arms muscled like old rope dangling from a shirt with the sleeves raggedly torn off, long knife brandished, sitting like a pampered child in the midst of six middle-aged (and older) women: the women who wielded social power in Gerlach. He charmed his way into most of their hearts, and talked Joan Grant, a big landowner on the outskirts of Gerlach, into making him her partner in running the Black Rock Saloon. Joan agreed to a sixty-forty split (sixty for Flash, forty for her), as Flash tells it, because the joint had heretofore been pulling in almost nothing, and she had little faith it could ever do better since it was just thirty feet or so down Main Street from Bruno's.

Flash thinks many Burning Man people approached Gerlach with too inflated a sense of self-importance about their world-changing missions. Gerlachians didn't really cotton to that. "But I just came in and said, 'Let's party down!'"

When Flash set up shop in the saloon, well, he *Flashized* the place. He bussed in bands and customers from Reno and prostitutes from the Mustang Ranch. "It's Girl-lack," as a local joke goes. Soon, says Flash, money was pouring in, and Joan Grant began resenting the split in Flash's favor. Flash became giddy with the desire to shake up the old town, began scheming to buy out some of the other bars, and set himself against the mighty Bruno just for shits 'n' giggles. Flash is a man who needs to *move*.

When he noticed Gerlach had no chamber of commerce, he started one and named himself president. When it looked like the BLM might keep Burning Man out of the area through early 1998, he and Larry amused themselves by carrying on a public conversation in the press, not as old friends, but as the head of Burning Man and Michael Hopkins, concerned president of the Gerlach Chamber of Commerce, who very much treasured the business that Burning Man brought to his town. Flash swears a Washoe County commissioner owes his job to his savvy politicking. "It's easy to get political clout in small towns," he tells me. "There's not a lot of competition. Most people just want to be left alone, so if you want to get involved in politics, go right ahead. Nothing's going to stop you."

Flash was host and helper in '97 to Sir Richard Noble's land-speed record team, and he treasures his fax from the queen congratulating the whole squad for its achievement and for promoting the greater glory of the empire.

But imperial glory must fade. By the time Burning Man rolled around in 1998, plenty of locals were unhappy with Flash. He had thrown Joan Grant out of her own bar and fired one of her friends for her inability to properly cook a chicken. Flash decided that Grant owed him money and for revenge began cooking all the restaurant's food supplies and throwing huge free parties for his friends.

A few days after Burning Man '98 was over, Flash, as he remembers, was walking home down Gerlach's main street very late one night. He heard a very particular noise.

"I've been around guns my whole life. I know that sound. I looked out from the corner of my eye and there was [the inferior chicken cooker]. I said, 'You fucking bitch,' and threw myself on the ground, and she started to unload. The bar was still packed inside. I stumbled in and said, 'The bitch just shot me. Give me some whiskey, boys. I wanna die like Eli Wallach.' I wanted to go out like a cowboy."

Flash lived but felt wounded again by Nevada justice after the trial of his shooter. "It's full of Holy Rollers; everyone in the place looks like Mother Teresa or an ex-president, and they all hate you. 'Where you from? You ain't from around here, are you?'" The alleged shooter's lawyer got another Gerlach local to testify that he knew the alleged victim not only by the name of Flash, but as *Papa Satan*.

"Everyone gasped. I knew I was sunk. Of course it's all right to shoot Papa Satan! Why, if he had a gun, any God-fearing man would shoot Papa Satan!" Despite Flash's testimony that he knew full well

who shot him, that he *saw* her, the jury in her first trial did not con-
vict. That about wrapped up Flash's adventures in Gerlach.

Years later, he's philosophical about the whole thing. It increased his
social capital among some of Burning Man's more rough-and-tumble
citizens. Surviving a shooting? *Dude!* And he recognizes that if you
spend a lot of time in a place like Gerlach, well, what do you expect?
"Guns get pulled a lot out there. It's very popular, to pull a gun in the
Wild West. Guys and guns, well, I feel I can speak on this subject. I've
been around a lot of that. I've been around every side of the guy with
the gun. This side [feigns aiming gun at me]. This side [feigns aiming
gun at himself]. 'Should I?' Guys talk about it—'Fuck, I'm gonna kill
you man!' 'Should I fucking kill him?' 'I think I'm gonna dust him
here, boys, what do you think?' Guys talk.

"*Girls don't.* By the time she picks up a gun and aims it at you, your
name is on every bullet. Every decision has already been made. Guys
get killed by women with guns like this"—he throws open his arms
and thrusts his body toward me—"'But honey-.-.-.' You're a dead
man, Jack. You're a dead man." He laughs his raspy laugh. "That's lesson
number one. Trust me on this one. If your wife—a lovely woman!—at
any time pulls a gun, just remember all the decisions have been made.
There is no talking at that point."

Justin Atwood had shown up at Burning Man in 1997 at the tail end
of another grueling Circus Redickuless tour, a failed attempt to bring
a more well-rounded Burning Man vibe to the parking lots of small-
capacity punkish clubs in America's second-tier great cities.

The tour was supposed to combine Plundertown's failed Burning Man Mousetrap with Circus Redickuless and Minneapolis's
Hard Times Bike Club, the pioneers of punk-engineered goofy trick
bikes—absurdly tall bikes for jousting, bikes on which the wheel you
pedal turns another wheel that makes you go backward, bikes on
which steering one way makes the wheel turn the other, propane-fire
spitting bikes.

The Mousetrap got abandoned in Phoenix, and most of the Hard Times kids quit in New Orleans, but at the end, some of them made it to the Hualapai. In the meantime, Justin—who grew up in L.A. and knew nothing of nonmotorized transportation—was won over by the allure of the trick bike. It was democratic—almost everyone could afford one, could ride one. It was low-tech—no motors or electrical systems to master. OK, he didn't know much about bikes, but no one in Circus Redickuless knew much about performing either.

Chicken John had deposited Justin and the rump Hard Times crew on the Hualapai Playa and left them there, penniless and helpless. They formed the nucleus of what became the DPW—the men willing, for whatever reason, to spend months in a hateful desert for usually no more than food, beer, and maybe enough cash to catch a bus back to wherever they started, to set up and then clean up Black Rock City.

The original pitch for Pedal Camp—bringing the Hard Times trick-bike aesthetic to Burning Man and providing a needed public service in a city that, for the first time in its history, had banned automobile driving—had Chicken and Justin promising to build two hundred to three hundred cart bikes as public transportation, jitney-style. That didn't happen, but they did allow citizens to (mostly) freely borrow the bikes they were working on, and they helped fix other people's bikes.

Most of Pedal Camp's bikes came from a nearby abandoned ranch, which local legend claimed had been managed by an old hermit who was one day set upon by a marauding motorcycle mob that eventually had to be ousted by the National Guard. Scattered all over that ranch—why, no one knew—were dozens of old bicycles, which were used to build the foundations of an empire that pedals to this day, touring nationally and internationally, under the name Cyclecide Bike Rodeo.

Abandoned in the cruel desert, the peculiar aesthetic of Pedal Camp—rough, junky, resourceful, comic-aggressive—developed, says Justin, "out of necessity. We were like Neanderthals. The corrugated shelter wasn't the brilliant idea of a visionary genius. It was a vision of 'We need fucking shade,' and there was all this corrugated steel out at the ranch where we found the bikes. So we stripped it all off sheep pens and scavenged wood, and I became really good, let me say, at siphoning gas from vehicles."

Pedal Camp was filthy, raw, and rude, and its builders came back to do it again at Burning Man '98. Again, they were the first to arrive and the last to leave. Their junk-punk ethos aggravated some in the Burning Man organization. Their music was loud trash metal, punk, and even some improvised rap; their begging robot often verbally abused passersby (depending on who was hiding up on the tower running the remote control and giving the robot its voice). When told their tower was too close to the road and would have to be moved back, they instead, in the dead of night, moved all the spires defining the road and pretended they'd moved the tower. Pedal Camp was that era's version of the Official Bad Element at Burning Man, which is always around in some form. (Later versions have included the Thunderdome Death Guild and the Chupacabra Policía.) Since Pedal Camp comprised most of the clean-up crew in both '97 and '98, they were blamed in a pissy Internet posting war for any mess left behind—especially by people who didn't realize that the home base and processing center for a whole city's garbage was going to look trashed up to the very last minute.

Feeling betrayed by that sort of talk—again, the very people spending weeks picking up others' junk cannot escape calumny!—Justin submitted the following as a grant proposal in 1999 to Larry (all eccentricities of style here preserved):

> Let us discuss time, this year's Burning Man theme. Turn the clock back; Burning Man 1997: 666 altered bikes built for public consumption. 8,000 bikes repaired, including 6,666 flat tires… Oh, and 58 dumpsters of human waste and garbage removed…6 months later…Pedal Camp accused of renting playa out as New Jersey landfill. 'Trashing the playa' quoted by on-line idiots who have never so much as picked up a cigarette butt, let alone their own garbage.
>
> Burning Man 1998: Pedal camp provides an average of 1½ bikes for every man, woman, and child as well as providing bicycles for

orphans in Malaysia, as well as to troubled and at risk urban inner city youth and also provides needle exchange and HIV testing for ugly, pregnant Black Rock strippers...6-months later. Pedal camp accused of over consumption of everything, anti-social behavior, arson, indecent exposure, hoarding and stealing of Burning Man property and once again, fucking up clean-up through a drug induced voodoo that inevitably caused the 10 day downpour of rain, all putting Burning Man at risk.

Now how about the future...OUR PROPOSAL. In light of the past we members of pedal camp are eager to give something back to the Burning Man community. A community that has nurtured us. A community that has made us better people. All inspiring us to make a better world.

This year we begin to ask ourselves: 'What can we do?' What can we do to make a kinder, gentler, friendlier environment for the citizens of Black Rock? Absolutely nothing.

That's right, nothing means something. Not wanting to be cut out of the creative process, yearning to see the advancemental evolution of a desert civilization we have collectively come to the conclusion that our participation elsewhere is a much, much greater contribution to the community as a whole.

We ask that the Burning Man project help us help ourselves help others. Your taxable contribution of $2000 to the pedal camp project will guarantee our involvement in the Burning Man project to not exist. Not participating is participating. It's the least we can do. Won't you help us, Larry?

Despite the bitter ending to Pedal Camp's official relationship with Burning Man (one of the Burning Man organization's charms is its forgiveness, as long as you don't tell them openly to fuck off—Justin and his crew got a grant in 2001 to bring some of their homemade bicycle-based carny rides back to the playa), Justin remembers that "a lot of people loved us. We had crazy music, different from the hippie-dippie fucking drum-jam element. We were the real thing. We came out with generators and did our thing out there. We didn't make our projects in some studio in San Francisco and then bring [them] out. We did it right there in front of people's eyes.

"And I think in the end we had a profound influence not just on Burning Man itself—which is now totally filled with altered bikes and other bicycle clubs and repair shops and bike rodeos. I think we had an impact on the bicycle itself. I was initially pissed off when I saw a Honda commercial where they were jousting tall bikes, but now I've come to think of it as the greatest form of flattery: to not just have an effect on your subculture but the mainstream. That's cool. I can take that to the bank and laugh.

"But when Burning Man started giving money to artists, it changed the event for the bad and for the worse in a lot of ways. And I'm biting my tongue here, because I've been the recipient of Burning Man's money every time I've been affiliated with a project, because it takes a lot of money to accomplish anything out there, even if it's like Pedal Camp, just a bunch of crazy junk bikes. It's no joke. It's a real hostile environment. People aren't supposed to be there. There's a reason why it's flat with no trees and no water. That's reality, and everything else about Burning Man is *not* reality. Though that's what's kind of cool about it."

Burning Man claims full intellectual property rights over everything that occurs within their fence, and effective ownership over pieces they fund—if the piece is sold, the grant is supposed to be repaid, at least up to the sales price. To Justin, an old L.A. vet, that smells like pay-to-play. "Who provides what to whom, who makes what an event? Burning Man does provide a venue, but ultimately that playa belongs to you and me anyway. It's public land. For them to say they own the rights to your art [just because they covered some of the cost] is fucking crap. Anyway, I didn't sign that contract with my real name. I never sign anything with my real name. Jarico Reese, who's that?"

Justin and the Pedal Camp crew got trapped on the playa during the Flood Year of 1998. On Monday, the last day of the event, the rains began and did not let up for days. By the middle of Monday night, you couldn't escape the playa. The dry cracked alkali of the Black Rock becomes grasping batter-thick muck when pounded by constant rain. Vehicles were sinking into it up to their axles.

In 2000, a bunch of us were sitting around a fire barrel, indulging in one of Black Rock City's greatest pleasures: shooting the shit about marvelous adventures of the past, on the playa and elsewhere.

"I am just *waiting* for a strong rain on some day when there are thirty thousand of us out here. The newbies will be freaked. It will be impossible," said one guy.

"Impossible is fucking right. We're talking National Guard situation—troops massed in Gerlach passing us food," another added.

"Were any of you out here in '98, last day of the event?" asked Chicken John. "When it started raining?"

"I got out, last possible moment," I said. "The car was skidding *zhoom-zhoom-zhoom,* back and forth, the whole way up to the paved road."

"It didn't stop raining after you left. It kept raining. For days. Total cholera threat—water everywhere, no one cleaning up what few porta potties were left. We were on a tight clean-up schedule that I was responsible for. I had this crew of a dozen bicycle mechanics and gutter punks from Minnesota and enough drugs and booze for a whole city. In fact, it was exactly a whole city's worth of drugs and booze.

"I went around the last morning, as everyone was packing up and leaving, as they were stuck in traffic waiting for over ten thousand cars to get out one bottleneck to one two-lane highway, shouting through a bullhorn. Used whatever trick seemed like it might work best. For the friendly-looking ones, just the 'Aw, man, cut us some slack' deal. You know, we're gonna be stuck out here and all the chicks have left and all the fire's gone and we'll be bent-back digging cigarette butts out of the ground while they were all going back to their office jobs in Walnut Creek. Give us all your food, all your booze, all your drugs. Your party's over. Our nightmare's beginning.

"For ones that looked more uptight and nervous that this smelly crazed motherfucker was shouting at them through a bullhorn, I'd tell them, 'Hey, be careful man, be smart. The Highway Patrol is totally targeting us. Lots of stop-and-searches. It would be a real dumb idea to take anything illegal out of this place. Leave it with us, man. Hey, no problem, we're totally glad to help. That's what clean-up crew is all-about.'

"Vials of liquid LSD. Heaps of pot. Blizzards of cocaine and speed. And a bunch of edgy, scrappy freakazoids who'd already been crawling in the dust out here way too long. And we've got nothing to do, and lots of drugs to do it with. We ended up putting on a variety show to amuse ourselves where we pretended to be characters from the *Wizard of Oz*."

It's hard to imagine, survivors tell me, exactly what it was like to spend more than a week stuck in the mud with nothing to do and then another month and more out there lifting tens of thousands of people's debris tiny piece by tiny piece. One quickly loses track of any reason for *anything*. Civilization frays, the center cannot hold, anarchy is loosed, etc. The most prominent theme art that year was a roving device called the Nebulous Entity, conceptualized by Larry and executed by a team of artists, including Michael Christian and Aaron Wolf Baum. It was like a giant mechanical alien squid rolling awkwardly and crankily through the city, loaded with sound and light equipment. It was, in theory, meant to be an entity living off information plumbed from the humans who interacted with it, processing-it and projecting it back out. It was a fun, strange thing to see galumphing down the narrow streets of Black Rock City and knocking over road signs, at any rate.

After the event, it was set on fire. It wasn't intended to be. Elements of its frame were reused for the Bone Tree, designed and built by Dana Albany and Flash, in 1999. Justin told me in 2003, "It was kind of funny spending all this Burning Man money on a piece of art that wasn't supposed to burn. It didn't make sense. Someone set it on fire. It was a big mystery. Who did it? I don't know."

A few sentences later, "So we lit it on fire, and they were all pissed off. Burning Man, duh? What do you expect?" After a pause, more soberly: "I don't condone burning anybody's art…I guess. Yeah, I do! It's fucking Burning Man, burn it, burn my bicycles, I don't care, I wouldn't whine about it. If someone lit all the bikes from the Bike Rodeo on fire, I'd be laughing my ass off. It'd be like, 'Great, can't do the show! Someone burned all the bikes.'"

In 1998, the Man did not so much burn as explode. For the second year in a row, the Man was lit by an actual human being set on fire, who ran up the stack of straw bales the Man was standing on by then and grabbed the statue and ignited it. Kimric Smythe had been a bit excessive that year, larding the Man with lots of military-grade explosives, illumination grenades, magnesium, and the like. The flaming human inadvertently lit not just the wood but some fusing, and for some reason nearly every goddamn explosive stuffed in the Man went off at once and this transcendent apparition burst forth, a sun-white cloud of roiling smoke twice as wide and quite a bit taller than the-Man. We all held our breath, and it was a miraculous, patriotic moment that after that cataclysm Our Man Was Still There, standing and burning, not reduced to splinters.

The man on fire looked up and saw the Man exploding and ran for his life down the steps of the bales and toward the safety crew that was supposed to put him out. The safety crew, meanwhile, was running away from the explosion and away from him, so the flaming man chased them, an angry ghost. (He was put out safely before the protective coating burned away.)

The gradual exodus of some of the old guard from the Burning Man Project continued. Chris Campbell, one of the Man's primary builders for most of the nineties, was pissed about some of the same things that drove John Law away. The event's growing size, he thought, had changed its feel and apparent purpose for the worse. By 1998, the return to the Black Rock, more than ten thousand people were there, and there were new amenities for some, like the power grid the organizers trenched and wired around Center Camp. If your artwork or theme camp was lucky enough to have been sited there—because with the city grid came zoning of a sort, for artworks and camps who had prearranged their presence with the organizers—you had free access to plug-in electricity. This bothered Campbell. To his mind, a certain imaginative frugality was key to why he thought the event important, what he hoped it could teach the world: how to use the fewest resources possible to accomplish the most.

But something sillier finally caused him to publicly break from the new Burning Man consensus. In 1998, the Donner Award, instituted by Michael Michael to commemorate stupidly self-destructive behavior at Burning Man, was granted to a DPW worker who got his truck smashed by a train on the tracks bordering the playa. Campbell saw this as a dangerous sign that the new organizational structure was either losing its sense of humor, covering its own ass, or both. Because Campbell thought the award should really have gone to Joegh Bullock, then still a member of Burning Man's owning LLC.

Bullock, you see, had burned down his own camp that year with his regrettable choice of straw bales for structure and tiki torches for illumination. (I was one of the people frantically shoveling barely useful clods of playa on the blazing tents. I had dashed toward the fire from one hundred yards or so away, where I was trenching wire. It was still a few days before the event officially began, so I figured the fire was accident, not art.)

"I thought, really, who best epitomized the Donner spirit, which is, how many ways can you kill yourself?" asks Campbell. "When Joegh burned down his own camp, that to me was number one. If you burn down your own structure, that's it, other than stabbing yourself in the eyeball. I mean, you earned the title. I said that publicly at a postevent meeting that the LLC obviously wanted to just be a lovefest. And they all stared at me, like I'd forced their hand on something they didn't want to talk about.

"Joegh stood up and said, 'I'll share it,' but I'm like, 'No, man, it's *yours.*'" Campbell insists this made the other organizers leery of him— he was cut out of discussions and had budgets that had been promised him arbitrarily reduced, he says—and after 1999, he began making more public complaints about the event's increasingly heavy damage to the desert's skin. "Why are we digging holes? Why are we trench-ing? Why don't we call up some solar people and some wind people and subsidize installation of low-voltage light, low-voltage transform-ers if you need a PA? There are ways to draw huge amounts of energy out there without internal combustion generators, and they didn't do a goddamn thing about it.

"A lot of individuals were bringing solar and bringing turbines and setting up small-scale solar and wind power. And Burning Man was ignoring them in favor of this fucking convoy of generators. This upset me because I dumped all this energy into this with the belief that we were doing something better. I believed to my fucking core that this was bigger and better than anything that had come to date and with the right kind of energy we could set up a large-scale alter-native living venue. What it became instead was a giant rave with the same generators, the same blinkie lights, and all that crap." After nine years, Chris Campbell stopped building the Burning Man.

Everyone in 1998 survived, even the wounded Flash, though he's mostly stopped doing business in Gerlach. The mud dried and the playa got cleaned up, mostly, and the Man rose again and he's been coming back to the neighborhood every year since, staring blankly and glowing neon over crowds that just keep getting bigger.

Someday, almost inevitably, rains and floods like those in 1998 will happen when Black Rock City is in full raucous, glorious communal-artistic swing with thirty thousand and more people, and what the hell will they do then? I ask Larry Harvey.

He just laughs. What could they do? Generally, people really over-pack, so it's unlikely we'd starve or run out of fresh water even if we were stuck there a full extra week.

"It would sort the wheat from the chaff," says Larry. "The true survivors would never let anyone who followed them forget that they were at Agincourt, that they faced that and survived."

In 1999, Black Rock City took on its current shape, a closing circle (getting closer to closed every year) with the Man at its center and the gap behind him. From the beginning of the desert event, Larry rejected the idea of placing the Man among the rest of the encampment. "I said no because at the beach it was against this great horizon, and I wanted it to belong to something beyond us because that was so integral to the original experience. My aesthetic intuition told me it should be that way—beyond the fact that burning a giant in the middle of camp is probably a bad idea."

Larry noticed that the entire city had—without his thinking about it, or its planner, Rod Garrett, knowing it—emulated the shape that the first small band attracted to his and Jerry's burning figure on the beach formed more than a decade earlier, a natural half circle, contemplating the wonder of that protoman.

So now there are more than thirty thousand people trucking through Gerlach the week before Labor Day and maybe buying some of Bruno's ravioli, or at least his gasoline, and then heading out to the playa and building and inhabiting Black Rock City.

But what are they *doing* there?

Part Three

NO SPECTATORS

Chapter Seven

THE WORLD'S MOST DANGEROUS DRINK BLENDER

A swirl of claims, some contradictory, runs through the endless conversation that Burning Man engenders in its devotees and detractors. You'll hear them over and over again at parties, jubilees, raves, fund-raisers, late-night welding sessions, tugboat soirees, intimate desert rituals: Burning Man creates artists; Burning Man is self-indulgent play; Burning Man renews lives; Burning Man destroys lives; Burning Man changes the world; Burning Man is a dangerous catastrophe.

For six years Jim Mason was one of Burning Man's most tenacious and excessive artists, living out all of those dichotomies. He has a wide, babyishly blank face (even when covered in a few days' unshaven beard, as it often is) beneath his dirty blond hair (usually longish and-tangled). His characteristic outfit is a dull-silver full-body fire-protection suit, which he has taken to wearing even during those (rare) moments when his catching himself on fire is only a remote possibility.

Mason is not a scientist, but his day job has been written up in *Scientific American*. He's creating a database of all of the world's surviving languages, a Utopian-linguist scheme known as the Rosetta Project, which is part of Stewart Brand's Long Now Foundation. Brand was one of Ken Kesey's Merry Prankster pals and the impresario behind the January 1966 Trips Festival (the apotheosis, or selling out, of Kesey's Acid Tests), one of the first public ticketed events in America to turn life into a theatrical happening and vice versa, to embrace incongruous and chemically enhanced freaky community publicly as a viable and even holy pursuit. Brand's Trips Festival and the Kesey movement from which it arose struck devastating blows that made chinks in consensual reality; Burning Man is now bulldozing boldly and heedlessly through those chinks and building an entire mini*civilization* around some of those same impulses that inspired the Kesey scene.

The threads of cultural rebellion and social evolution wind through American history, tracing strange coincidences and karmic connections: Stewart Brand to Jim Mason, the Acid Tests to Burning Man. Mason got his job not through the *New York Times* but through Burning Man. His supervisor, Alexander Rose, a fellow Burner, told a reporter from *SF Weekly* profiling the Rosetta Project that he recognized, after watching Mason achieve the absurd and improbable at Burning Man, that Mason was "someone more than willing to try desperately audacious tasks."

In 1995, Jim Mason was not an artist. He was an anthropologist supervising a cross-cultural art exchange between the people of New Guinea and Stanford University, organizing a sculpture garden of New Guinean art on Stanford's campus. Then he discovered Burning Man. "I first heard about it as a rave," Mason tells me. "I went out there because I like the desert. I spent most of my youth destroying the desert in Southern California with various motorcycles and dune buggies. While destroying it, I developed a tremendous appreciation for it. Deserts have always been my most strongly felt landscapes.

"I also spent much of my youth around machines, and as an anthropologist I had an interest in cultural appropriation. So the notion of taking curiosities from urban environments and employing them in the blank desert with these curious new readings on them appealed to me greatly. A combination of deserts with improvisational anthropology and machines pretty much summarized my life. I had made motorcycles and dune buggies before—functional things. But Burning Man helped me realize there was this thing called 'installation art'—which I came to realize was basically conceptually motivated building. I went to college to be a mechanical engineer, but I ended up doing anthropology because I became much more interested in cultural interpretation."

Mason, with his six-figure Stanford education behind him, is more bourgeois-intellectual in background than many of the machine workers and radical grease monkeys who build crazy shit at Burning Man. He's spent a good part of his life in a world where Burning Man's particular combination of qualities is very unusual indeed, a fact that helped him develop a well-honed sense of irony and ridiculousness about the whole business. He tells me about how Burning Man turned him from an anthropologist to an artist.

"By the time I decided to go to Burning Man in 1995, I was clear on the notion that you were supposed to bring bullshit there and build. In true Jim Mason form, I rented a piece-of-shit single-axle U-Haul and stacked it with an unbelievable amount of steel—three thousand pounds on a truck built to handle around fifteen hundred pounds. Of course the axle broke, and it took fourteen hours to get [to the playa]. I had the notion of a community welding camp. I thought I'd bring a bunch of steel and people would show up and we could all weld things. All I brought was an oxyacetylene torch. I didn't realize then that if you weld things together seriously, you are supposed to have arc welders."

From that inauspicious beginning, he leaped the next year to what he still considers his favorite project at Burning Man.

"I brought a bunch of rusted steel water pipe and made a desert forest spread out over two miles of the Black Rock Desert. It was like a minimalist Zen garden, with the pipes forming the shapes of cacti. It was a very spare arrangement, done visually in relation to the sides of the mountains and valleys surrounding the playa. I did it ten miles away from where the rest of the Burning Man encampment was, so very few people saw it. But the people who found out through word of mouth drove out to find it. I didn't care about the audience. I was having an *art experience*."

Back then, before Burning Man's reputation became inextricably linked with that of the Black Rock Playa, the playa was mainly known for being that enormous, utterly empty place where people set land-speed records in jet cars. Locals out to blow off some steam—and BLM law enforcement—were used to driving carelessly and swiftly through Black Rock's trackless vastness.

"Of course, people ran into it," says Mason. "They might be driving a hundred miles an hour in the desert, and suddenly there's a steel tree sticking out. Some good ol' boys from Reno took one out. They were all pissed off and came and found the guy responsible for the damn metal trees. They came to my camp with guns trying to find me, and I wouldn't come out. So they completely trashed my Bronco. They wanted to discuss the damage to their truck, and when they weren't able to have that discussion, they expressed their upsetness on the wires and vacuum system of my Bronco.

"It's the biggest thing anyone ever did out there, although it had a very slight visual weight because the individual trees were so small and so spread out. But the BLM got pissed about it. Michael Michael wasn't very pleased. I mean, everyone liked the *idea* of it, but the practical reality bothered them. I was calling the piece the Forest of Meditation. People were calling it the Forest of Death.

"I've thought about redoing that project as a proper permitted thing and doing much larger pieces over a larger part of the desert. Have it be sort of a Christo project at Black Rock. As is often the case, that first thoughtless, naive thing you go out there and do is the best thing you ever do. And it cost Burning Man zero and cost me about a thousand bucks."

Although it did not end in fire—the ultimate statement of passionate ephemerality that epitomizes Burning Man—Mason's steel forest was still *for the moment,* for those who were there to experience it. Mason has no aerial photos that capture the entire pattern. And shots of the single trees—well, they miss the forest. Mason has me clamber up a makeshift ladder to the loft where he sleeps, where a photo of one of the trees is on the wall. It looks like some alien insect's quivering, questing antennae breaking through the extraplanetary crust of the Black Rock Playa. But the photo is ultimately just dots on a page—only a shadow of an experience.

After '96, Mason began attending Burning Man community events in the Bay Area and slowly inserting himself into the then still small social circles surrounding the festival and its planning. In 1997, Mason executed another in his series of absurdist follies, huge assertions of self that command attention because of both idea and execution. One wonders what inner neuroses are being fed by what Mason calls his "obsessive ambition." Explains Mason, "[It's] almost dysfunctional— -I find a great need to justify myself through uniquely large and excessive productions, which Burning Man certainly encourages. It's typically self-destructive and highly narcissistic in some ways—like, I'm-going to sacrifice everything around me out of some need to *do that thing.*"

His 1997 piece was called Temporal Decomposition. It was a twelve-foot-diameter ball of ice with 200 timepieces frozen inside of it. An aluminum pipe extended from the ball, acting as the gnomon of a sundial. It was constructed on-site at Hualapai, in the August desert sun, then left to melt, releasing the timepieces. This art did slowly and deliberately what so much Burning Man art does quickly and chaotically: It used temperature to cause a change in form, an ancient alchemy. The four compass points around the sundial were marked with hollowed obelisks of ice that surrounded pipes spitting fire.

The Burning Man organization gave Mason $4,500 to create the piece. "I wrote my first annoying Jim Mason project description, the first time I tried coopting Larry's writing style," recalls Mason. "The art theme was fertility that year, so I wrote a bullshit mythic narrative relating solar cycles to fertility. It was pitched as a solar temple thing because of the sundial aspect. That was the first Burning Man project I got funded for. I was the first anonymous person who wasn't an old friend who came to them saying I'd like to do an art project that's ambitious and costs lots of money. Back then, all the funding decisions were made in the International Café on Haight Street. That was Larry's office.

"It was actually an interesting high school physics problem, making Temporal Decomposition. I got out the books and figured out how many calories I had to remove to draw the temperature of x units of water down x number of degrees. I did all the math, and all the math turned out to be irrelevant. Well, it sort of helped me figure out what ballpark the solution existed in. And in the end I made it work by hauling an obscene amount of ice from Reno out there.

"We built a fiberglass mold with an insulating building around it, and we had a junky refrigerator unit off a diesel truck. The first big problem was making the mold. We needed something to lay the fiberglass over. We tried weather balloons, but the thing we got to work in the end was rebar and chicken wire. Then we built a building around it, a big wooden frame, then foam on the frame, then plastic on the foam and expanding foam to seal all the joints and corners, so we had a fourteen-by-fourteen-by-fourteen-foot building around the piece for insulation. Then we surrounded the building with hay and stuck the refrigerator unit inside the hay and ran it for two weeks. But I still had to haul twenty thousand pounds of ice from Reno. I found a company with old blocks sitting around that were unusably dirty and misformed, and they sold them to me cheap. I got to work breaking the ice up and putting it in through a hole in the foam and through the top of the fiberglass.

"The idea was to peel off the mold at the beginning of Burning Man and have the piece decompose over the course of the event. But of course I didn't get it finished until the next-to-last day. Like all Jim Mason's failures, it turned out more interesting than the original plan. I desperately cling to that hope.

"What ended up being interesting was that there was this thing, and no one had any idea what it *was*—this huge mound of hay in the middle of the event is all people saw. Then I started peeling off the hay and foam, and I hadn't slept in days and I was a screaming hysterical wreck, falling over, peeling off this fiberglass, and then it was a beautiful thing that most people saw. The way it ultimately melted didn't look that good, so I'm actually happy I didn't finish it as I planned because it would have looked horrible in a couple of days. It was better to do the unveiling the night of the Burn."

Burning Man art is inherently, and by necessity, communal. No one person could pull off stunts of this nature by himself, and there is almost never enough money involved to pay helpers. The constant maintenance needed on Mason's awful, truculent junkyard refrigerator unit came from a local machinehead who was fascinated by the idea and miraculously came up with replacement parts from Gerlach-area yards for every element of the unit that failed. Quick trips to the hardware store are impossible at Burning Man; the nearest Home Depot is a four-hour-plus round trip.

"The building of the mold and the walls was mostly girlfriend labor and good-friend labor. Hauling the ice up to the top was gutter-punk labor, and that's where the beer came in. Every time I'd get a load of ice in Reno, I'd get two cases of shitty beer. I'd park the truck, lay out the beer, and say, 'Anyone wanna help?'

"The project had a powerful effect on people. One woman saw the proposal online and came to Burning Man all the way from Florida because she saw some vision in the art, something very important to her, and she had to be a part of it. She came out and did all sorts of stuff to help."

Temporal Decomposition was not all Mason brought to Burning Man in 1997. He also brought the Vegematic of the Apocalypse.

The Veg, as everyone affectionately called it, was a long drill, mounted on a pair of rusty metal tractor wheels around six feet tall. It also sported a fire cannon, capable of spitting flame jets one hundred feet or more. While experimenting and putzing around, Mason managed to ignorantly come up with the standard old-fashioned design for military flamethrowers. The drill was a relic of the Stanford-/ New Guinea sculpture garden, meant to dig deep, narrow holes for sculptural supports to rest in. The machine's look of decrepit rusty decay, and the fact that it was pedal powered, combined with its unprecedented and utterly unnecessary destructive power, made it an archetypal toy for midera Burning Man, the epitome of the oft-mentioned *Mad Max* vibe.

Burning Man 1997 was actually the Veg's second year at Black Rock. In 1996 it showed up unannounced and inadvertently became part of the big Burn. Mason innocently pedaled it around the Man and created the circle beyond which the crowd stayed to ensure the Man's cindered remains didn't fall on them. In 1997, the Veg was his toy for when he wasn't tearing his hair out over Temporal Decomposition.

"Chris DeMonterey came up to me late on the night Temporal Decomposition had been unveiled, and he said, 'Jim, I was wondering why you built this giant ice ball, and I realized that you never had anything to really shoot the Veg at, and now you have its natural enemy: ice.' I had never thought of that at all, but when Chris said it, I thought it was the best idea I'd heard in my life. I reloaded the Veg with fuel and attacked Temporal Decomposition."

It was a sight that cemented affection for Burning Man into the most jaded of hearts: this reckless and unprecedented device coughing jets of flame and grinding its drill bit into a twelve-foot ball of ice embedded with dozens of windup clocks and watches. With each fiery growl, the ice ball shed another thin layer of watery, steamy skin. A crowd gathered, excited as only people seeing something thrilling they could never have imagined before can be. Mason remembers that "this woman from Amsterdam got so excited by the sight of the Veg fighting the ice ball that she grabbed some random guy and started fucking him on the playa." Karie Henderson, an anthropologist studying Burning Man who hooked up with Jim's crew and has worked with Burning Man ever since, now as a video documentarian, says, "I have had people tell me they saw God in the Vegematic–ice ball fight. Their whole life shifted forever."

In the primal battle of fire versus ice, ice won. Temporal Decomposition lost some inches and the Veg's drill dented its frigid shell, but the ice ball outlasted the flamethrower's fuel.

Very late Sunday night, 3:00 AM or so, during Burning Man 1999, Jim Mason's fire symphony was about to be performed. Mason fiddled with five tall tanks to make them shoot pressurized kerosene jets in the air nearly one hundred *yards*. He arranged them in a four-tank circle, one hundred feet in diameter, with one tank in the center. He composed a three-movement symphony with musical notes represented by flames of different height and intensity bursting in planned rhythms and patterns from the five tanks. It is a perfect example of an art project that could only be pulled off within the space and emptiness of Black Rock. Mason conducted by speaking through a headphone radio to the five tank operators and their fire-extinguisher- bearing spotters, one of whom, at the center tank, was me.

I was not then, and am not now, an experienced fire-safety maven. My presence there was a good example of how Mason earned the semi-affectionate nickname of Jim "Safety Third" Mason. He barely knew me then; I was just a passerby he realized he'd seen somewhere before. Yet he asked me, not ten minutes before the show was to begin, if I'd be interested in running one of the fire extinguishers for the performance. Four years earlier, I had been intensely nervous about even staying two nights in the Black Rock Desert. With most of five Burning Mans behind me, my sense of what I could handle was grander. I said yes.

"The Impotence Compensation Symphony will now begin," Mason joked. It went off impressively for the first two movements, though falling kerosene lit small fires on the tanks, the cracked playa, and a shirt left lying near a tank. A couple of the ground fires seemed threatening, and I dashed from my spot on the center tank to help others with my water-pressure extinguisher. I slipped on a sheet of kerosene, righted myself frantically. The flame jets, well over one hundred feet tall and only ten feet from me, were a hot weight crushing down on my skull, palpable, like a heavy brick of fire balanced on my head. I kept patting my long tangled hair, certain it was on fire.

Streaks of flame poured down the tank fifty feet behind me. I rushed to empty my extinguisher on it, futilely. Someone grabbed the extinguisher from my hand. "Run, run, run! It might blow," Mason was shouting. Performers and crowd formed a circle a hundred yards wide around the tank, perhaps secretly hoping for one more colorful explosion. Luckily, or alas, the tank, with its nozzle left open, ran out of kerosene before the pressurized liquid could explode.

Mason began to doubt the value of the fire cannons. They came out to Burning Man for years and were, for a time, a fixture in the actual burning of the Man, surrounding him and shooting their gushes of flame and smoke a football-field length in the air. But Mason came to think there wasn't enough *art* to them—no concept, just pure explosive power. "I decided I hated them and gave them away for other people to operate. But recently I had so much fun watching Mark Pauline of SRL play with his huge terrifying machines that I got excited and unembarrassed about the cannons again. It's OK if I just want to play with them because they are big and scary. If I can keep making them bigger and scarier and operate them while drunk, then I'm happy. Maybe they aren't art, but they are a very fun toy for boys."

In 2000, Mason tried something even more ambitious—and ultimately less successful. With his reach far exceeding his grasp—or even any clear idea of how he could possibly grasp what he was reaching for—he decided to prank the obsession with stock prices among the digerati and yuppies who had come to dominate San Francisco, and who were by then a huge presence at Burning Man as-well.

The idea was dubbed the G-7 Stock Puppets—a series of oversized fiberglass human figures dressed in giant suits and tethered to a series of twenty-five-foot-tall pulleys on a frame. The idea was that the puppets would be mechanically manipulated via real-time computer feeds of stock prices. In some way, each puppet was to represent one of the G-7 nations. An elaborate game show was somehow to interact with it, with Chicken John as host. Passersby at Burning Man would be recruited as players, and then "their" puppet would react to data on stocks owned by the contestant. As the stock prices rose, the puppet would rise. If it reached the top, it would shoot fire.

Actually, as the idea shifted and evolved and the people of Burning Man watched Jim and some occasional helpers erecting the frames and fiddling with the computers and dragging around the puppets, no one knew what was really supposed to happen, and no one knew what the fuck Jim was thinking, even though he'd been granted a huge budget from Burning Man and the most honored spot for an art project: the "keyhole," located at the point at the Center Camp of Black Rock City where the promenade to the Man begins. Anyone walking from Center Camp to the Man—which would eventually be almost everyone in the city—would pass by this piece.

Mason had begun the Stock Puppets project, like all of his projects, with a pure faith that somehow, through tenacity and the love and support of the community, his dreams would transmogrify into reality. Such wonderful alchemy actually does work at Burning Man more often than a hidebound capitalist skeptic would anticipate.

As Mason says, "All these projects are claims of faith. I have this idea, and I'm stupid and delusional enough to believe it can actually happen, even though it far exceeds my own capacities to do it. But if I just set it in motion, once I am out on the playa, people will want to help, and come in and save the idea."

But that communal magic wasn't strong enough this time to conjure the physical and programming miracles necessary, under broiling sun with unpredictable windstorms and inadequate tools, with an already-baked crew (they had spent months in San Francisco fruitlessly trying to make the puppets work) who didn't even make it out to Burning Man until two days after the event had begun.

One night late in the week during Burning Man 2000, I was sitting around the communal fire barrels at Happyland, a theme camp that was home to many of Burning Man's most ambitious metal sculpture artists. Mason, a guest, was looking surprisingly undefeated. No one had seen him for a day and a half; turned out he'd been crashed in a sleeping bag in the back of the battered, barely functioning panel truck he'd driven up from San Francisco. By now it was clear that it was all over. The giant fiberglass puppets would not rise, fall, jerk, shimmy, and shoot flames in response to real-time data on stock price fluctuations.

"How you feeling, Jimmy?" someone asked.

"I feel good. I failed big. I failed the biggest I've ever failed. I think I failed bigger than anyone has ever failed out here. Over twenty thousand dollars and five months of failure."

"How's Larry feel?"

"Larry understands. I think. He's not yelling or threatening to cut my head off or screaming for his money back at any rate. What can he say? He saw me out there crawling in the dust and throwing wrenches and crying."

Dan Das Mann, another of Burning Man's sculptors, walked by. "Jim, everyone's asking me when your puppet show is going to happen."

"Tell them it already happened. Tell them it happened very late Friday night. Tell them how earthshakingly awesome it was. Shake your head about how sorry you are they missed it. Best shit out here, by far."

"Hey, Jim," someone else suggested, "tell everyone there was a typo on the program. Tell Larry he misread your proposal. It was actually the G-7 *Sock* Puppets. You needed the twenty grand for some very high-quality silk socks. Imported from China."

Larry Harvey commented on the Stock Puppets' failure three years later: "Jim had me snowed on that thing. He told me he'd delegated it all out. And I see him outside my trailer for three days working alone, and the third time I see him he's got a puppet on his shoulder, trudging it around in a dust storm. The project is four days overdue. I can see it's not going to happen. I stood beside him in the dust, and the puppet looked like a cross on his shoulder. He loves that kind of drama. I said to him, 'Jim, it's not enough to be Jesus. You have to have some disciples.'"

Jim was humbled, but only for a while. He spent most of the *next* year trying to make the Stock Puppets work. He finally succeeded, at SIG-GRAPH in summer 2001, a high-end professional conference dedicated to cutting-edge computer graphics and interactive technology. "The Stock Puppets were a one-line joke that destroyed my life for two years," Mason says of the project now. The whole ordeal did teach him that he has far more fun working amid Burning Man's inspired and inspiring amateurism than among the slick, highly funded professionalism of SIGGRAPH.

Because the Stock Puppets ate up all his ridiculous-project energy again in 2001, Mason never managed to get his idea for Burning Man 2001 off the ground: the Ascension Machine.

Jim Mason is serious about Burning Man because it's *fun*. He bandies about the word *bullshit* to refer to the stunts he and other artists pull off out there, but he doesn't mean it in a bad way. When Larry Harvey announced the art theme for 2001—the Seven Ages (originally the Seven Ages of Man until feminists in the Burning Man community complained)—Mason bridled at what he saw as an attempt to impose spiritual meaning on the Burning Man experience.

The theme became the framework for a game that Burners were supposed to participate in every stage of (though few did). It was vague and encompassing enough to cover almost anything. It was derived from Shakespeare's famous "All the world's a stage" speech from *As You Like It,* about the stages every human life progresses through. Larry's explanation of the theme said that "the object of this game is the attainment of wisdom. In order to achieve this goal, participants must pass through successive stages of life. The theme of our game is choice, striving, trial, and transformation."

Mason, suspicious of modern spirituality, sniffed a rat. "One thing that's annoyed me about Burning Man lately is the earnestness that has come into the core, an attempt to forcibly increase its impact and meaning. But the reason Burning Man had meaning to begin with was that it was always deeply comedic—it has always been a spin through jesting and farce and absurdism. I try to imagine my projects as spiritual farces."

Thus, the Ascension Machine—a way to turn the quest for ultimate wisdom and inner Nirvana into something Jim Mason could understand: a competition. "The Ascension Machine will be a contest of meditative skill and competitive concentration—a race to enlightenment. It will consist of two towers built in a Japanese-pagoda style, twenty-five feet tall, each with a platform base upon which one person can sit lotus style. The two competitors will have EEG sensors on their temples to monitor their alpha and beta waves, and you will attempt to *quiet your mind* faster than your opponent.

"The flatter your brain waves get, the higher your platform will rise up the tower, and then when one of you reaches the top, bells go off and you're the winner. I can reuse the electromechanically controlled puppet technology with people, only instead of reacting to stock market averages, it's reacting to brain waves.

"The challenge will be the terrible negative feedback loop in trying to maintain concentration, because as you get higher, the music playing will change from a soothing ambient drone to Tibetan chanting and then to didgeridoo and there will be driving techno as you approach Nirvana. You'll have pressure sensors on your fingers, and if they leave that fingertips-touching position, flamethrowers on the side will go off. And it will be mechanically rough, so every time you move, you'll be thinking of the creator of this tower and the previous things he's made and the mechanical challenges they've faced while you are twenty feet in the air dependent on something Jim Mason designed."

The Ascension Machine didn't happen. Selling off the bulk of his life just to create another absurd catastrophe in the desert has taken a backseat the past couple of years. Mason has instead been marshaling his energy in a serious attempt to create a slice of Burning Man in Berkeley at what he calls his Shipyard.

Mason and I get together there one Sunday afternoon, in a few spare hours he has among his months working to satisfy the city of-Berkeley's code requirements for the bizarre ghetto of shipping containers he's built on an empty lot. (In late 2003, he finally got the requisite permits.) This is the Shipyard: Mason's gift to the artistic community that has grown around Burning Man. It's meant to provide a breeding ground for large-scale, Burning Man–style art projects— many of such a heroic and Brobdingnagian scale that they couldn't be-built indoors anywhere smaller than an airplane hangar. All morning he's been planting shrubs to add a touch of beauty—and futile camouflage—around the ugly hulking containers.

"All the plants I'm planting here, I'm stealing from the sculpture garden I helped design at Stanford. And when I planted them there, I stole them from elsewhere around the Bay Area. I'm always propagating the transfer of interesting plants. That's one of the main narratives of my life."

We settle down on rusty folding chairs in front of a giant over-turned cable spool, standing in for a table. Mason, again the anthropologist, tells me about the cultural effects of Burning Man.

"It's a radically unusual idea that has overtaken a large group of people in one region. This notion, propagated by Burning Man, that you *should* create something. That you should notice the world and make a comment on it and express that comment through building something—and that you should do this in a very unusual, very harsh environment, under the worst imaginable conditions. Burning Man has infested the Bay Area with the notion that *people should do creative work*. And that it's not just a right but a responsibility, in order to be a living, breathing, valuable human being."

Mason loves this idea and decided to help sustain it year-round. So along with continuing his day job preserving all the world's languages, he built an unprecedented live-work space out of modular shipping containers, just so the Burning Man spirit can spread. Dozens of friends and fellow dreamers bought in to help him make it work, with money and/or labor. Similarly inspired, Burning Man artists Dan Das Mann and Charlie Gadeken created another container art space in San Francisco, called the Box Shop.

The weary Mason eventually suggested we move to someplace more comfortable. Now we are slumped on a pair of couches pushed together front to front in a corner of the only non-shipping-container structure on his site. He gestures around to the piles of tangled wiring, the half-built fountain, the tall robotic wheel out in the courtyard that can be mounted and moved by a human driver strapped in like an astronaut in a capsule—and which, of course, sports flamethrowers.

"This wouldn't exist if Burning Man didn't exist. I think the main accomplishment of Burning Man is creating a broad sense of participatory, collaborative, creative work. This isn't a notion that generally exists in most cities, but it uniquely exists in the Bay Area because this is the main center for Burning Man. I constantly get comments from people I know in other cities—'What do you mean you can put an idea out on a computer Listserv and people come out and help you build it and you don't have to pay them an hourly rate?' People from

L.A. particularly get freaked out by this. It's like Burning Man sent an idea virus around: that you can have a big idea and be confident that the material resources will show up and the people resources will show up to help you build it."

The Burning Man community works, then, like one of the emergent systems that get *Wired*-type intellectuals all aflutter—an unexpected and rich order that arises not from central planning but from the myriad choices of seemingly disconnected individuals. Those choices create highly complicated results that no individual, however brilliant or driven, could have planned.

With that meme in mind, Mason told me of his plans to propose to Larry Harvey a project that would create such an unplanned order while clearing "a vibrant and rich new ground for exciting creative work at Burning Man: the porta potty." Yes, the necessarily ubiquitous pale-green-and-blue shitboxes littering the playa.

"Given Larry's interest in monumental community-based iconic architecture, I proposed a carillon made of large metal bells hanging in the middle of the café in Center Camp that are fired with pneumatic hammers triggered by the opening and closing of porta potty doors all across the playa via a system of light sensors and a computer network."

Mason suddenly seems lost in the deepest levels of heavy-duty artistic theorizing. "I'm sure some interesting self-organizing phenomenon would start to develop; all this distributed activity across the playa transformed into sound in this one location should make for a fascinating emergent-property work of sound art. It would help to make people more consciously, directly aware of the impact of what they are doing in the café—drinking. The inevitable result of that consumption will be made manifest as they listen to the bells. It will make people more aware of their impact on the planet. It will be a very positive project."

He says all this with great gravity. I think about it for a second. I reply, "But really, it sounds like it would just result in a lot of horrible loud noises going off *constantly*."

Now he's smiling. "With no discernable relation to anything, yes."

☼

The Porta-John carillon hasn't happened—yet. Just because it was clearly conceptualized as a self- and event-deprecating bit of whimsy doesn't mean it will never be built. Lots of Burning Man art has that same feel, of amusingly absurd intellectualized nonsense, the kind of ideas that slightly skewed creative people brainstorm about in late nights at cafés and around the hardwood living room floor after the fourth glass of wine or third bowl of pot, but *actually executed.*

Burning Man uniquely invites and brings together a supportive and enthusiastic audience for smart silliness. One slogan circulating through the community, originally coined as a cynical joke by Chicken John, refers to Burning Man as the "Special Olympics of art—where everyone plays and everyone's a winner." Mason thinks there's a kinder, more important truth behind the jibe. "Everyone can go out with their impossible idea and try it and fall on their face, and everyone can kick them in the ass about it a couple of months later, but ultimately everyone smiles and everyone gets hugged in the end. I've certainly blazed new trails in aggressive failure on the playa, so I can appreciate the affirming and gee-whiz good feeling aspect of that." Anyone from the bitterly cutthroat (in proportion to how small the stakes are) world of "normal art" could certainly appreciate—even be envious of—the opportunities the Burning Man community provides for artists.

Burning Man's vibe, though, is not all love and encouragement. It tiptoes on a knife-edge between two dominant alternative outlooks in American underground culture. They can be roughly characterized as punk and hippie. (Of course, I'm naming attitudes, not pigeonholing people. One person might easily slip into either tendency at different times, and people who might self-identify one way or the other will never be pure exemplars of the attitudes as I'm defining them here. Living among the people of Burning Man is an efficient way to learn to mistrust sweeping generalizations about human types.) "Punk" is the attempt to transgress perceived limits of acceptable and proper behavior and comportment through a sometimes cynically mean absurdity (redeemed by being often hilarious); "hippie" is the belief that "love is all you need" and that the proper response to American mainstream culture is a manic togetherness and all-encompassing acceptance that's all sweet and no sour—it can be inspiring but can also seem disturbingly soft and gelatinous.

Burning Man is full of people openly embracing either possibility—and also many, like me, torn between an attraction to the aggressive wit and piquant tomfoolery of the punk mentality and the warm sincerity and endearing openness of the hippie one. One must not make the mistake of categorizing by appearance or lifestyle. Many a couch-surfing sunken-cheekboned blond young man with wispy facial hair, a Phish jones, and a pale-tan fringed vest with no shirt can have a punk disregard for others' person and property; and the greasiest spiked-purple-hair-and-dog-collar kid can be filled with nothing but a noble and honorable respect and affection for all people of goodwill.

But despite differences about properly improper behavior, you'll find at Burning Man a remarkably cheerful live-and-let-live internalized ethos that keeps thousands of people coexisting in a deliberately stressful *extremis* surprisingly peaceful, both physically and psychically. Though you can find more and more opportunities as the years go by to engage in serious and spirited discussions about what sort of behavior is or is not Burning Man, these conversations end with no more than, at worst, hurt feelings.

Still, it isn't all social harmony in the experimental community at Burning Man. There are tensions, aggravations, fault lines. Some of them—like arguments at hip parties, and among the many things it is, Burning Man is the hippest party around—are over music.

The dominant musical culture at Burning Man is post–rock 'n' roll—the beats and drones and throbs and hums and bleeps of electronic dance music in all its styles. Many, many Burners love and cherish the presence of dozens of miniraves at Burning Man. Many others resent the fact that the presence of the ravers makes many people carelessly assume that Burning Man is nothing but a giant rave.

Raves are noisy. Fueled by the ecstasy of musical communion, and often by the ecstasy of the drug ecstasy, the ravers frequently go on and on 'til the break of dawn. The would-be DJ kings of Black Rock City frequently keep the music banging and lights flashing even past the dawn, often to an audience of no one but themselves. City zoning in Black Rock, such as it is, has tried different ways to balance fairly between your freedom to rave on and someone else's ability to sleep without it sounding as if a mountain-sized dryer containing a giant's steel-toed boots were churning fifty yards away.

For a few early years, the ravers were physically segregated a mile or so away from the main encampment. This was viable back when Burning Man was small and had to do less maneuvering and planning to satisfy the demands of the various government agencies that think they have a stake in what happens on the Black Rock Playa. But since the chaos and hazards of 1996 spawned a mostly enforced no-driving rule (except for the omnipresent art cars), that was no longer tenable.

Then one year they tried zoning, defining a quiet side and a noisy side of Black Rock City. As in any city, zoning produced political conflicts that the solons of Burning Man chose to resolve—or at least remove themselves from responsibility for—by declaring that sound zoning would be self-directed. They invoked the overarching Burning Man rule of "not interfering with anyone else's direct experience" and hoped that people could resolve any conflicts peaceably without generators being sabotaged, wires chopped, or turntables smashed. Nowadays, sound systems of a certain size are restricted to the edge of the city, with speakers directed toward the open playa.

Still, it's pretty hard to get away from the noise. The only solution is cultivating insensitivity to it. I don't like most electronic dance music—and years of forced exposure to it at Burning Man haven't helped. Sure, I have some fond memories of occasions when a puckish desire to beard the beast in its den brought me and some friends into a rave "scene." Like the night an overfull load was raging in the Directioner—an old Toyota Celica with its trunk torn out for more sitting/standing room for the gangs of friends who crammed into it every night, with a giant rotating arrow dangling overhead, attached to a pipe slid into a fitting drilled into the floor of the car. The Directioner only drove backward, and its gas pedal was stick operated, allowing the driver to stand on the hood and drive it. We showed up at Bianca's Smut Shack, Burning Man's most popular erotic dance club in its day.

Mateo, the car's bullhorn-wielding designer, pushed his way through the dense crowd of ravers barking, "I lost my glowstick! Has anyone seen my glowstick? It's short and greenish," between deadpan recitations of the lyrics of "Play That Funky Music." Rave scenes are ultimately impenetrable to parody or joshing. Our gang's intentionally ridiculous spasmodic jerkings and arms (and legs) thrown in the air fit in all too well. It's hard to fight against something so innocently, so mindlessly, well meaning that it's willing and eager to assimilate *everything.*

I mostly don't even notice how omnipresent the beats and the bleeps are out there. But when I listen to audiotapes of conversations from Burning Man, what I might remember as a quiet scene of talking around the fire is revealed to be a conversation in what sounds like the bathroom of a discotheque.

Jim Mason has thoughtful opinions about almost every aspect of Burning Man, forged through his many years and wide range of experiences there. He's never stopped being incensed that rave music, which he hates, is such a big part of an event he otherwise respects and loves. He once turned a Burning Man town meeting (held in San Francisco after the event to discuss community business), usually a hive of happy vibes, into a buzz of muttered disapproval by publicly requesting that Burning Man's organizers for God's sake do something to curb the ravers.

Mason was no do-nothing whiner. He resorted to the authorities only after he failed in his own attempt at a final solution to the rave question.

"You can't stop the music" is a belovedly campy phrase for dance-music devotees. On Burn Night in 1997—at the moment when the devilish, anything-the-fuck-goes atmosphere at Burning Man reaches almost palpable density (maybe it's just the smoke from all the fires)—Mason decided to test that maxim, using the Vegematic of the Apocalypse.

"I pedaled the Vegematic around for five hours that night," Mason remembers, "having very loaded, tense confrontations with the owners of various artworks as to what our interaction with said artwork should be. It's fun riding on the Veg, which inevitably attracts a very rowdy, screaming mob running alongside. It's obviously the most dangerous thing out there, and it can cause tremendous problems if everyone thinks you're some methhead who wants to destroy everything.

"Of course, in reality we are reasonably nice, taxpaying citizens. I didn't intend to really burn anything down. But the crowd wanted *everything* burned down. We did shoot down a weather balloon, and we did burn a giant duck. I had three hundred people following me, chanting 'Burn the Duck!'

"But the best part was when we rolled into the rave camp."

I was there. Not even one-hundred-foot flame jets could sway the DJ. He had been flown in that day from Goa, India. His mission was to groove the crowd, and by Vishnu, that crowd was going to groove. He stared, arms crossed, at the gang of circus freaks, sweaty bike mechanics, and dust-caked cheering hooligans who had dared invade his sacred space, the mini-arena where his people swayed and slid and jerked and elevated themselves to the beat he laid down. But right now most of the dancing had stopped, as the nervous ravers stepped back and gaped at this freakish device, simultaneously ancient and postapocalyptic, rolling heedlessly through their densely dancing bodies.

At the end of its drill snout, the Vegematic sported two rusty saw blades, attached by loosely fastened chains. They rattled menacingly when the machine churned its drill bit. The Vegematic's followers were chanting: "*Led* Zeppelin! *Led* Zeppelin! *Led* Zeppelin!"

It was a sharply defined clash of cultures—peace-and-unity ravers conjuring up a communal vibe based on music and pleasure versus the grease-monkey mechanics who built their weird, scary destructive devices and rolled them around shooting off one-hundred-foot-long flames for the sheer exhilaration of watching the fire arc, of feeling its pummeling heat, of seeing the darker smoke smudge the dark night sky. It had been a rampage of pure mindless release, until Mason and his marauding band heard a real target in the distance—this rave camp, projecting its mellow dance culture out into the vast night. Now, Mason thought, the Vegematic could perform a genuine public service—stopping that damned electronic *bompbompbomp.*

Mason pedaled the flamethrowing nose ten feet from the DJ in his elevated booth. It licked small flames from the snout, a restrained threat of infernos to come. Hadn't the DJ seen them out there, toasting flying objects ninety feet up? Didn't he *know* what this machine was capable of?

Still, he just stared. Was it a glower of defiance, or merely the sheer self-confidence of a man who knew that his crowd and the vibe he was creating were just too vibrant and energetic to be stopped? I suppose there is no standard pat reaction for confrontations with giant pedal-powered flamethrowing drills.

The rowdies stared at this *electronica-playing hippie* who stood his ground in the face of this machine of absurd, pointless destructive power. And they knew they'd met their match. With grudging respect, the Vegematic gave ground, its crew broke ranks, and Mason pedaled it slowly around, away, and back into the chaotic night, dotted with fires small and large and jammed with running, whooping crowds of mysterious purpose, or of no purpose at all.

As its nose rotated, the Vegematic's kinetic energy was turned to its most vital use: powering a margarita-filled blender back within reach of its driver. The Vegematic, this ferocious mobile flamethrower, was also the world's most dangerous drink blender.

The Vegematic, to Mason's astonishment, was *stolen* one night back in San Francisco a few years later, where it was parked around the corner from a Burning Man fund-raising party. He hoped it was just a prank. (Imagining what the thief would *do* with the non-street-legal machine that Mason spent inordinate amounts of time trying to find a place to store boggles his mind to this day.) It would have been a perfectly typical prank in the Burning Man art circles in which Mason was known as a top dog and was also notorious for fucking with other people's shit. During Burning Man 2000, after the failure of the Puppets had been (perhaps not completely) internalized, Jim, in a drunken fit, "borrowed" an art car—a van with its shell ripped out and replaced by a splitting DNA molecule made of wrecked bumpers stretching about twenty feet in the sky, dubbed the Chromazoom by its creator, Robert Burke. Before Jim was through with it, three of its tires were flat.

Mason and I discussed the delicate issue of otherwise decent human beings' occasional enjoyment of acts of completely fucked-up chaos. Looking quite serious as he reflects on his sins, Mason says, "I'll give a dubious justification via the words of Chris Radcliffe: He said, 'Jim, you're the only one out there willing to have fun—like, fuck you, I'm gonna steal your art car and I'm gonna crash it.' He was very affirming of my transgressions.

"But still, I don't like breaking things. I *was* upset I hurt Robert's car. I don't even know how it happened. The stealing of art cars was never a willful idiom I took up."

The rush of justification, though, can't be stopped. "You see, *my* stuff gets stolen all the time. The problem is, I have very few boundaries—everyone uses my stuff and breaks it, and I'm completely fine with it. So I make the incorrect assumption that others are fine with me using their stuff. So while I'm not pleased I hurt Robert's car, in general I am in full support of more elaborate chaos in the desert. The event has become very nice in the last several years. It's very pleasant there. I do think there should be some things that are a little less pleasant."

Not everyone agrees. "The Vegematic was *un*invited back," explains Mason. "After 1997 they had a lot of permitting issues with the authorities, and Pershing County's Sheriff Skinner would refer to the Veg by name at meetings when explaining why this event was too dangerous to happen. He actually had pictures of it and used it as a symbol of why Burning Man had to be stopped.

"The only reason it didn't cause any genuine problems was the decisions [and judgment] of the operator. Nothing else could guarantee that some disaster wouldn't happen. We always looked maniacal and drunk and out of control, and everyone was always convinced we were on the verge of killing someone. And we were always convinced we weren't."

While Mason accurately notes the gradual imposition of order and rules over Burning Man's originally formless chaos, he still marvels at what is possible out there for artists. "They have been amazingly successful at creating a space that allows all sorts of basic illegality and dangerous behavior in a somewhat regulated environment. The stuff I do with the fire cannons—there is not any other regulated environment on the planet where I could do that. It does not conform to any existing civilian pyrotechnic code. We can make great arguments that we know what we're doing and that we've tested it, but it's essentially military equipment, and you don't get permits to run stuff like that."

Mason's experiences with his Shipyard, and his discussion of how Burning Man is a space for rituals of inversion where the normal rules of behavior are overturned or suspended, made me think of a short story I had once read and loved but not fully understood: Argentine fabulist Jorge Luis Borges's "Tlön, Uqbar, Orbis Tertius." I began to see that Larry Harvey's experiment was achieving the shape and heft of the experiment related in that tale. It's about a squad of intellectuals who create an intricately designed, fantasized alternate world, and about how that fantasy world mysteriously begins transforming the real world into itself. Burning Man is not only growing, it is growing outside its own bounds, creating a space almost magical in its implications and its ability to make the unlikely happen. Every year, more artists take advantage of the world Burning Man creates— and Burning Man takes advantage of human beings by turning them into artists.

Chapter Eight

"THE ASS HAS SPOKEN!"

Art at Burning Man crosses genres and defies classification and doesn't fit comfortably in the standard academic and gallery worlds that dominate the "real art scene" in America. Burning Man is an almost purely outsider-art festival, generally ignored by the real art world (with a couple of rare exceptions among art professors) until 2003, when a small flurry of art press coverage appeared—in *Art Papers, Modern Painters,* and *Leonardo,* an arts journal published by MIT.

Although most generalizations about Burning Man are ultimately misleading, it's fair enough to think of the art there as mostly outsider, executed by people with no particular credentials from or love for the gallery or academic scene. While many artists at Burning Man would be happy to sell the work they've done out there after Black Rock City evaporates, it hardly ever happens.

In the old days, when so much of the art burned, that wasn't even an issue. But most of it doesn't burn anymore. After 2000 or so, new restrictions on art burns had settled in: the piece must sit on a burn blanket so no fire directly touches the playa; what's going to happen, and how, has to be preplanned and approved by Burning Man officials, in collaboration with actual fire marshals. (Someone on Burning Man's inspection team, however, tells me that the marshals usually bow down to Burning Man's greater expertise and long history in art burns, allowing whatever Burning Man says is OK to proceed.)

One will find artistic gestures and productions of all varieties out there, in all mediums from metal to plastic to stone, lots of them incorporating light, many of them incorporating sound, some solemn and dignified, some outrageous and bizarre. A fair amount of them, though not quite most of them, involve fire, even if they don't burn themselves down.

Burning Man has provided a palette for certain art forms that could almost be considered indigenous to the city, that play out and evolve on the playa in great abundance year to year. Like the performing art of fire-spinning—dancing and swaying with fiery balls on the ends of staffs or chains, and spinning the flames, creating instantaneous, evanescent, and ever-changing images and figures of red-orange hot swirls, with yourself the paintbrush, and fire the paint.

There's also electroluminescent wire—el-wire—a thin, portable copper wire coated with phosphorus and wrapped with transmitter wires, powered by batteries and tiny inverters, that allows artists to create all the delightful effects of neon light but with a medium that's portable, malleable, and thin. People at Burning Man do amazing things with it; its range of colors and the ability to switch it on and off make it perhaps the most phantasmagoric art form man has yet invented. The user can make actual objects, not just images on a screen, appear, disappear, and change colors. Dolphins of el-wire break through the playa's oceanic surface and disappear; hopping kangaroos of light cavort behind bicycles; twirling hypnotic circles adorn hats and the backs of people's coats. The horizons of Black Rock City are a constant gorgeous panorama of light because of fire-spinning and el-wire.

The art at Burning Man is bound together by an unusual, at least for our culture, emotional reality. Its audience knows the work is all there not to sell you anything, or even to sell itself, but as a gift. The pieces aren't marked with plaques; you wouldn't necessarily have any way of knowing who did a particular artwork or what it is "supposed" to be, adding to both the purity and amusement of people's reactions. A very hardworking crew from New York at Burning Man 2003 built a giant homage to Duchamp in the form of a urinal lying on the ground, dozens of feet both tall and long. You entered the inside of the bowl through a long pipe. Because the urinal wasn't oriented up on a wall, many people who crawled inside had no idea what it was supposed to be. And who the hell would *guess* that someone would build a giant urinal at great expense and effort—especially one so meticulously carpentered? (It was some of the most professional work I'd ever seen out there.) I sat around inside it for a few hours one night, amused at the speculations I heard. My favorite was that it might be a hockey arena, since the giant glowing plastic urinal cake seemed like it might represent a puck.

You do get a booklet when you arrive—which most people, as near as I can tell, deposit on their dashboard for the duration of the gathering—that has a map and identifies the names of the pieces and the artists, and often gives brief descriptions of the work, but even with that in hand it's often hard to tell exactly where you are in reality in relation to the symbols on the map. Even the stuff the Burning Man organization helps fund is still a gift from the artists—because that grant almost never covers the entire cost, either in dollars or in sweat, of the project (nor is it intended to). The grants themselves are also essentially a gift from Burning Man, even though they come out of the ticket money. Burning Man doesn't *have* to spend the money funding art.

Longtime Burning Man photographer Leo Nash got me thinking about something important regarding Burning Man art: its honest, rough-and-ready quality. The seams are exposed, the mechanisms open and obvious. If you show up early enough and care to pay attention, the very act of construction and fitting the pieces together can be seen in daylight, in public. These are almost indecent acts of artistic shamelessness, the garret and the gallery and the studio be damned—this is something human beings do, and dammit, they are all there *doing* it.

You can not only *see* it being done but also, in almost every case, help make it happen. It is extraordinary how many different stories I've heard from large-installation artists of how just the right technically skilled person came by and was willing to kick in anywhere from two hours to four days to help a stranger assert his or her Self. This sort of thing has, over time, entered the lore of Black Rock City: "The playa provides" is a popular Burning Man epigram. (The playa can also, of course, wreck and ruin.)

People talk about "self-expression" when it comes to art—people name that as one of Burning Man's glories. But I think there is something subtly different going on out there. Whether they're works whose creators I know nothing of, or ones by people I've spent more than a hundred hours with, I find art out there doesn't seem to be so much arising from something deep and unique in the individual creator; rather, it all seems particularly civic, particularly risen from some Black Rock City group mind, expressions of the collective awe and confrontation with material reality we face out there, and of idea-viruses that float around the Burner collective unconscious. One year, say, you'll see lots of lily pad gardens by different, unconnected artists executed in different styles and media; and every year, you witness continual evolutions and differentiations of such popular Burning Man mediums as propane jets and el-wire. And all of it is uniquely *corporeal* in a way you might not notice with, say, sculptures in a gallery; everything gets hot in the middle of the day, so you can't touch it, and no matter what it is, it's got the look, color, and feel of playa dust.

Volunteerism is vital at every level of Burning Man, from specific artworks to the festival as a whole. In choosing whom to fund, Burning Man explicitly considers whether the artist-in-charge has a community on which he can lean in order to execute the piece.

Every craftsman must become a Tom Sawyer, convincing the doubting that hell, painting the fence is actually *fun*. It helps that most of the time, at Burning Man at least, it really is. Beyond fun, it's fulfilling in an old-fashioned sense of satisfying a civic responsibility that most of us have rarely known, growing up as we have in an age when a hypertrophied government tries to finesse most civic obligations and community needs through taxing and spending.

My favorite pieces at Burning Man, the ones that fill my own mind with wonder and make me glad both to be in Black Rock City and to be a member of the human race, are the absurd assertions of human will, the stuff that takes full advantage of the vaulting sky with only human imagination as the limit—in other words, the really big, spectacular, you've-never-seen-anything-like-this-before, often dangerous stuff.

Grand examples of huge and spectacular—and of pieces brilliantly designed to capture one's emotions and reach for a grand communal catharsis—are the tall, filigreed, and airy soaring temples built in successive mutating shapes for the past three years by David Best and an extensive crew, mostly from industrial scrap woods and cardboard tubes. The temples have been dedicated, in turn, as monuments to death, joy, and memory. All week, the temple invites and embraces thousands of citizens' thoughts and energy, all directed toward its stated purpose, and then it ignites, transforms, and dissipates those energies in a quietly intense Sunday-night burn ceremony that has come to mean more to many than the burn of the Man himself.

Another particular favorite of mine appeared in 2003. Atlanta's Zack Coffin pushed "huge" and "dangerous" to the limit with his Temple of Gravity. It was a pair of crossed arcing metal pieces from which hung five fucking enormous slabs of granite. It covered fifty feet of ground, rose twenty-four feet, and weighed seventy *tons*. People climbed on it and surfed on the granite slabs that swayed and jerked from gigantic chains, and woe betide you if your head was in the way. You experienced the awe of knowing that this thing could and would snuff out your life without a second thought and that it was up to you to keep your eye on it and make sure it didn't.

As its name suggested, it made you contemplate the core forces in this universe, weight and solidity and their undeniable reality—and the equally undeniable reality that we are clever enough to defeat these forces, to keep the tons of stone suspended for our contemplation and play. It all added up to a mighty victory for the spirit of mankind. When I was lucky enough to get to clamber to its pinnacle and help my friend Joe Joe the Clown, a lighting wizard, install the beacon on top—displaying a series of diode lights that blinked in sequence, making a light that appeared to fall at the speed of a falling object, thirty-two feet per second—I looked down at the swaying brazier filled with smoldering logs hanging from the piece's central joint and at the dozens of smiling lovely people touching and staring and playing with the piece and—do you know what it's like to be around so many people who are *happily amazed* for a week? —I was in every way possible on top of the world.

Contemplation and mastery of universal forces is a common theme at Burning Man. In addition to gravity, electricity has been used for artistic play in spectacular ways.

Austin Richards is a pale, tall, man with a standard close-cropped haircut. He orders milk with his meals. He frequently refers to women as "gals." He wrote a highly technical book on exploring the electromagnetic spectrum through computerized imaging technology. Austin is an industrial physicist. Yes, Austin is a bit of a geek.

Still, women frequently e-mail him nude pictures of themselves— unsolicited. Because Austin Richards is also a superhero. Under the lambent moon of the Black Rock Desert, a marvelous transformation takes place. Austin Richards becomes…Dr. Megavolt! Master of the Living Lightning!

Austin has had a passion for the Tesla coil since he was eight years old, when a techhead neighbor introduced him to a three-foot-tall coil that emitted two-inch sparks. When he grew up, he decided to start making them himself. The Tesla coil is an arcane device perhaps most associated with planetarium displays—or old horror movies in which mad scientists create lightning in their labs. The coil is the product of the theories and experiments of classic nutball scientist Nikola Tesla, Edison's greatest rival, who envisioned a wireless world of free electricity broadcast through the air. Tesla is the patron saint of those who like to mix their science with occult conspiracy theories. Some of his devotees believe he was an alien visitor, crushed by the sinister forces of Edison because Tesla wanted a world where people didn't have to pay for electricity.

While Tesla's dream of unmetered broadcast electricity failed, he did succeed in creating a device that makes for one of the most dramatic shows around. It looks like a giant doughnut elevated on a bronzed column. It takes one of the universe's weirdest forces—I mean, what *is* electricity? It ain't solid, it ain't liquid, it ain't air, it can appear from nowhere, it can kill you (no wonder myths about fickle gods always arose around it)—and half-tames it. The technicalities are maddeningly complicated, but the coil basically steps up, at four different points, voltage from a generator, transferring it at the last stage into purely resonant megavoltage that reaches toward radio frequencies and broadcasts the power through the air. As the voltage grows toward the top of the column, wrapped hundreds of times with thin wire, the hum it generates gets deeper and thicker.

As the charge reaches critical mass on the coil's doughnut head, its energy begins to leak, then spit, its jagged, twisting, churning purple-white bolts crackling and writhing and stretching for the sky and the ground simultaneously. The frequencies in the air can illuminate fluorescent bulbs for dozens of yards. The eerily refreshing smell of ozone emanates from the lightning bursts.

On its own, it is an irresistible attraction, at least at first. But Austin Richards, scientist, holds within him the secrets of Dr. Megavolt, showman. The frequencies that the coil produces flow by their nature on the top layer of what they hit, so Austin knew that a man could stand in a metal cage next to the coil and not get hurt by the lightning. Then he realized the "cage" could be shrunk to the size of a metal suit and worn. A man in this suit could receive and even seem to conduct the lightning—adding a human element to the elemental force.

Says Austin, "Coils are fun to look at for a few minutes; then people start to get bored, for the same reason people are bored with NASA when they send up unmanned space probes. Nobody cares because there's *nobody there.* You need the human element. People want to see the guy in the suit who looks like he's gonna die from the electricity. People never get tired of that."

At Burning Man, Austin took to mounting a nearly nine-foot-tall self-built coil—and then a second one—on top of a tall panel truck and driving around, with himself and his friends wearing the Dr. Megavolt suit and dominating the cityscape with their apocalyptic lightning flashes. Friends with megaphones would shout mock-religious rants, inviting the people of Black Rock to bow down and worship the might of Megavolt. It became an integral part of the scene, especially on Burn Night, after the Man went down and the city went nuts.

During the show, Austin, jerking like a funky robot, challenges the coil, effortlessly palms its stabbing bolts, teases it with long wooden sticks that become transfixed and glow and burn, but that goddamn robot guy is still there, dancing way too close, striking poses, taking all this megavoltage with panache and without a flinch.

The truck the coil stands on becomes highly electrified itself, and Austin had to think about how to ground it properly. He settled on chains rattling off the truck and onto the ground. But for a while the truck itself was holding 500 volts—some of which was once discharged into a careless kid running alongside the panel truck and touching it. Remembers Austin, "I shouted, 'Dude, you can't *do* that.' He shouts back, 'It's OK, I'm on ketamine, I can't feel a thing.'"

Megavolt's performance amazed people, but the fact that it was a-pure show made it a little unusual at Burning Man, where interactivity—pieces one could use, touch, play with, make come to life—is both catchphrase and reality. So in 2003, Austin let audience members get in the suit and get zapped themselves.

Austin himself didn't realize at first how great being in the suit could be. When he first brought the routine to Burning Man, with "a funny-looking suit that looked like a fifties science-fiction movie robot, with dryer ducts for arms and legs," Austin thought it more important that he be running his coil—taking care of the technical stuff he understood better than almost anyone else in the world—than wearing the suit and conducting the lightning. Until "a beautiful girl in a cat outfit came and kissed [the suit-wearer]. I thought, that should be *me* in the suit. It was my first inkling that this might be something to make me popular with women at Burning Man."

Austin is refreshingly ingenuous about some of the subterranean realities of what motivates men to pull off grand stunts—at Burning Man, or anywhere.

"I love Burning Man for itself," says Austin, "for all the things people are doing there. I love to see other people's creative stuff. I'd never been a popular kid. I was pretty shy and withdrawn, doing my physics and electronics. No one appreciated that. Megavolt allows me to be one of the alpha dogs at Burning Man and do something I really like doing that not many other people can do and become popular in a place where I *care* about being popular.

"Being popular at Burning Man means coming into contact with a lot of fascinating and wonderful people who come seek me out and tell me about what they are doing. They're not just praising *me*. I don't care about being popular in Santa Barbara or Los Angeles, but I-do want to be popular at Burning Man. It's a huge compliment because I respect people with lots of integrity and creativity and I want to be their hero in a way.

"Burning Man really has given me this incredible social framework—it has showed me by example how people should interact in a perfect world. I'm now selective about who I hang out with—only with people who are creative and fun. When I was in high school and college, I went to parties, and no one was *doing* anything. People were just all bored, drinking and looking for something to do. Burning Man is full of people who need to be *doing* something all the time, obsessive-compulsive creative people with this hyperactivity." And that, saith Megavolt, makes for a party worth attending.

Kal Spelletich's workingman's body is covered with a fair amount of-weird cuts, lumps, and uncategorizable wounds. Still, he moves through the world smoothly and exudes an effortless cool that's not unapproachable but radiates the fact that he knows some things you don't know, and wouldn't it be great if you learned?

Kal's in his early forties now. He grew up on the Mississippi River in Iowa and would regularly take to a homemade raft and try to conquer the Mighty Mississippi. He was tearing apart and rebuilding cars before he was legal to drive them. He ran away from home at fifteen, and after finding out that factory work sucked worse than he imagined college might, he ended up at the University of Iowa, where he discovered Re-Search's *Industrial Culture Handbook,* sparking his interest in how electronics and robotics could be incorporated into "art."

That interest led him to where he is today, in a tall square of a dusty warehouse in San Francisco cluttered with machines in all stages of construction and deconstruction dangling from the ceiling and filling the floor. He lives down near the docks in an area that the city is constantly threatening to tear down in order to make room for a new bridge. Kal now teaches robotics and electronics meshed in an artistic context, his self-created passion, at San Francisco State. While he did not invent the notion of publicly exhibiting destructive and fiery machines for the sake of art, he and the art collective he manages, called the Seemen, were the first to bring such machines to Burning Man. Kal and crew's crazy machines became one of the things everyone would talk about when they talked about Burning Man, and the Seemen added greatly to the event's aura of bizarre and unexpected cool.

Kal's friend John Law—they met each other through Survival Research Labs, the original machine-art-destruction collective—had told him about this weird thing he and his friends made happen in the Black Rock Desert and suggested it would be cool for the Seemen to do their thing out there. In 1995, Kal agreed to go see what all the fuss was about.

A Seemen show provides interactive experiences during which audience members are forced to deal directly with the devices Kal and his gang make—to become their operators, their masters, the stars of the show. They have to get in the fire shower and have jets of flame spin around them, framing their entire body on all sides, forming a curtain of swirling red-orange that makes them look as if they are teleporting away. They have to strap on the flamethrower that pulses along with their heartbeat. They have to sit in the clanging, jerking, living bed.

It's a sign of Burning Man's fervent pull on the imagination that people like Megavolt and Kal would dream of bringing valuable, sometimes delicate machinery out there—but where else could they operate it? The dust, which instantly and hopelessly coats everything within about ten seconds of arriving on the playa, plays hob with any kind of engine, gear, wiring, anything that needs to move or conduct or transmit anything. Dust in valves and air cylinders in electric motors "just wreaks havoc, can destroy it in no time," Kal tells me. "I've spent most of a month cleaning my gear after Burning Man, and it's not fun. It's not an enjoyable process to stand there with a nice DC motor and take it apart and blow it all out and put it back together, and even then you can't really ever get it all out. It just never completely washes off."

Also indicative of the miraculous spirit of Burning Man is the fact that relationships of any sort—especially working ones—survive out there. As Kal notes, "You're always working at an impaired level. Lack of sleep, terrible environment, dust, filth, a million things on your mind, never enough food, water, temperature control, hardware. Everyone crashes and burns at that festival. So you have to be infinitely forgiving out there."

This is true. But equally true is something former Burning Man media team member Candace Locklear said to me about why she loves it: "You see people at their sparkling best out there, at their most creative, engaging, aware. It makes you believe there is good in everyone. You don't get that much beauty in one place in our world."

This is the Zen of Burning Man: It is almost unbelievably difficult and trying, and almost unbelievably wonderful and fulfilling. For that-reason, people manage to both hate and love Burning Man as they've never hated or loved before. That sort of intensity is something people will go a long way and pay a fair chunk of change to experience.

After his Seemen show in '99—a year in which he was momentarily taken in by cops for having too many explosives and operating dangerous devices until Crimson Rose told the cops to leave him the hell alone—Kal decided the magic might be gone for him. He didn't think he'd go in 2000, but the pull was too strong and he showed up on a last-minute whim. He improvised a quick art car with flame-throwers on the front and tiered seating in the back. Late one night, he and a water truck began playing a high-speed game of swerving cat and mouse, the vehicles floating along and jabbing at each other and squealing off through darkness made lighter by the clouds of dull-silver dust motes raised in their wake. Kal could shoot balls of fire almost thirty feet, if upwind from his adversary. Kal's car would loop around behind the truck and shoot, circle around and do the same thing from the front, and his ridiculously overstuffed crew would laugh and hoot and sometimes fall off.

Chris Radcliffe stood in the front seat barking orders to Kal: when to swerve, when to fire. The water truck was feebly firing back from its rear with its water jets, coolly and playfully keeping the shots above Kal's bow. Kal and Radcliffe weren't as kind. They swooped in beside them, turned the jets sideways, and fired at the water truck's cab. The driver's and passenger's heads ducked and disappeared. One jet went through the passenger window and out the driver's. Triumph!

The peace broken, the water truck swung its ass around to face Kal's car and let slip the floods of war, dousing the flamethrowers' igniters. It was 2:00 AM in the cold desert night, and Kal and his wet-rat crew retreated quickly to the nearest fire. As they opened the car-doors to leap out to the warmth, a cartoonish flood of water gushed out.

What, I ask Kal, is the secret of people's attraction to these clunky contraptions with all the seams showing—and some of them cracking—that burn gases and clank and crash and crush? What is so compelling about his machines, and those of fellow roboticist Christian Ristow of L.A.-based RoboChrist Industries, whose belching, grunting killdozer, known as the Subjugator, has also been a hit at many Burning Mans?

Kal replies: "Some people are always dancing around some cliff edge or running right up to the edge of the railroad track. I think a hundred years ago [his art] might not have been that interesting. Now life has become more passive and white-collar, and most people in America don't work dangerous jobs that beat you up. You can't expect people to go from hunters and gatherers for millennia and then for this hundred years, oh, we're going to be office workers! And everything is going to be all right, and there isn't going to be anything pent up from that. But there is obviously a lot of pent-up shit. And people need release. And fear is never boring."

Burning Man frequently becomes a place to create a fearful situation for yourself, just for the fun of it. Like dragging a canister of flammable liquid *into* a fire.

Chris Campbell had contributed his own art piece in 1999, his last year working on the construction crew for Burning Man. It was called Orbicular Affect: four elevated balls composed of hundreds of interlocked pieces of scrap wood, stationed around the Man. They were supposed to burn, but one of them didn't catch fire as planned. It occurred to someone: Jim Mason's fire cannons from the Impotence Compensation Symphony should be able to finish the job. This was in the days before scheduling, planning, and preapproval of dangerous fire art were required, so Mason's crew just rolled one on over.

The straw beneath the unburned ball was on fire, so the cannon—essentially a pressurized kerosene bomb—was sitting cozily in a live fire. Michael Christian, one of the tank operators, was wearing his own signature parody of fire safety: a loud, multicolored polyester suit. "If you're going to catch fire," he figures, "you should really do it right."

The flame spigoting from the cannon wasn't aimed quite right, so Christian and some buddies physically bulldogged it to a 45-degree angle. Then a fireman approached.

"Is there anything I can do?"

Only one thing occurred to Christian: "Tell us not to do this!"

Not surprisingly, a lot of the fire workers and cops out there are as mightily impressed as the next American man with excessively destructive machinery and find duty at Burning Man pretty damn cool. If Michael and his companions had fucked up, if the cannon had slipped from their grip and fallen, a fair number of onlookers would have been engulfed in a jet of fire, resulting in injury and pain and ambulances, and a heavily oppressive buzz kill would have landed on them all, and on the whole city once everyone heard about it. But it worked, and everyone around, tank operators and onlookers, shared an extraordinary experience of chaotic fun, with adrenaline expended in joy and exhilaration, not panic.

Months later, back in San Francisco, Christian was hanging out in front of a nightclub when a friend approached and said, "I want to introduce you to this woman." His friend introduced Christian by telling the woman, "This is one of the guys who set that ball on fire at Burning Man."

The woman grabbed Christian's hand, looked him in the eye, and thanked him. "We had the ashes of one of our friends in that ball. It was the only one that didn't catch fire, and it all seemed like a bad omen. Then you all came along and made it work, and it was wonderful, and thank you."

Michael Christian—blond, strong chin, friendly, and puppishly exuberant—came from Texas and marveled at the people he saw at his first Burning Man in '95, thinking, *Man, these guys seem like they're having fun. I wanna know where these guys live. I wanna hang out with these-guys.* Within a year and a half, he was, and he contributed a sculpture—a throne made of simulated turds—to a weekend art party out at Flash's Placerville property in 1997 that celebrated the old Feast of Fools. From then on, he was part of the family, and he has made big, funded theme-art pieces at Burning Man pretty much every year since.

He started with the Bone Arch in '97, made from the remnants of John Casey's unlucky bovines, then the Nebulous Entity in '98. In '99, he was placed in the keyhole by Center Camp, and he created a treelike sculpture of spinning balls made from spacily wrought metal, nestled one inside the other. He succumbed to big-art hubris in 2000—the same year that Jim Mason humbled himself with his failed Stock Puppets—with an overengineered, too-many-moving-parts pipe organ that didn't get done until the event was over. Those still around on Tuesday got quite a kick out of it.

Then in 2001, he and his crew gave birth to the tallest metal sculpture ever to grace Black Rock, called Flock. Flock was a delicate, Daliesque headless cat-/horselike creature whose legs, as they tapered and curved down to the playa, became a twisted forest of supple metal.

Relatively late in the process, he made the decision—an aesthetically proper one, I'd say—to not add skin to the skeletal piece so moonlight and dust-mist could thread through the beast. It added an eerie elegance to the Black Rock landscape.

Like most of the core crew that pull off huge things at Burning Man, Christian strives to make this whole…thing…this art-celebration-community thing…a reality year-round, not just for a week, or a few weeks, in the Black Rock Desert. (Most of the bigger art pieces and theme camps are done by groups who are likely to show up at Black Rock a good week before the event's official beginning, and often stay a week later for a leisurely, tranquil breakdown and cleanup.) Christian throws regular warehouse parties at his studio in Oakland; his specialty is theme events designed to aid and abet strenuous physical play, like his Spin Party, with all the furniture on casters, allowing for rolling and 360-degree twirling; tires hanging on ropes from the ceiling; a large circular board for people to lie on and be, well, spun.

Christian, one friend said admiringly, "shows a lot of promise for a six-year-old." One night at Burning Man 2000, at our mutual camp, Happyland, I came home from an evening's wanderings to discover Christian in the midst of initiating not a pillow fight but a *couch* fight. He also helped invent the playa game of catapulting flaming logs with an improvised seesaw; the logs would land wherever gravity and fate dictated, maybe hit a tent or two, or a moving art car. Everyone would cheer while the log flipped through the air, and friendly bets would be placed on what it might land closest to, or hit.

Christian remembers being interviewed by a *Rolling Stone* reporter for a story on Burning Man. "The guy seemed pretty bright, but he said to me, 'Seems like Burning Man would be a good platform for an agenda.' And I wondered, Have you ever seen a group of artists agree on anything? That idea is so contrary to the whole concept to me. I've never been into cooperatives. What would be a cooperative spirituality, a cooperative personal experience? Sure, an agenda—we'll form the League of Flaming Log Tossers, develop a platform on the proper techniques and write a book."

Christian earns his living doing custom metalwork and sculptures; he's a full-time professional artist. Burning Man can stretch professional artists' conception of *what is art?*—or make them wonder whether the question is even worth asking. Christian remembers seeing one of Chicken John's horrendous absurdities at Burning Man '98—the installation/performance *The Wizard of Ass,* in which supplicants skipped down a few dozen yards of carpet remnants sloppily painted yellow to address questions about life and love to a twenty-foot-across grotesque, hairy papier-mâché-on-chicken-wire-and-bent-pipe pockmarked ass, elevated on a three-story scaffolding. (Chicken, annoyed that Burning Man refused to fund this monstrosity, deliberately placed his Ass where Larry would have to see it out the front door of his trailer.)

Church of the SubGenius pastor Rev. Howland Owl (Hal Robins) was the hidden voice of the Ass. At the end of his oracular pronouncements, he would declare, with an ominous booming echo, "The Ass has spoken!" and two of Jim Mason's fire cannons would squirt their liquid high in the air and set, well, *most* of that liquid on fire in a frighteningly loud, hot, and bright column. The rest of the kerosene rained lazily down on anyone unlucky enough to be sitting within fifteen yards or so around the kerosene tanks. While at the time it merely made him laugh, afterward Christian realized it was the experience that year—precisely because of its unexpected and brazen absurdity—that stuck with him the most.

What Christian creates—ultimately sculptures of various sorts, forging material into shapes meant to say something or express something—would at least be recognized by art-world people as unequivocally art. That might not be so for Kal's machines or Megavolt's Tesla coil romps. Or for one of Burning Man's most distinguishing features: the art car.

Robert Burke has built a bunch of them at Burning Man, striving to contribute a fresh one every year. Burke and Pepe Ozan, the major-domo of the Burning Man opera through the nineties, shared some mysterious nautical past, gadding about in the Virgin Islands, sailing the seven seas; there are hints and allegations of pirating and running blockades, who knows, but both became men who, Burke tells me, could walk down a swaying gangplank and stay perfectly centered themselves.

Burke had been building nonpractical devices since he was a kid— a common trait in many whose souls vibrate in tune with Burning Man—and let Pepe talk him into a hegira to this weird desert in Nevada for the first Desert Siteworks, whatever *that* was. There they built the first fire lingam. John Law—"intrigued by all things new and alarming" —told them they really ought to go to Burning Man, a few months later.

They did, and the lingam shape became the center of Pepe's Burning Man operas, a star attraction all the way through 1999, when Pepe mostly retired from Burning Man. But Burke moved in a different direction. The towers and opera were all right and all, very tribal and primal, but Burke was a child of Western civilization and the Motor Age and he liked things to *move*.

Burke has a rap, and it's deep and long and hypnotic. He doesn't shout or emote, but draws you in by keeping his voice low and sonorous and continuous, and you lean in and you start listening and it's like Bob Dylan liner notes coming to life or a visit from the ghost of Neal Cassady, a mode of expression that's highly energized and highly stylized, conversation as a bewildering show. He's talking about the attractions of Burning Man and of the necessity of art cars. Among other things. "Nothing's more attractive than somebody having more fun than yourself," says Burke. "It doesn't matter what you're wearing; if you're naked having a good time, people assume nudity's part of that good time so they get naked. People attracted to Burning Man come from really adventurous lives, and why did they end up in Burning Man and not anywhere else? I became supercharged, gassed up, full tank, you know this is original, you didn't have to fake it, just felt this is beyond anything you thought about before and any other setting you've seen. I try to go at Burning Man like an inventor every year. They know you drink Miller in the bottle with no glass, so you gotta come up with a fresh contention, you wanna wow yourself and wow others, same coif maybe but a different cut."

We are walking and talking at a Burning Man street party in San Francisco, and Burke stops me to point out "that crystal palace down there...it's a pallet-wrapped thing. I love this shit; I started playing with pallet-wrap tape when I did the Banana Car. It has evolved as a medium of choice because of what it can do for so little. Everyone got a little taste of it; I still see it celebrated as a technological standard, like red sienna out of a tube of paint. Got to keep yourself amused with new ways, new material. I like to pick up from the industrial world all around us; you don't notice all these computers wrapped with this shit, it lasts forever. You try to touch as many people with as little as possible, walk over that beach without leaving footprints. It's not really attractive seeing someone struggle, reloading under pressure with sniper fire all around you, but to walk out in the gunfire and light your smoke and rejoice yourself...You're out there dealing with the history of art; you've gotta know what you are doing, not be redundant. What's it gonna take to have a good time after you've had all the good times? We're all in the trenches of boredom...after touring the world you want to do something else, even at an art freak fest enclave of a scene—I lived in New York, London, Paris; I love art but I really feel bad when it just *sits* there, doesn't get out...My influence is in the art-car scene, seeing it converge with Burning Man, seeing what art can do if it moves...I like cruising; I wanna see everyone in the petri dish of biological exchange, go to the end of the street and turn back; it's all about movement, seeing shit go by you and finding a chance happening, and did you see that?

"I was just into junk. How can you throw anything away? I wanted to put it back out there; everything's alive, the cup's alive, the beer's alive, the tennis shoe's alive, not just the culture growing in them; junkyards are astonishing, landfills—this isn't *debris!* It all has something left to do. I chose to let those discarded things say something one last time...I'm actually best outfitted to be on a deserted island; everyone should have that mentality, think when you throw shit out, when you give up on that relationship—this has become such a shifty society. You've got to pay homage to older things, older people, the old monuments, old gestures, old understanding—I chose trash 'cause it was free—that resourcefulness comes if you've ever been without, had not much to work with, like the Cameroonian people make bikes out of wood. That's such a polite mentality to have, and Burning Man helps with that resourcefulness. Burning Man actually gets started when it's over; incredible shit gets built during the last hours of activity when you're running out of cheese.

"If you're inspired, we could probably do anything. Those who aren't become very difficult, and it's company that I can't keep for long. I always wanna sit in the company of people who are under their own gases—those are people you wanna break down with in the middle of fucking nowhere or have a screaming party with on a deserted island. Versus someone that's not sure—they haven't thought about what their soul's work *is*. Sure, you're trapped in a body, it's nauseating, you get hot flashes and cold calls, but dude, what are you *doing?* Your soul's work? Some people don't even wanna go there. That's why I traveled for years, looking for that. I hung out with Pepe, he had it, those people I was attracted to. John Law. Larry Harvey. All these people impassioned about their work."

Burke's first Burning Man art car was the Terror of America, a forced welding together of the military/industrial complex with the People's Car: the jettisoned fuel tank of a military airplane over the running gear of a VW bug, so the fuel tank alone appeared to be cruising the playa. He then made the Buffalo Car, a rebar-and-mesh buffalo sculpture rising from a chopped car: a shamanic resurrection of the mighty beast of the plains in the form of one of its greatest enemies, the automobile, whose paths destroyed the buffalo's own trails.

Burke conceptualized the notion of the Car Hunt back in the mid-nineties, executed by him with John Law; Chip Flynn, of the machine-art collective Peoplehater; and various Cacophonists. They'd drive madly across the playa emptying out round after round of weaponry, some automatic, at a remote-controlled armor-plated '65 Olds Sierra Vista. Talk about an American art form, goddamn. The Buffalo Car was perfectly designed to be hunted, refiguring and reenacting the ancient Indian rituals of survival and adulthood in the only context in which they make sense nowadays: the automobile. Burke thinks, and the Buffalo Car is meant to embody this belief, that the automobile plays an all-encompassing role in our culture similar to what the buffalo did for the Indians of the plains.

My favorite of Burke's creations was the Lighthouse Car from '99. It was simple, visually elegant, a fully functional lighthouse. It provided a very useful service in the Black Rock night, where distances become hard to discern once you get even fifty yards from where you thought you were. It certainly helped to have a tall, lighted beacon to help orient yourself. Black Rock City at night can be confusing, too many colored lights in peculiar shapes barely limning shade structures and domes, in weird patterns, one mysterious, unpredictable creation blending into another one and all just a bit too dizzying to memorize.

This lighthouse was built on top of a car and rolled jauntily about the city at night, perplexing any lost soul who relied on it for stable guidance. Late Sunday night, a friend tells Burke excitedly about a young lady asking him, hey, which direction was the lighthouse in? Because she had left her friends over there, knowing that she could find them later using that shining beacon as her guide. "I had to tell her slowly," the friend explained. "Didn't she realize the lighthouse moved? She couldn't quite grasp it—'But it's a lighthouse!'"

Some art-car snobs only favor the ones that are relied on in everyday life on regular city streets, whose owners let their freak flags fly in a sometimes hostile and uncomprehending Normal world. Those are great, of course, but I also treasure the strictly playa-worthy ones, the ones so excessive and huge that the only place they could make sense—or fit—is rolling along the desert floor. Like Lisa Nigro's perennial Draka the Dragon, a chopped van dragging three trailers coated with chemical-green and rust-red scales, the front of the van projecting a proud dragon's head with proud dragon's fire breath, and the back trailer dragging a mighty, lean tail, with ominous black wings that sometimes unfurl. It rolled and crawled along the playascape, summoning a deep aura of fear and fascination, seemingly bred in our genes, millennia of myths of grotesque reptiles on the hoof.

Then there's *La Contessa,* an elaborately and insanely detailed reproduction of a sixteenth-century Spanish galleon built around a bus, with its masts and sails and crow's nests and prow and weathered woodwork hewn and nailed, and foredecks and aft decks and every detail so convincing that there is no play involved anymore—you *are* on the deck of an ancient ship and drifting across the still, sealike playa, and the moon is behind the masts and you are *there,* on the high seas, in another time. It is a sweet and powerful dream.

La Contessa was built by the members of the Extra Action Marching Band, longtime Burning Man favorites, a troupe of drums and horns and flag girls making a raucous noise, reinventing jazz like time travelers from 1902. Three of their number—Anna Fitch, Kelek Stevenson, and Sara Hankin—composed a ballad, singing out the glories and travails of their task, and the band would gather on deck and sing it. Part of it goes like this:

They toiled for a thousand white nights, to build the ship they sailed
bound together with sweat and spunk...buckets of bloody nails
They thought that the task would be easy
They learned their lesson well
So no let it never be foolishly said
That the countess is easily wooed into bed...
They sailed to the end of the ocean
the sea turned into sand
They battened the hatches and took at the acid and sailed across the
*   land*
Who would have thought in this desert they'd find such gallons of
*   women and pleasures of wine?*

La Contessa often hunted the Whale—the Great White Whale, child of Flash and art-car superstar Tom Kennedy, who has been bringing such motorized creations as Ripper the Friendly Shark to Burning

Man for years. The Whale is also built around a bus, lit from within the white-sheet skin for a gorgeous, ghostly glow, with a fully articulated moving tail and a blowhole that spits propane fire.

I remember riding on top of the whale one especially vivid night, my ass balanced precariously on a thin bit of metal piping, two feet from the blowhole that shot fire tall and hot. The Whale's spew would wave unpredictably with the wind—everyone within ten yards needed to bend his or her body 45 degrees to the horizontal to avoid being scorched when she blew.

We started zooming toward *La Contessa* at fifty miles per hour or more, swooping and gliding with inexorable smoothness and then twisting around a tight arc to miss her often only by yards. We saw from too close the faces of her passengers and crew turned to burnished metal by the blowhole's fierce light as they crowded colorfully at the railing, all in pirate finery and ball-gown elegance. We were all bathed in glory there, doing something we'd never done before, and knowing that even if the two colossi collided and sent us all off to some reward—some reward we all felt would pale in comparison to this—a mighty ballad would forever sing of how bonny *La Contessa* went a-hunting for the Whale, and of the marvelous tragedies that resulted.

One night, some BLM rangers took exception to the Whale's carefree speed and tried a cutoff maneuver, squealing their truck in front of the cetacean conveyance. Driving the Whale was a madman's task; Captain Kennedy stood on top of the Whale's head and steered with a wheel attached to a long bike chain stretching down into the bus's cabin. But the gas and brakes were operated by Flash in the bus, who couldn't see a damn thing, his view blocked by the Whale's face over the bus window. They communicated by means of plastic funnels attached to a length of green garden hose, shouting at each other, then moving the funnel to their ear to hear the return shout.

"When those cops pulled up in front of us to stop us," Flash remembers, shaking his head with his dry, raspy laughter, "if they had any idea how we drove that fucking whale, they wouldn't have pulled that Starsky and Hutch move!"

Chapter Nine

"THIS ISN'T WHAT THE REAL WORLD IS LIKE"

The gift economy thing—it really does work at Burning Man. Many of the people there give what seem like the biggest, most elaborate, most expensive gifts, but when you break it down, it still seems as if they are getting more than they give.

Charlie Smith is a huge man, a character of mighty joys and mighty cholers. He's a metal sculptor from Atlanta, Georgia. I've been around him a fair amount; he's got almost superhuman endurance and strength, appears to require sleep only every third day, and has survived both scorpion and snake bites in various Burning Man– inspired adventures bringing his art to the people. I've started to suspect his dad might be named Zeus.

Charlie's Burning Man adventure started when his old friend Syd Klinge, a builder and actor living in Los Angeles, told him about Burning Man after 1997. This weird little city in the desert was, at last, Syd said wonderingly, a home. So Charlie came in 1998 and took a look around. His reactions—often shifting and contradictory—provide an interesting insight into how Burning Man can strike a newcomer.

On his first day, after dumping his tent out of the rental car he'd picked up after flying into Reno, "I go running around to check shit out. People are building a giant spiderweb hammock next to me to live in. Everyone I meet is like, 'Hey, how you doing?' Lots of smiling going on. Wow, this place is a trip. What the hell are we doing in this dusty place?

"I see a big temple, all beautiful melted plastic, with colors like stained glass, and then I see a giant Tesla coil. I'm hearing people talk about Dr. Megavolt. I'd never heard of such a thing. Who the fuck is

Dr. Megavolt? What do you mean he gets in something and gets elec-trocuted? Is he gonna die? What the fuck is that all about? You're going across the desert and hear this crazy ripping sound and see lightning striking right near the ground—let's go! You go running-across the desert and see him getting hit by lightning in his robotic suit.

"Then I hear a bullhorn, someone saying you can Molotov-cocktail your favorite politician. They have figures of likely suspects of destruc-tion, and I'm throwing a Molotov cocktail at Ronald Reagan. These guys I don't know hand me a glass container with a rag and gasoline, and I'm gonna throw it! My God! This is the tail end of really serious danger at Burning Man. I'm glad I caught that tail end.

"I take a tour down to Center Camp and see this huge copper tree shooting water; then I go by at night, and it's all on fire and I'm think-ing, *Woo, nice.* I felt like a kid the first time he goes to the circus—all butterflies, wondering what amazing thing is going to be next, the whole time on pins and needles with a little bit of a fear factor. Who do I trust? I could get killed. There is some dangerous shit going on."

This was 1998, the year the Man exploded. "I couldn't believe the brightness of that fire. I mean, I'm used to bright lights from welding, but *this*…I'm looking around at the crowd, thinking, *Who am I with here? This is intense; where are we going with this? What's really happening here? Am I gonna get thrown in this fire? Do all these people* know *each other?* And I'm seeing myself everywhere, not literally, but a reflection of myself in other people's eyes. It changed dramatically my way of relating to other people.

"I dropped a lot of money on food on the way out and ended up giving most of it away. Every night, I'd get invited to have dinner at someone's camp. 'Can we feed you? Can we give you a bath?' Oh, God, sure, I'd love to be scrubbed. This wonderful Hawaiian woman I met through Syd, she said, 'Charlie, come with me, I'm giving you a bath.' Then I'm standing behind a VW camper with three girls getting scrubbed down, getting my armpits shampooed, and I'm scrubbing them and I'm not even getting a woody, for God's sakes. Just people taking care of each other, like, 'I'm gonna wash you.' OK, I'm gonna wash *you*. Yeah, I really do need a shower. Of course, ten seconds later you're dusty again—even before you're dry."

For a while he could talk about little else but Burning Man. It made people who had been close to him further away but brought him closer to something he hadn't realized he'd been looking for.

Previous plans with his then-girlfriend kept him from Burning Man in '99. (They are no longer together.) Then in 2000, he and his friend had nearly simultaneous impulses—Syd was struck with a vision of a burning heart while hiking through the Hollywood Hills; Charlie, in Atlanta, had been idly drawing orbs with flames that looked like Syd's vision. With some financial support from Burning Man—they were some of the first artists from outside the San Francisco community to get a major art grant—they built their heart.

It began in their heads as a ten-foot-tall propane-fed piece; by the time they were done, it was an almost twenty-foot-tall wood-burning one, made of steel and set in a large tray to catch the ashes. Large-scale fabrication for Burning Man is always an experimental process— there are no blueprints from experts or previous experience to guide you. Their piece represented the heart within 2000's art theme, which was the Body. They called their sculpture Hearth: the place where heart meets earth.

On one level they saw it as a strictly practical gift to the people of Black Rock City. Syd remembered in 1999, an especially cold year, how hard it was to find warmth on frigid nights on the open playa. By then at Burning Man, there were no more open campfires allowed because of concerns about damage to the playa surface and fires going wild in the increasingly dense campsite; only contained blazes in "burn barrels" and planned art burns were allowed. So a sculpture that also gave off sustaining heat seemed like a lovely idea. Indeed, Hearth's pulsing, sweet hot-metal glow drew thousands, mothlike, wandering toward it through the Black Rock night.

It was...it was beautiful, is what it was, both the object and the experience that grew around it. Making it do its thing required the help of anyone around; Charlie and Syd themselves touched every log in twelve cords of wood at least three times (off the delivery truck, onto their van, out of their van and into the Hearth). Lines of friends and strangers would gather every night around sunset to offload and toss wood through Hearth's hinged door, whimsically naming each log as it slammed into Hearth's insides. The herky-jerky booming percussion of log-slam on metal became a wild music; and shared labor, even in play, really does build community ties. It was almost like a Mass, the logs a sacrifice, releasing their energy, their stored life, to succor the humans.

Hearth allowed for no cynicism, really. It warmed all who came to it, and the rough, weathered metal skin glowed and bulged and aged and warped before our eyes and the raw reality of that—of the ancient truths of gods like Hephaestus (and how much Charlie started to remind you of him, really, when you thought about it) and their gift to mankind—well, it was not something one would experience in an average visit to a city park. As Charlie, who stood watch there 'til dawn each night, a household god guarding his Hearth, said, "Watching people, watching strangers fall in love, watching people smile in the radiant heat...I never thought it could do *that*. How could we build such a crazy gift?"

Burning Man is, at its best, heartwarming. That—as much as the opportunity to act like an unbridled lunatic—is why it grips people. That is also why it repels people—those who refuse to open their hearts to that warmth, often because of a protective shell of contempt for the perceived deficiencies of the "type" of people they meet out there, and a feeling that those people are merely being pathetic by indulging in this sort of creative play. But it unquestionably provides for those who love it a space for the giving and receiving of gifts— unprecedented ones—that you will probably never be able to repay even though you'll be inspired to try.

One night at the Hearth, I saw a young woman, crying, burning her driver's license and a one-dollar bill. She was saying something to two people surrounding her—old friends? people who just happened to be there? I couldn't tell—about new beginnings and transcending the past, but her act was far more articulate than her words. She laughed through the tears, saying how she thought she ought to be burning a hundred-dollar bill but just wasn't ready for it yet.

Burning Man can help you burn through far more than just a hun- dred- dollar bill. To explore the extent to which the lure of Burning Man can not only grip you but in some ways crush you, I visit Dan Das Mann—on whose crew I'd worked for two large-scale projects, at Burning Man '98 and 2000—at his workspace and home in a burned- out liquor store near an old naval waste dump in San Francisco. You ring the doorbell by sticking your hand in an empty light socket, completing the circuit and getting a slight jolt.

Dan's relationship with Burning Man turned ugly after he produced some of its biggest, most ambitious, and most noted pieces of art. His first solo work out there was the One Tree in 1998, a twenty-foot- tall sculpture of welded copper. The tree was thrust through a slatted wooden platform, beneath which was a twenty-five-foot-diameter, three-foot-deep hole in the playa, dug mostly by me and Philip Bon- ham. For our own amusement, we'd chain ourselves together while we dug.

The tree was veined with two sets of internal tubing; one set, dur- ing the day, circulated (and recirculated) water stored in the hole below, which was lined with plastic sheeting. The pump was solar powered, and the tree made an inviting, and heavily trafficked, public shower. This was my fourth Burning Man, and if there was any chance that I might ever tire of being there, this killed that chance: seeing so many people laughing and squealing and rubbing wet hands over one another's dusty backs and just squirming with delighted relief because of this weird, unexpected thing that was there *because of my sweat* (would it have gotten done if I hadn't shown up? Sure. But still, *I did it*), well, I pledged my eternal fealty to Black Rock City. County Health Department agents, though, were not so warmed, contemplat- ing the recirculated water's funkiness. Two years earlier at Burning Man, there would have been no one to raise a fuss.

When night fell and it was too cold for showering, propane gas pulsed through the other set of tubes, which when lit turned the tree into a burnished metal candelabrum. Dan gave me the honor of lighting the tubes the first day. He was impressed that I, until then a total stranger, had spent a week digging a giant hole for him after idly walking by his truck as it arrived and asking if he needed a hand. I was pleased and proud, but the makeshift torch I cobbled together—a gas-soaked burning T-shirt on the end of a fifteen-foot pole—was underengineered, let me say. The burning T-shirt, not fastened very well, came sliding, on fire, back down toward me. Dan, gentle to the desk-job guy who didn't work with his hands much, granted me the dignity of allowing me to try again.

In 2000, Dan contributed the Faces of the Man—three twenty-five-foot-tall masks of welded metal, one plated in copper and weeping fire, one coated in grass and weeping water, and one covered with driftwood that was supposed to weep sand, only the (not fully tested) vacuum pump couldn't shoot the sand all the way from the ground to the eyeholes. After the event, these faces, like many huge pieces at Black Rock that the artists had no way of storing, were dragged to and kept at the DPW's nearby ranch, which functioned as both a storage and construction site for Black Rock City's infrastructure, vehicles, and art. While stored there, a couple of the big faces got bent out of shape—ruined, in Dan's estimation. He was told they were elevated and had fallen over in a storm; he is convinced some recklessly careless DPW worker drove into them with some heavy equipment. When Burning Man refused to recompense him for the damage, he threatened to sue. Mindful of what such a move could do to his own reputation in the tight-knit San Francisco art-weirdness community, he ultimately chose not to. Still, he was no longer one of the organization's favorite sons.

He was angry enough to take a year off from doing big things at-Burning Man in 2001, and—not coincidentally—he launched a rapidly growing business selling his flat metal carvings as wall hangings. Hundreds of thousands of dollars were flowing through his practically-a-squat (and now a squat metalworking factory) on a bad side of town;

dozens of pals and scene hangers-on were hired to make metal carvings, ship metal carvings, and sell metal carvings at trade shows.

The business flourished through 2001 and the first half of 2002; then Dan caught fire with the notion that he wanted to return to Burning Man in style, though without any funding from the organization. He planned what he thought of as the ultimate community-building piece, one that would leave the largest footprint of anything ever sited within Black Rock City's fence.

He called it the Last Stand. It consisted of dozens (hundreds, in the initial conception) of mostly three- to five-foot-tall flat metal cutout sculptures. The various designs were provided by dozens of different artists, or nonartists, within the Burning Man community. Anyone who could sketch a shape in simple, solid black lines could play. Dan and his studiomates would cut out the shapes, bring them to Burning Man, and set each one up on its own pole amid a field of 16,000 square feet of sod. In a touch that was, depending on whom you asked, either a deliberately punk *fuck you* to Burning Man or a commentary on how we separate ourselves from art and our own artistic temperament in this world, Dan built a double layer of barbed-wire fence around the whole deal.

Anyone who wanted to actually lounge in this impromptu desert sculpture garden had to navigate the walkway between the two layers of fence, the equivalent of four city blocks around a huge square. One late night, riding my bike past the Last Stand, I came within a foot of pedaling directly into a sprawling glob of excess barbed wire, lurking unmarked and unlit. As the Man was burning that year, Dan-and his crew tried and failed to set the garden on fire by tossing Molotov cocktails over the fence. All they managed were small guttering flames that choked, coughed, and died after about thirty seconds.

The project cost Dan tens of thousands of dollars to execute, ship, and install, and it was all his money—or that of friends from whom he had borrowed to buoy his high-cash-flow, but not always solvent, business. The Last Stand also distracted him from actually attending to the company's needs. Around the same time, a truck full of his studio's work—pieces that cost a total of $50,000 to produce and had an even higher market value—caught fire, ruining everything inside. And then he decided to buy a tugboat—yup—and a friend hurt herself falling from it. Things were going south for Dan Das Mann.

His business—still crawling along after bankruptcy—was both a creation of and a victim of Burning Man, its community, and the queer mania to create, contribute, impress, and exceed that it generates. In the midst of a disquisition on the uniquely experimental quality of large installations at Burning Man—experiments driven less by knowledge than by ego and faith—Dan suddenly notes that "there's always a wreckage of your life on the other side. Burning Man has entirely absorbed all the financial gain I've ever made in my life and left me poor and destitute. It's great to create the pieces, but what is the benefit versus the cost—emotionally, intellectually, financially? So why are we doing all this again? Is it all ego? Because we can? Because we *can't?* I knew from the start it wouldn't lead to any real financial *gain,* but if anything, it has actually left this giant hole in the ground.

"As much benefit as I've received from Burning Man, it has also destroyed me in a lot of strange ways. Hey, I'm thirty-three. I can start over anyway. But [Burning Man] promotes an unstable lifestyle where you throw everything away for the good time, for the moment, rather than build stability. I see so many people wreck their lives year after year to make the art, make the statement. In dollars spent by me that I'll never see back, it's in the neighborhood of one hundred thousand.

"But the funny thing is, I can't imagine life without it. It's such a gift that we all share. I've gotten tons of relationships from it—love, hate, all of it. There's nothing else I could even imagine that would begin to offer all that, and for that I'm deeply thankful."

One thing Dan got out of Burning Man was Chris Radcliffe in his life. Radcliffe thought that Dan's behavior in the wake of his financial troubles was undignified and that some of his unpaid loans amounted to taking advantage of friends. So when he saw Dan for the first time in months, he punched him in the face. A mercurial character, that Radcliffe, but obsessed with his own unique conception of justice and righteous behavior. When I first tried to get Radcliffe to talk to me about Burning Man—I had only met him there once myself, but everyone who had had anything to do with the event pre-1996 would tell me, with something approaching awe in their voices, that I *must* talk to Chris Radcliffe if I wanted to understand Burning Man—he soundly rejected my overtures. Radcliffe talks with a lazy, comic-contemptuous drawl, his face sensuous and thick. He baited me and teased me and hazed me and eventually relented, but at first he would only grant me one comment: that he had a streak of Howard Roark in him.

He was referring to one of the acts of awful, inexcusable mischief that have made him a legend to his friends, and have also made some of the current organizers of Burning Man think that they'd be glad if he never crossed the threshold of Black Rock City again.

Radcliffe was a skilled builder, and often pals and acquaintances in the community would ask for his help and advice on projects for Burning Man. In 1999, he tells me, he helped Steven Raspa with a project. Raspa is a favorite Burning Man–world MC and raconteur, and has the coolest beard I've ever seen—long, elegant, dark, and wiry and always crafted into striking, imaginative hair sculptures. That year, Raspa designed a structure called the Futura Deluxe Bubble Fountain and Porta-Temple that, to Radcliffe's horror, ended up being labeled with the words: *hope, wish, dream, pray.*

This was positive and inspirational to Raspa. To Radcliffe, it betokened a mealy-mouthed dependency that implied one must look to something else to find fulfillment rather than take active responsibility for one's own happiness, creativity, life. Radcliffe's motto comes from Captain Ahab: "What I've dared, I've willed; and what I've willed, I'll do!" The words on Raspa's piece were antithetical to what Radcliffe thought he and Cacophony and Burning Man stood for. And worse, he had helped build it. The Howard Roark in him came out.

"I snuck into Ranger Camp and stole a couple of uniforms and a golf cart and picked up a can of gas," he tells me. "There were a bunch of people sitting around [Raspa's piece] doing TM [transcendental meditation] or something. I drove up, shouted, 'Guys, we're Rangers.

Everything's all right, but you have to back up. There's going to be a fire here.'

"They weren't moving very fast. So I tossed the gas all over it. 'Can you smell that? That's octane. There's about to be a fire, so move or fucking die!' I had a hard time getting the thing lit—I specced it too well. Had to crawl underneath it and splash gas under it and throw match after match 'til I got the fucker lit. Then I jumped back in the golf cart with a few other people I can't name and rode around it a few times cackling, shouting, 'It's OK. We're Rangers.'"

Radcliffe's ideological arson wasn't the only unplanned art burn that night. Steve Heck, who had returned to build a boat of pianos (a piece less huge and ambitious than his '96 contribution), was also assaulted by unwanted arsonists.

"When I found out someone had burned Steve Heck's piece, I felt like I had lit a firecracker that blew up in my ass," Radcliffe admits. "He had produced another magnificent piece of monumental art, and for someone to burn it…I felt I had intellectual reasons to justify my act, but looking at the larger picture, maybe I was just creating permission for other people to go fucking nuts. So, I'll never do it again. But I stand behind my act."

Tyler Hanson, the prophet of the Holy Moment at Burning Man, was a Reno teenager and Deadhead who first came out to the playa in 1995—expecting nothing and understanding nothing—and was blindsided by Holy Moments through the sights and the situation and the way people talked and acted. It triggered in him a sense of possibilities wider than northern Nevada, prompting him to leave Reno and thus miss Burning Man in 1996.

As Labor Day weekend 1996 approached, Tyler was setting sail in the Bering Sea, cooking on a fishing ship. But his mind was on the playa. He cut out a two-foot-tall cardboard figurine emulating the Man from Black Rock and grabbed some charcoal lighter fluid from the kitchen. On the first day of throwing nets on the ship, with a captain stressed out from the rough seas and the fifteen- to twenty-foot waves battering the boat, Tyler went to the back of the trawl deck, doused the figure, and tried to set it aflame.

With the wind and spray, it just wasn't happening. "So I threw him overboard instead," recalls Tyler. "He twirled down among the thousands of birds that follow fishing vessels, hit the water, and disappeared. The Drowning Man."

Tyler looked up to see the captain at the helm, glaring at him. He was summoned to the wheelhouse. "For fifteen minutes he chews me a new asshole. He's beet red, telling me how stupid I am, and Jesus, what was I thinking, trying to start a fire on his ship? I tried to explain what I was doing, tried to explain Burning Man in these broken sentences between his barking, but he didn't wanna listen. He kicked me out of the wheelhouse and said [he'd] decide [my] fate later.

"From what I had tried to explain to him about Burning Man, the rumor spread around the ship that I was part of this weird cult that burned people in Colorado once a month. At that point I would have been perfectly happy to be kicked off the ship and sent home. But the Norwegian first mate, the son of the owner of the shipping company, comes down and, in a thick accent, tells me that the only reason I'm not firing you is because you were following the dictates of your little religion and that if I have to I can burn my little man in the ship's incinerator."

Tyler returned to Burning Man after his exile on the Alaskan fishing boat. He had internalized the message that it was both possible and appropriate to make big things. In 2000, he worked on a set of thirty-three cloth cutouts in the shape of lamps hanging off guylines between towers he and his friends erected. "For one moment it looked pretty much like it was supposed to look," he remembers fondly.

Then the winds came. His project went down, uneventfully; the next art piece over was a set of taller-than-human dominoes made of one-eighth-inch-thick plywood sheets. They were suddenly swooping perilously everywhere. To amuse themselves, Tyler and his buddies rode with the wind on their bikes to fetch the wood, then had a friend drive a van out to retrieve them and bring back bikes, riders, and dominoes.

"I remember this woman huddled in the back of a twenty-five-foot Penske rental shouting through a bullhorn, 'Fuck the art! Save yourselves!' She was actually pissed at me because we were still moving, driving, trying to retrieve the pieces. 'Fuck the art! Those are hurricane-force winds!' What do you mean? This is the best time I've had so far. What am I supposed to do? Stop everything and come participate in your freak-out?"

I remember my own experience in a similar windstorm—struggling to unload the truck containing L.A. Cacophony's project for 1999's Burning Man. It was to be a scale-model replica of the Disney ride It's a Small World After All, which would blast that insidious song twenty-four hours a day. After a week in which people could "enjoy" it, it would be demolished and immolated after a sick little ceremony involving a long string of people dressed as offensively overbroad ethnic stereotypes, handcuffed together in enforced unity. This was meant to jab at the one-world, we-are-all-together mentality that united both Walt Disney and many of the gooey political progressives in the Burning Man audience who might think they hated everything Disney stood for.

Black Rock is a city with no reliable news source, and lots of pranksters, so the rumor mill's grindings are heeded at your peril. That day, the rumors were of rain—always a reason for potential panic on the playa. The thick, dark, roiling sky and punishing winds made those rumors believable. I was with Steven Carthy and Al Ridenour, majordomo of L.A. Cacophony. We started out jammed into the back of a crowded panel truck, in the only spare space, a small rectangle about two feet deep and ten feet long in front of carefully stacked piles of painted wood, provisions, and explosives.

By 1999, burning your art was no longer anything-goes. Instructed sternly by Burning Man to not burn plastic—environmental damage, you know—L.A. Cacophony had disguised the plastic that formed various grates on the facade of the fake Small World by painting it to look, unconvincingly, like wood. In the inferno that would consume the entire contraption, they figured no one would notice the telltale acrid stink of burning plastic mixed in with all the burning wood, paper, gasoline, and gunpowder.

We listened on a small battery-powered radio to the Black Rock radio stations, powered and run by pirates who dragged transmitters out to the desert, the Federal Communications Commission be damned. More than twenty of them broadcast that year. The one we were tuned into alternated warnings of storms and loops of electronic dance music at mechanical intervals. Carthy, who would rather do anything than nothing, paced as best he could and talked back to the radio. He was a radio professional.

"That's dead air," said Carthy. A box rolled by in a cloud of fast-moving dust, leaped, then flew.

"You don't refer to the audience as 'you all out there.' Radio is all about the intimate illusion of one voice talking to one listener."

Two pieces of man-sized poster board skidded and flipped past the-back of our truck. A cowboy hat followed them, chased by a baseball cap.

Carthy could sit still no longer. "We gotta start unloading this truck," he said.

"The pieces will be pretty vulnerable once we get them out of here," I volunteered. "Maybe we should wait to see if the wind dies down."

"The wind could blow for the next five days. This morning is shot. I want to get something good out of today."

Carthy carefully dislodged the wooden flats—all at least ten feet tall and either four or six feet wide—and handed them to Al and me as we stood on the truck's lift gate. We jumped awkwardly to the ground and into the wind carrying wide, flat planks of wood that functioned surprisingly well as windsails.

The instant we cleared the truck bed, we were swept yards to the left of the truck. We wrestled the pieces flat by throwing ourselves atop them. As Al staggered over to the pile with his third flat, he was clocked in the back of the head by an empty cardboard box propelled by the wind. His glasses hit the ground and began scuttling away. He hunched over, hands to his head. I dashed after the glasses, the flat I was struggling with scraping down the side of my shorts-clad leg as I let it down too fast.

Al continued, as he had been ever since getting out of the truck, muttering to himself.

"Fuck, shit. Shit, shit, fuck. My fucking head. Did you get my fucking glasses? What the fuck hit me? Shit. This fucking sand blowing in my eyes. Fuck, I'm tired of this. What are we *doing* here? This is like being condemned to build something on the fucking moon. It's fucking unlivable in this fucking never-ending wind. My fucking God. Christ. Burning Man causes Tourette's syndrome."

The rain never came. Later I hear Mateo, the best of Burning Man's omnipresent bullhorn comedians, bringing the news to the citizens: "I have just received word from some geologists back in Reno. An earthquake is very solidly predicted, probably a six point nine, strong chance of even a seven point one. Everything now staked to the ground should be suspended in the air *immediately.*"

"I learned how to weld," Amacker Bullwinkle (yes, that's the name her parents gave her), a former "senior technical evangelist" for the Adobe Corporation, tells me. "And that changed everything. I've overcome my fear of large things I can't control. I'm not afraid of engines now. I realized I could control fire as well, and make my own personal fire art. Women who weld—they create this big sexual energy. All our lives we were powder-puffed and made up, and now I can take two big thick pieces of steel and some fire and make things with them."

Amacker—a tall, buxom woman, equally at home in boilersuits and hippie granny dresses, who is unnecessarily shy about an old dog bite that has slightly scarred her face—turned this talent and confidence toward mutating her motorcycle, a Honda Nighthawk S 700, into a winged dragon. Fire-breathing, of course. She named her Justice. And Justice can be harsh.

"Someone totally brained herself on one wing," remembers Amacker. "Justice's battery was dead, and we were sitting in the dark in the middle of the playa except for the el-wire that articulated her wings. Someone rode her bike right into the tip of the wing any-way. Her friends ran over but were quick to tell me, 'This is not your fault, and we know this is art and we remember what it says on our ticket.'"

A large portion of your ticket to Burning Man is taken up by the phrase *You voluntarily assume the risk of death or serious injury by attending.* Still, some people aren't ready to completely take care of themselves. Justice can spit her fiery propane breath a good long way. "We incin-erated the wings of a fairy that went close by," says Amacker. (Gossa-mer wings are one of the most prevalent whimsical accoutrements at Burning Man.) "When you shout 'fire in the hole' and send someone out to tell everyone to get back, something dangerous is about to hap-pen, they don't always take it seriously."

I, too, have noted that too many people bring an overregulated American's mentality out to Burning Man—a notion (completely false, out there) that everything has been designed to ensure it couldn't possibly hurt them, no matter how careless or unheeding they are. But Amacker thinks that "this personal responsibility thing grows you up really fast out there. In the middle of all this seemingly childish activ-ity, there's this huge adult thing that happens."

Burning Man has taught her that she is both freer and more respon-sible than she had guessed. "You can be *anything* you want to be. You make choices, and you have experiences and you give the experience to everyone around you. And whether you know it or not, it makes huge changes, whether it results in 'I never wanna do that again' or 'I want to live this way three hundred sixty-five days a year.' I will not say no anymore. I will say yes to everything, and I may get hurt, but it's all just as real. Now playa time is real time."

I'm sitting in an unfinished second-story room in a Bay Area ware-house art space, one that masquerades, for zoning and code inspection purposes, as a theatrical set-building shop, talking to another welder, Rosanna Scimeca.

I'm looking at her as we talk, naturally, which is both hard not to do and hard to do—she's profoundly gorgeous, golden face, obscenely wide, thick, and lively mouth, wildly clumped hair dyed fiery red, and she's rocking the leather and the lace with equal panache. But one doesn't want to be rude by staring, by adding to the social burden of the superattractive. Rosanna has the hesitancy of the unearthly beautiful woman who wants naturally to be open and friendly but is aware of the hazards—which adds to a vulnerability that is all the more attractive, which she might not realize, and it all becomes an endless loop and it barely matters because she can conceptualize and execute things that would make even the hungriest man look at her creations instead of at her.

She first heard about Burning Man while taking a computer graphic design course in New Jersey in 1999. She found her way out to the desert, and although she loved everything about it, she didn't think she'd be back. Something about it told her it couldn't go on, couldn't have a place in her life. She thought, "This isn't what the real world is like. It's not happening."

But her doubts were mistaken, and she changed her life in order to make room for Burning Man, and things like it. She started spinning fire and hooked up with New York City's Madagascar Institute, a troupe of guerrilla fabricators and theatricians who build crazy devices and put on violent-fiery shows everywhere from California to Berlin. At Burning Man in 2002, they built what looked like a giant metal sea creature—some sort of mysterious giant squid that no human has ever seen—undulating over and through the playa surface.

"Nothing against Burning Man," says Rosanna of the Madagascar philosophy, "but the whole idea [behind Madagascar] is that we can do these sorts of things anywhere and anytime, not just one week of the year. So it happened. We did the big fucking parties. We made the thing. We made the other thing. We hurt the people." One of her favorite Madagascar events was the running of the bulls, in which they chased (invited) people down crowded New York City streets, riding and pushing an army of jerry-rigged bikes, carts, and floats that were all made to look, kind of, maybe, like bulls and, of course, ran down the people who didn't get out of the way.

She grew up in Jersey and wasn't raised, she thinks, to value "making my own decisions, creating and living as just *me,* and sharing that with others and getting them to do the same thing. No one does it, and it's sad to me.

"We aren't taught it's OK to feel that way. I didn't think I could at all. At all. Didn't think I'd go back to Burning Man because I thought it was too good to be true. Didn't think I'd be an artist. The idea of being called that is…pssh, no way, no fucking way at all. But slowly, subconsciously, [by entering the world of Burning Man] I was sent in that direction because that's what I wanted deep down inside.

"I was stubborn as hell since I was little…so I decided either I'd-be happy, or if I'm not, I'll die trying to be happy." Her parents may not understand what she's doing, but they are at least impressed she became a regular on cable's Learning Channel program *Junkyard-Wars,* fabricating crazy Burning Man–style shit to meet TV challenges.

Rosanna moved out to San Francisco after a couple of Burning Mans and did informal apprenticeships with many other large-scale Burning Man artists. In 2003, she launched her own huge project. It has a weird mythological backstory, to fit into Larry's theme for the year, which dealt with faith and the divine. But physically it's a giant, thirty-foot-tall, gorgeously rococo red chandelier that looks as if it has crashed down from heaven, attached to a ceiling fixture and a plaster chunk with trailing wires stretching about twenty yards away.

She solemnly informs me, when I ask a lame question about what inspired the piece, that it "arose from my desire to-.-.-."—serious, thoughtful pause—"electrocute people."

One thing she loved about Burning Man is that it gave tacit permission to unleash her wildest impulses—"I get to be an aggro bitch girl out there, scream, cause trouble. I love to make people react, to test them. Because people aren't usually challenged. I don't know what place I have to [provoke] another human being like that, but…*I* needed it; someone did that to me, and I think people need it in general."

She had thus taken to behaving like an unholy terror at parties, running around zapping people with handheld Taser-like devices. She'd make sure she was always dressed in skimpy clothes, running around flirty and happy, then *zap!* run! It was hard for people to take offense.

"I'm at a dinner party a week after one of those parties, dressed like a normal-looking lady, and someone comes up—'It's *you*.' [I say], 'Do I need to be apologizing for something?' She says no. At first she thought I stuck her with a needle and was pissed off but later realized [the shock] totally stimulated her, and she felt more alive for the rest of the night."

Rosanna's chandelier was wired so that if you touched it for more than just a moment, you'd receive a medium electric shock, feeling like you'd been quickly and forcefully punched.

The fabrication of the chandelier's delicately lovely arms, the red fiberglass resin that lined the insides of its welded-metal hollow globe body, and the various pieces that all slid down a central pole like a shish kebab to form a complete giant chandelier that had fallen from heaven and lay here in the dust was mostly done back in her Bay Area warehouse. Putting it all together on the playa was pure, exhilarating punk-rock construction in the crazy heat—we don't need no contractor's license!—with huge heavy poles swaying from cranes and people spraying WD-40 frantically in the faces of the other people trying to hold the big ball in place as we tried to jam it down on the pole, hold it so it didn't just spin around and take out the head of one of the many other people poking around inside trying to figure out why the fitting wasn't sliding down the pole like it should.

The problem was solved Burning Man style—on the fly and with whatever is closest at hand—by quickly attacking the ball with a grinder to cut the fitting ring open, and then down it went. Assembling the chandelier offered lots of moments like that, all to the most insane soundtrack—endless repetitions of that "I'm in reverse" beeping of the crane (could it not be stopped? Did no one notice but me? One doesn't want to be the first to *whine* about anything out there) and the almost subsonically low rumble of the generator. The two tones of the backward beep after the two hundredth repetition started to reveal a whole range of frequencies, not just the two. It was like a microtonal minimalist symphony, and the generator rumble was as funkily rhythmic as any bass player and the stress and heat must have driven me mad because I was actually starting to really *get into* those sounds.

You can visit, or work at, plenty of these art-construction sites before Burning Man starts and, the chaos of Burning Man being what it is, often on into the week of the event as well, where you can watch the crew guys in their crew-guy stance, crouching, ready for action, lanky, not tense but always observant, waiting, skin past leathery on its way to mummified, big shorts filthy with lots of pockets for tools, a bandanna of some sort and dark glasses or goggles, desert rugged. After we spend more than a week out there, the Black Rock Playa is either killing us by swift degrees or turning us into some kind of indestructible Next Man, and we'll only know which by the way we feel inside.

The chandelier was a big hit at Burning Man 2003. When I debrief with Rosanna afterward she is quietly humming with satisfaction. She did it, she might even sell it, and now she knows she can do whatever it is she imagines again. As she tells me, she now knows nothing is-standing in her way but herself. A permanent change in outlook—a-nice payment for a tense summer and three weeks of welding in the-dirt.

Aaron Muszalski made those taller-than-human dominoes that were tossed around in the windstorm. He and his pals decided to turn one of them into a makeshift bar in 2000—with no planning, no intent. It was nearly a mile away from the main encampment, out in the deep playa toward the plastic trash fence. They played some sophisticated jazz—you don't hear much of that at Burning Man—and dressed snazzily.

Their impromptu Domino Bar became a "fluidly authored group theater piece," Aaron remembers, as people picked up on the swanky vibe and returned in gowns and tuxedos. "Some priceless things happened, [things that] speak so much of the caliber of imagination of the people at Burning Man: people would walk right up to the bar and say, 'Give me my usual.' Perfect. You get it. You're not a person who walks up and says, *What is it? Why?* Clearly haven't been around Burning Man long if you're asking why. So, I'd say, 'Good to see you again…Rick? Steve, sorry, been a few days. Whiskey? Straight or rocks? Oh, I'll get it right next time.' You can drink here all night with that attitude."

It got Aaron thinking about consensual reality and the ways our own behavior and attitudes transform physical space into whatever we believe it to be, from a church to a smoky jazz nightclub. "If you get enough people playing along, it stops being make-believe. It becomes in every meaningful sense an actual nightclub, except we don't have a building."

Aaron worked for George Lucas at Industrial Light & Magic, and he and his friends—many of them also technogeeks from the special-effects world—decided they enjoyed being proprietors of a bar and did it again on a far more detailed level in 2001. They built what looked by day like just a giant pair of dice, far out from the encampment near the trash fence. But at night, hidden doors opened and inside was a fully equipped, swanky nightclub.

Aaron was thrilled with how his cohorts rose to the occasion, with no central planning. One man built a functional slot machine that dispensed prizes and chips, with Burning Man iconography for graphics. After years at Burning Man, Aaron was frustrated he'd never really found what he felt was his own community out there. Now, by creating (at great effort and expense—he sunk well over ten grand of his own money into this stunt) an atmosphere that amused him, that community of like-minded souls gravitated far out into the playa night to find *him*. It became an enormous hit, the Porn Clowns always hanging, everyone playing along, lines out the door most nights.

Since money isn't supposed to change hands, these Burning Man bars work by barter. Maybe you bring some booze, ice, or mixers, or just a special gift from yourself, and you get a drink. Once a girl offered to speak in tongues and ended up creeping everyone out so much with her eerie ululating and unearthly tongue that the proprietors begged her to stop. Sometimes this whole bartering thing means the barkeeps go home with more booze than they started with. "But it's not some scam," Aaron assures. "Yeah, I spent fourteen grand to build giant dice in order to scam everyone out of their liquor. What a genius plan!"

The bar had many nooks, crannies, and secret places; in one of them, Aaron found a couple of strangers furtively snorting coke. They look at him sheepishly, caught. "This is backstage at a jazz nightclub," he told them. "I should thank you for helping complete the picture."

The Dice Bar became more than just a location—it became a theatrical piece. Aaron and his cohorts developed an absurd mythos, this concocted backstory that they spread through one-page newspapers that they dragooned youngsters from Kids Camp into distributing in classic old-school newsboy style, wandering around shouting, "Ex-tree! Ex-tree! Read all about it!" The phony drama stretched out over the course of the week, with unexpected outbursts of public skits in the Dice, having something to do with the bar's proprietor ending up on the wrong end of a deal with the dreaded Hawaiian mafia and their overboss, Don Ho. Floral-shirted goons pulled off theatrical fake hits in the middle of the crowd, and the whole plot ended in a karaoke contest for the fate of the bar in which the proprietor beats Ho with a stirring rendition of Ho's own signature hit, "Tiny Bubbles." It can be a pretty goddamn silly place, Burning Man.

And then it can stop being silly. At the end of the week, the Dice Bar was dismantled, and the pieces burned. The following account was written by a man who was there, Peter Christian. He had been the last person to play the piano at the Dice Bar. He played a tune he'd composed, and he found people accompanying him and dancing to the music he made. He had never played piano in public before.

But now the nightclub was gone, and the dawn was arriving; the magic spell of the bar had been dissipated, though its fans and last audience were still hanging around, savoring the afterglow, with Sinatra music blasting as they watched the pieces of the dice burn as the sun dried away the ink of the night. Christian remembers: "I turned toward the Dice fire just in time to lock eyes with a burning man walking out of the fire and toward me. I will never forget the look in those eyes—eyes that were looking directly at me, eyes that said, 'What did I just do?' I looked back into those eyes and let out a long breath, and my mind bent around the fact that I was actually witnessing a naked man walking out of a fairly large fire, walking toward me, trailing flesh. The group of us there to welcome the new day intuitively realized that a fellow human being had just sustained a fatal injury, the way a sudden change in direction passes among a school of fish...This man before us, this melted man, he was not surviving the night.

"Someone cut Sinatra; people sprang to action. A man from the Death Guild eased the burned man down to the ground (no one knew where to set his melted skin down—a dusty piece of carpet, the bare playa, where? Was this really happening?) and talked to him gently, trying to calm him. 'What you have, it's like a really bad sunburn. Hell, I get horrible sunburns out here. You've probably got a third-degree sunburn, that's all. Happens to all of us. I got sunburned real bad out here, earlier in the week...' The burned man looked on with huge eyes...You could see deep into his body, where the fire had burned away the skin." He was taken away from the playa, and he died. He had walked into the fire deliberately, for reasons no one will ever know.

Working at Lucas alone, one man, one computer, fiddling on Photoshop in the dark, crawling up his own asshole, made Aaron finicky and antisocial, and Burning Man was a way out of it. Despite the dark pall cast by the Dice burn, he and his crew came out with a bar again the next year. The Dice's small size and the resulting lines out the door and the bad feelings that result from anything that smacks of exclusivity in the Burning Man community taught them a lesson. So they made a huge open public space for this bar. It took the form of a gigantic building-sized yellow duckie to gently rib that year's aquatic art theme. And once again, at great cost to Aaron and other contributors, lots of strangers and good friends had a grand time. The world works this way sometimes.

Aaron was originally inspired to try something ambitious at Burning Man by Steve Heck's Piano Bell. He was awed and amused by its improbable majesty and just stood wondering *why?* and *how?* and the world seemed a mysterious and wonderful place.

He found after building the Dice and the Duck that people approached him with that same sense of "stupefied wonder—'How did you…? Why did you…? I dig this!'"

And Aaron would say to them: "You think this is cool? Thanks. But you can totally do this. Whatever dumb-ass idea you have, get friends together and do it. This event is a place where you can make these things come true. And once you realize that, then life becomes a place where you can make things come true, too.

"The lesson for me from Burning Man was, at first I just thought the playa was this magical place, that *only* on the playa could you make your dreams come true. But once you learn the method of making stuff happen, it's the same everywhere."

And he'd tell them that they better do it because he was getting tired and soon he'd just want to bring his lawn chair and a case of beer and watch their cool thing because he'd be broke and disgusted.

What gift does the Burning Man bring? As Aaron says, "The whole landscape of what was possible just changed."

Part Four

ANARCHY AND COMMUNITY

Chapter Ten

"YOU CAN BURN YOUR OWN CAR"

Burning Man's allure has always been not just creativity but freedom. That freedom is real, but it is often misunderstood, by both those who overestimate it and those who underestimate it. Some old-timers, or people just seduced by the myth of the old days, may still harbor old deep-playa-fueled fantasies of an exploding *Mad Max* wonderland where the blue of authority never mars the playa's profound blankness. And some cranky old bastards think that just because there are cops around, any implied promise of a liberatory experience at Burning Man is a vicious lie, undoubtedly told to put one more gold bar in Larry Harvey's hidden vault, somewhere far, far away from his dingy apartment.

The freedom at Burning Man is not *legal*—the laws of the United States and Nevada are enforced. Of course, if your crimes are victimless, even in cop-ridden Black Rock City, you'll get away with violating certain laws more often than not. But where you are free is in what I've come to understand as *social* freedom—freedom from the negative judgments of those around you, or at least from your anxieties about same. The social freedom at Burning Man is wide, and it is inspiring.

Most of what keeps us from doing what we want to do in our day-to-day lives, after all, has little to do with fear of legal punishment. We are generally motivated to keep ourselves in line by fear of social ostracism and of negative reactions, even if they are not violent and would never result in our being locked up or fined. People at Burning Man enjoy wandering around dressed like silver aliens or princess warriors, sporting outrageous names and outré glasses and funky hats and diaphanous sarongs and being almost aggressively friendly with everyone they meet. They go a long way and spend a lot of money to experience this. Why don't they do all this wherever they come from (which most of them, I've found, don't—and if they do, it's in explicitly designed Burning Manesque scenarios, local burns, decompression parties, and the like)? It's not because they might get arrested for it. It is because such behavior in most cities in America will probably lead to unpleasant interactions with fellow citizens.

In Black Rock City, one's eccentricities are cheered and encouraged, not mocked or derided. It is not entirely accurate to say that no one judges you at Burning Man, or even that no one judges you uncharitably. But enough people don't that the few who do are bearable and might even seem ridiculous enough that *you* can easily dismiss *them*. Not all of us are strong enough to act as we please, and fuck other people's judgments. Burning Man gives us the chance to live one week in a world where our own inclinations can be indulged with no fear of negative repercussions, and gives us the strength to realize that we needn't live in fear of what others might think. We don't; but most of us need practice to realize it.

Certain people's judgments, though, must be heeded—like the ones by the men who can have you sent to prison. Ever since the event's return to the Black Rock Playa in 1998, lots of police patrol Burning Man—local, state, federal, deputized from faraway places. There's a plethora of police, a cop cavalcade. Ask Seth Malice.

Burning Man has developed a reputation—one its organizers are always fighting against or trying to suppress—as an illegal-drug free-for-all. It wouldn't be accurate to say that everyone at Burning Man is high on some crazy illegal drug. However, compared with any randomly selected group of thirty thousand Americans, the number of people at Burning Man partaking in psychoactive substances is unusually large. There are no scientifically valid polls or statistics proving it. And the legal citation rate at Burning Man isn't commensurate with the idea that a significant percentage of those thirty thousand are breaking the law.

Still, from informal surveying of the people I've known, talked to, and played with on the playa, the number of people at Burning Man ingesting some sort of illegal drug could well top 50 percent. Don't ask the police though—they don't believe there is that much drug use either. When discussing such politically sensitive issues, it's hard to tell who is speaking the truth of his heart and who is just covering his ass. If any police officer admitted to believing that there was *that much* drug use out there, he would need to explain why there are so few arrests for it, relatively. (The Fourth Amendment is one big reason.)

But you can't say it's a free-for-all. The laws of the land that deny Americans the right to eat the substances they wish and play/experiment with their minds as they please *are* enforced in Black Rock City, though not with Draconian efficiency. There is no TAZ anymore, not really. Or if there is, you can't buy a ticket for it.

Seth Malice has been going to Burning Man regularly since 1995; he has worked for DPW and contributed an absurdist art car called the Grassy Knoll. He also made a Web site ridiculing Burning Man propaganda in the late nineties, emulating the precise look of Burning Man's own site. Following is a sample from the site, from a second-person narrative meant to sum up the experience of arriving on the playa:

> You're here to huff art, and beer-bong culture…you crash land in the center camp, with 15,000 naked computer programmers dancing around your flaming wreckage, greeting you, neon and benevolence, watching you. You're here to build a community based on *Lord of the Flies*. They need you; you have toothpaste… You've built an egg for shelter, a suit made of human skin, a car that looks like shit. You've covered yourself in dirt, you're sporting a mullet, and food stamps, or maybe a shirt for the first time. You're broadcasting desperate rays to thousands.

Seth is also a proud federal drug offender with thirty days in the federal penitentiary behind him, where he served some quiet, rewarding time with a guy involved in fencing stolen Norman Rockwell paintings.

Seth is an original slacker, formerly of Austin, Texas (he even appeared in Richard Linklater's cult classic, *Slacker.*) He drifted out to San Francisco in the early nineties, where, out of a general inability to work for others, he makes a meager living selling homemade shirts and stickers out of his backpack in San Francisco bars. Customers are treated to absurdist wisecracks delivered in a self-deprecating and unyielding rhythm, and the joke usually ends up being on him. He insists I buy him a steak in San Francisco's business district before he'll tell me his story.

He's wearing a workingman's blue button-down that identifies him as a member of the Honolulu police force. He takes me up a glass elevator to the top of a ritzy hotel, where a pair of tight-dressed society matrons coo over him because of the police thing. He carries on with grim aplomb, even—it seemed—convincing them that I was a prisoner on my last night of freedom, being given a special treat.

He tells me a tale of his own days as a freelance writer, about interviewing a car thief regarding his techniques. "'Really? You can bend a typical car window back how far before it breaks? Seven inches?' My goal was to turn everybody into a car thief by the end of reading the article," says Seth.

Seth tells me all the things he got out of his Burning Man experience: "A year's probation, a month's jail time, a month's stay at a halfway house, this number I have to call every day to see when I have to go all the way across the city to pee in a cup, free drug counseling, a new mom in the guise of a probation officer, the right not to leave the northern district of California, to not own a gun, and to not hang out with my friends because they can get high and I can't."

Seth was cruising along in his car by the trash fence one dawn at Burning Man 2001, idly picking up flotsam, and well, he had a packet sitting in the car with methamphetamine residue in it. You aren't allowed to drive off the city streets in Black Rock City these days without a special permit from Burning Man's Department of Mutant Vehicles certifying you as an art car or a vehicle otherwise necessary to the functioning of the event. The cops saw the packet when they pulled Seth over for unauthorized driving. He was arrested. He sold more drugs, he tells me, to finance the many trips to Reno for court dates as his case progressed.

His favorite saying regarding Burning Man: "How can something so much fun be so annoying?" So, why did he go every year until his probation officer told him he couldn't? "It was lonely in the city when everyone was gone. When people go to Burning Man, they take all the drugs with them and there are none left in the city. I like seeing all my friends naked." Seth had come to see himself—and his friends, such as Flash and Robert Burke—as a court jester in the Burning Man kingdom, with a certain unstated license to act out, act up, misbehave, drive recklessly, and do fuck-all. "It was like, I'll do anything—get in the car, pop a beer, and drive on, flipping off all the cops. 'What are you gonna do, pigs?'

"I found out."

Burning Man simply provided a particularly concentrated and dusty version of a life Seth tries to live every day. "In real life I push as many buttons as I can find, see how far I can go, because it's fun. Why be at the Exploratorium and watch some kid push a button that gets a machine going? Why not be the kid who pushes the button? Or better, the guy who makes the machine that the button turns on."

Still, contemplating Seth's life makes one wonder about the costs of living that way. But he bore them, and bears them, and is still laughing.

Some years there are lots of drug arrests at Burning Man, and some years fewer. It seems unlikely that the amount of illegal drugs being done has varied that widely. Until 1999 or so, the police simply felt too outmanned to put much effort into the matter.

The police presence at Burning Man includes officers from Pershing County, Washoe County, and the BLM, as well as the out-of-towners whom both Pershing and the BLM have to ship in and deputize, since they don't have enough law officers native to the region. The BLM usually has one law enforcement ranger for 13,000 square miles of territory out there, and Black Rock City more than quadruples the population of Pershing County during its brief life, thus overwhelming the resources of its tiny police force.

From the BLM's 2003 post–Burning Man press release:

> Law enforcement at the event is conducted primarily by BLM and the Pershing County Sheriff's office in cooperation with other State and county law enforcement offices. State and federal laws pertaining to illegal drug use are strictly enforced. This year BLM rangers issued a total of 177 citations and made five arrests (down 25% from last year). One of the arrests resulted in a federal grand jury indictment for distribution of ecstasy. Of the total citations, 102 were for drug related offenses (also down by 25% from 2002), 53 for violations of closure orders (down 10% from a year ago), and the remainder for miscellaneous violations.
>
> The Pershing County Sheriff's Office issued nine citations to eight individuals (up from the four citations issued last year) and made five arrests. Three of the citations related to possession or use of unlawful drugs or drug paraphernalia, one for simple battery, one for destruction of private property, one for unlawful trespass, and three for fireworks violations. The arrests included three for sex acts in public, one for trespass, and one on a failure to appear on a warrant from the Nevada Highway Patrol.

"Sex acts in public" (mostly oral) provides an opening to contemplate the ways in which Burning Man feels like a TAZ without really being one—how a sense of social freedom can be liberating even when laws are still in full effect. Outside of Black Rock City, I daresay, none of those people arrested would likely have engaged in a public sex act. And if they had, there is some likelihood someone might call the cops on them if they were discovered.

At Burning Man, it is almost certain no one would intentionally call the cops on you. However, they might well attract a cruising officer's attention by gathering around or even cheering you on.

And since the cop-per-yard ratio at Burning Man is higher than in most other American cities, the chances of your accidentally being fallen upon by a cop while engaging in public copulation or oral sex are far higher than they would be in, say, Santa Barbara.

Still, most people would be more likely to engage in public sex at Burning Man than outside of it simply because the cops are not usually a primary concern when making decisions regarding how to behave in public. How other people will react tends to weigh on us more (along with our own sense of what's right or proper, which of course develops in a subtle feedback effect with other people's judgments and the law). And if you decide to get carnal in public at Burning Man, other people will, most likely, either politely tiptoe by you or interact in ways you might enjoy.

A very popular theme camp at Burning Man in the late nineties, run by people from the *Wired* magazine world, was known as Bianca's Smut Shack. It served grilled cheese sandwiches, had plenty of comfy oversized couches, and invited open sexual play. (Strangely, the results of this year's informal Black Rock City Ministry of Statistics poll indicate that more people have *seen other* people having sex at Burning Man than have had sex there themselves, whether public or private. This both seems improbable and says a lot about the accuracy of the information you'll get when polling a community of pranksters.)

After a few years, Bianca's, by all accounts, got a little overrun by-creepy people—though I confess I'm not sure what separates the-"cool" people who want to have a place to engage in (and watch others engage in) public sex from the "creepy" ones. (I suspect weight, gender, and cameras might have been factors.) So Bianca's went more underground and by 2003 had, as far as I could tell, disappeared completely. (At least no one reported a sighting to me—in 2002, their surprise one-night appearance ended up being next door to my camp.)

Social space is a malleable thing—Black Rock City on the whole is a little like a Bianca's Smut Shack writ large, where people feel free to presume they won't risk public shame for having sex among others. That knowledge becomes a social attractor for people who want to do that sort of thing. There were no aphrodisiacs in the grilled cheese at Bianca's; sure, some porn was lying around, but nothing other than a social agreement that *this stuff is OK here; no one will mind* made Bianca's the "sex place," when any given camp that had room for fifty writhing bodies might have become that.

People don't tend to *do* things like that unless they've been given the social signal, sometimes subtle, sometimes blatant, that it's OK. And that's where Burning Man's true freedom lies: from public blow-jobs to any crazy act of performance art or costumery or random jackanapery or shouting silliness at strangers or arbitrarily visiting any and all neighbors, it's pretty much *all cool, man,* even a certain amount of comedic aggression is fine, and people know it. That can sound somewhat…unimportant, perhaps, no grand step in social evolution. But you'd be wrong to think so. It is powerfully liberating, and vital to Burning Man's strong hold on its devotees.

Those three public-sex arrests were probably on Pershing County Sheriff Ron Skinner's mind when I visited him in his bus toward the end of Burning Man 2003. He has been dealing with Burning Man since 1995—he's been around long enough to still remember John Law fondly—and he candidly admits that if he could wave a wand and not have to be the one to deal with it every year he would. He then painstakingly points out that of course he respects our right to gather as well as the BLM's prerogative to site us here. He knows that for now it is his fate to be in charge of local law enforcement in Black Rock City. And he knows that, as with most of his life experiences, he is getting something valuable out of it.

Skinner has seen Burning Man become simultaneously more of a family event—Kids Camp is a big, popular theme camp these days (for parents with kids, not kids by themselves, of course)—and more of a place for public lewdness. He would really prefer that Burning Man become an adult-only event.

Larry Harvey and Marian Goodell say that absolutely will not happen. Larry is happy to stress—as is already true, by the laws of Pershing County—that public sex is not permitted in Black Rock City. "I think it's in the worst possible taste," says Larry. "It's inherently uncivil. You don't want to get out of your tent and see someone fucking. Everyone knows this informally, but let's make it official." He knows the shit he'll get for saying this, and he is *so* tired of it. "They can add that to the litany of lost liberties—'You used to be able to shoot at random, fuck in the road, and drive over people!' Yeah, well, times change. [If the cops want an] overt ban on that, fine."

Jennifer Linx, who goes by the name Kamakhya Devi in the Burning Man world, has been wrangling Kids Camp for a few years and is not at all concerned with public sex or obscenity at Burning Man. Obviously, all parents have their own sense of what their children can handle or need to be segregated from, and Burning Man would self-select for those who share Linx's laissez-faire attitude. Intentional community, even one that strives to be as all-inclusive as Burning Man (to anyone who can come up with the ticket price), solves a lot of social problems; a tacit preagreement reigns regarding what sort of thing is permitted. Any parent who brings a kid to Burning Man and complains about lewdness would be, in legal jargon, coming to the nuisance. Still, when the cops in 2001 demanded that a wooden piece depicting two men having anal sex be taken down from a camp catering to gay men called Jiffy Lube, the art's proximity to Kids Camp was the stated reason. Linx tells me no one in Kids Camp could have cared less.

Sheriff Skinner fears, though, that the general aura of surprisingly complete trust and friendliness to strangers at Burning Man means that it will inevitably attract an audience of pedophiles intent on preying on the children there.

Well, you can't say it could never happen. But as Marian Goodell points out, there have already been sexual assaults and rapes at Burning Man, but that doesn't mean women should be banned for their own protection. As Black Rock becomes more and more a real city, it will increasingly have the problems of a real city, including crime. Any solution that would be clearly ludicrous in a city off the playa—like exiling a potential victim class—should not be imposed on Burning Man's population either.

The number of arrests made during the event is not necessarily a good indication of the number of crimes that take place, because most crimes at Burning Man go unpunished (at least by official law enforcement). An impression reigns in the city—which the statistics can neither bear out nor disprove because crime stats per se are not kept—that Black Rock is a uniquely peaceful and crime-free place for a city of thirty-thousand-plus hard partiers. The very fact that most Burners believe in their city's idyllic nature makes it a far more pleasant place than it would be if we chose to focus on really figuring out exactly how crime-free or safe it is, and wondering if every neighbor is a potential thief or attacker.

I've had bikes stolen twice out there, both times on Monday night, the event's last official day. I was heavily bummed for about an hour both times. But I still don't want to lock up my bike, or keep everything valuable locked up in my car. (In fact, I don't lock my car door either, most of the time, even though I keep some valuables there.)

This makes my life in Black Rock City happier and more fulfilling, even if it might be based on a naive misunderstanding of the facts. As long as we all *believe* we live in a trustworthy and safe community, we will be happier and feel freer, even if our beliefs aren't necessarily true. Often, to our detriment, we make the opposite mistake, letting potential problems and fears weigh on our minds and actions to an extent that's grossly incommensurate with the actual chances that any problem will befall us. It makes life darker, more limited, more frightened. Our mutual belief in one another's good intentions at Burning Man makes us all happier than we'd otherwise be.

Sheriff Skinner doesn't think Burning Man even comes close to creating a new, better way to live. He believes that if any approach to Utopianism is the goal, "they are failing miserably...I don't think the Burning Man community is any different from most communities; a small percentage of the population causes ninety-five percent of the problems. But we do have a lot of property crimes and crimes against persons, at a much higher percentage than you would find in a normal working community. Let's face it, this community is here to party and that's what they do, and when people party, there tend to be problems."

☀

Most people who've heard only a little about Burning Man know that there's lots of public nudity there. It's true, but early attendees from the days when it was still mostly friends and friends of friends recall that it wasn't until 1994—the year the population leaped to around two thousand, far beyond anyone's immediate degrees of separation— that public nudity became noticeable. It makes sense that the comfort level on the part of the nude person would rise when the social environment was loose and forgiving but was not made up of an immediate circle of acquaintances. When you actually *know* people, as crushes, past relationships, coworkers, you might have some obvious and understandable reasons to not want to be naked in front of them.

Harrod Blank, the art-car expert, is also a filmmaker specializing in documenting cutting-edge American art and experience scenes. To his mind, Burning Man is creating new images, new iconographies, fresh to human art and expression, at least in Western culture: The art car is one, the fully fluorescent-painted naked body might be another.

"It's like a new word in the language of art, or images...it's fresh, fresh art. It doesn't have a set meaning yet. It's being defined by us as we look at it," explains Blank. Most people, when talking about nudity at Burning Man, talk about it in terms of their freedom to *be* nude. Blank, the filmmaker, the professional voyeur, sees the nudity more interestingly: that it creates a unique freedom to *see* live, nude strangers in a public, civic context. "It's a beauty we not only don't get to express but don't get to experience outside a porn movie or enjoying your mate. It's not the same old thing; it's a whole other level of expression. It irks me when [the] Burning Man [organization] says [it doesn't] want to see nudity in movies [filmed at Burning Man]." (Burning Man claims total intellectual property rights over all images taken within its gates, and to market film shot there, the filmmaker must secure permission and meet certain requirements, which typically include tithing any income from the work back to Burning Man.)

As naive as I am about theft, I talked to many women who have an equally empowering naïveté about sexual violence. It is *not* completely unknown at Burning Man, but many women think it is. Several women have told me that this is the only city in the world where they feel completely confident and safe in being as sexual as they care to be in their dress (or lack of it) and behavior. And feeling that way is good enough for them. Humans live only partially in the world of facts; we live even more in the world of our interpretations. It is in the interpretive world that most of the glory of Burning Man lies. Our acts, after all, live only for the moment we live them; the meanings we ascribe to them survive and guide our actions and our souls forever.

Burning Man is not only more nude than most cities but also sexier. You can ask—and be asked by—relative strangers to walk off in the distance, or to your tent, to fuck and suck, and more than sometimes, the answer will be an inviting yes. It happens. That doesn't mean it will happen to you, and it doesn't mean it's an understood social norm that anyone owes you.

I ask Doyle, a leonine young giant from DPW whom the ladies clearly like quite a bit, why Burning Man is so aquiver with sexual energy and acts. Replies Doyle: "When you're doing what you like doing"—as most people out there are—"you're confident, and that confidence is attractive to other people. So when you're having fun, you are attractive to so many people and there are so many other amazing confident people all around you that monogamy suddenly doesn't seem like the right choice.

"It's wild and fun. That's why people love it, and that's why people hate it. You go there to let the monster out of the box, and there are how many square miles of flat monster-out-of-the-box land out there? You're driving stupid chopped-up cars with flamethrowers, acting invincible, and people die, cheat on their girlfriends, get hurt, do tons of drugs, or just come out as voyeurs to watch the whole thing."

Among the people watching are the police. The police didn't really want to discuss their techniques with me. A few people cited or arrested did, though, and it all sounds pretty basic: Cops drive and walk around looking, sometimes with night-vision goggles, and if it looks like you are smoking dope or whatever, they might try to pop you.

I've heard secondhand accounts that police at Burning Man have picked up on the event's gifting meme, and will entrap people (without meeting the legal definition of entrapment). They might give a gift to a passerby (this only works if they are undercover, as some of them are), and when that passerby says he's sorry that he doesn't have anything to give in return, the cop might hint, well, hey, isn't there something special you could give me? Maybe back at your camp? Legally, it's important the cops use only code words and never explicitly mention drugs. And sometimes people bite. Well, hey, I have some dope back in camp. Really? That might be cool...The end of this little drama is obvious, and sad.

The relationship between Burning Man and law enforcement is neither as tight nor as antagonistic as different parts of the community think. Burning Man cooperates with the law; it also sometimes pushes back, and will speak up for its citizens' perceived needs. Every afternoon of the event, Burning Man's senior staff meets with representatives of the many law enforcement agencies out there, but they all like to keep quiet about what exactly is discussed. I am told, though, that a few years ago, Burning Man representatives tried to educate the-cops about who they might be dealing with in Black Rock City by showing them representative photos of people police might encounter while doggedly searching for druggy miscreants. One, a hairy gentleman in drag, is identified as a Bay Area artist with an annual income floating around or often below six thousand a-year.

Then the police were shown a mostly naked potbellied middle-aged man painted a dusty blue. He, of course, is a specialist criminal attorney with an annual income of $240,000. It was a risky move, rubbing the cops' faces in the fact that they couldn't be confident of the subtle socioeconomic decisions they make that often influence, whether cops like to admit it or not, how they treat potential perps. Burning Man wants them to know that a Supreme Court justice's daughter may well be out here, and they better make sure they treat her properly.

Gerlach's local judge, Phil Thomas, candidly tells me that in his opinion the feds from BLM often don't respect citizens' constitutional rights. Unfortunately, he only gets to adjudicate arrests made by Pershing or Washoe cops. Of those, he tells me, around 10 percent tend to have procedural irregularities such that he'd be apt to throw the case out.

"What really scares me," Judge Phil says, "is that people don't know that they can't have [warrantless searches] done to them. We need to get back to teaching our kids the Constitution and Bill of Rights and all that shit. Anybody should be able to say, 'You can't do that. Let go of me; you can't touch me.' The fact that we as a people don't know our rights shows that we are fucking stupid."

The police at Burning Man have had to figure out what is private-out on this public land. For the most part, any fully enclosed structure, even if it's a tent, should be secure from unwarranted searches. Cops have violated that tenet at Burning Man in the past. Everyone involved says it's a learning curve, and that things are getting better. Burning Man sources often blame bad or overweening policing on a few specific bad cops, not the law enforcement system as a whole.

The fact is, it is in no one's interest to drive Burning Man away from the Black Rock with overzealous policing. In the early years of Burning Man in the desert, the BLM charged very small permitting fees; by the time the event came back to the playa in '98, they had switched to a full cost-recovery system, theoretically charging how much it cost them to deal with the event. In 2000 they switched to a $4.00 per person, per day fee, which has made Burning Man a vital source of cash to the Winnemucca branch office of the BLM, which collected around $600,000 from Burning Man in 2003. (And the money stays in the area, rather than just going to Washington.) All the other government agencies in the area, from the Nevada Highway Patrol to the Paiute Indian tribes up at Pyramid Lake, get payoffs (all perfectly legal, of course) as well.

Burning Man's organizers would like to see the cops mellow out on lifestyle issues like drugs and public obscenity and do a better job of helping them secure their borders against gate-crashers. Burning Man runs a remarkably tight gate; their gate-workers will and do pop open the backs of vehicles and poke around for stowaways.

Burning Man even has a boat radar system now, to detect cars dumping people off to hop the fence or trying to enter the back gate. From TAZ to panopticon in less than fifteen years. Burning Man has intentionally cut itself off from some of our culture's major sources of money—corporate donations, sponsorship, the selling of film rights to MTV, and the like. Thus, perhaps understandably, they tend to try to squeeze every penny they can from the cash sources they do allow themselves access to, like tickets. But a loose gate can be a valuable social lubricant and add to the overall pleasure of the event—as Chicken John once said, if someone can manage to get in, then they probably deserve to be there. When a structure is too rigid, the slightest shake breaks it; it has no room to adjust. One morning a few days before the official start of the event in 2003, I tried to tell all this to the Black Rock Ranger doing a ticket sweep—harassing every single person within Burning Man's fence and making them show a ticket stub—after the gate was already operating and checking tickets and searching trunks.

I know you are all trying to run a tight business here, I began, so let's talk business: The people here now who you are waking up at six in the morning and alienating are your core customers, and in most cases are essentially working for you—doing the things that make people want to pay $250 to be here. Certainly they aren't coming to watch Marian Goodell and Larry Harvey put on a show or admire Will Roger and Harley Dubois's sculptures. If some of the people here now haven't bought a ticket, you won't get your money; you'll kick them out, and their being here is most likely adding something of value to the community and…Dude, he shut me up, this wasn't my idea.

One man I know, a fabulously skilled contortionist, regularly foils Burning Man's gate search by folding himself inside a box that sits in full view on the passenger seat of a friend's car. No gate-worker has ever guessed that he or she could possibly need to examine that tiny box for a human stowaway.

☼

Burning Man has something more interesting and useful than police for its internal peacekeeping. It has the mostly all-volunteer Black Rock Rangers. (A small handful of higher-ups get salaries, but even those aren't much compensation for the time put in.) Mostly, mutual respect reigns between the cops and Rangers. Once, while I was riding around with a Pershing officer on patrol, he took what seemed a pretty clearly drug-addled guy who had sat down in a woman's passenger seat during a dust storm and refused to either speak or leave and, without asking for ID or running a check or whatever, just deposited him at a Black Rock Ranger station and asked them to take care of him for a while.

The Rangers, as they shout at their training sessions, "are not cops!" They have no power to detain or arrest. They are meant to assist and advise, serve as nonviolent conflict mediators between Black Rock citizens, liaise with medical staff and police, and serve as perimeter guards at big burns. They are responsible for certain coplike behaviors, however, even without official cop authority—enforcing Burning Man's no-driving rules, for example.

In some ways, the rules and mores specific to Black Rock City allow more latitude for individual expression and experimentation than those of the outside world. But along with that, as Michael Michael noted while contemplating the evolution of the Ranger function, is a more absolute authority than we are used to outside Burning Man. Summary justice can be and is dispensed, such as the arbitrary draining of the tires of insistent drivers, with a message from Danger Ranger left behind—"Tire pressure is a privilege, not a right."

In the nineties, Black Rock Rangers would perform the equivalent of arrests and property confiscation—and it was frontier justice, with the understood presumption that the Rangers were deputized by the community to do whatever was necessary for its survival. This worked surprisingly well. Many old-timers remember fondly a solution developed by Vanessa Kuemmerle, which was in essence the creation of a short-term jail in a place with no walls. A particularly truculent drunk was driven a couple of miles outside of camp, handed a gallon of water, and told that if you walk *that* way (back to camp) and drink this water and calm down by the time you return, everything will be fine; and that if you walk in any other direction, you'll die. Kimric Smythe tore out wires and tossed away keys from a pickup truck driver who was menacing the encampment in an early year. Justice—swift and personal—was handed down without much in the way of procedural niceties, and it worked. It was private, anarchist justice.

The official sheriffs, Michael says, are amused and somewhat envious of the authority the Rangers can wield. Many of the standards of the outside world, in Michael's estimation, have no place in the Black Rock community; at the same time, there are values unique to the Black Rock community, and the Rangers will sometimes impose them on that community for, as they perceive it, its benefit and continuation.

The Black Rock Rangers were founded by Michael Michael—Danger Ranger—in the old days, before the city had a well-hewn path depositing you directly into its closed fence straight from the 34. In those days, community members faced perils such as getting lost or stuck out on the grand playa. In the current version of Black Rock City, Rangers can seem less like heroes and protectors and more like nags or an excuse for people to not handle their own problems.

They provide what they call "nonconfrontational dispute resolution" and, in practice, spend a fair amount of time giving advice (sometimes gentle, sometimes not) to Black Rock denizens about what they ought to or ought not to be doing. Original Ranger philosopher Michael Michael likes to keep to an old-school Ranger spirit, one that, at its most radical, declares, as he once told me, "You can burn your own car" in Black Rock City as long as you are prepared to clean it up. He always wanted to ensure that Rangers did not instantly think no, but yes—and that any reason they had to say no should be unique and appropriate to Black Rock City, not mindlessly imported from the outside world.

Everyone's experience at Burning Man is individual; I almost never notice Rangers out there. When I tell one Ranger this, he laughs and says, "Good." But I've heard some stories of Ranger interference in other people's business (mostly along the lines of a Ranger telling someone not to do something the Ranger thinks is unsafe), and one year, wags from one of Burning Man's longest-lasting theme villages, Gigsville, printed up a card that read FUCK OFF RANGER. The Black Rock Rangers give the type of person that would print a card like that exactly what he wants: a casual, unthreatening, Potemkin authority to rebel against. After all, as Michael points out, they didn't print cards reading FUCK OFF COP.

Most Rangers seem to enjoy their job. It attracts a more intense and serious bunch than other areas of Burning Man's volunteer staff. Typically, the worst problem they have to deal with is calming down a troublesome drunk. Most of them get plenty of love from the people of Black Rock, too. But it's not always so pleasant. The current Ranger leader goes by the name Seadog; he's an ex–military man who came to Burning Man in 2000 from the Sturgis bike rally not knowing what to expect. He wandered over and helped set up the Man and realized Burning Man was a lot more fun if you had something to do. He didn't feel like continuing construction all week—he does that in his normal life—so he gave DPW a pass and out of curiosity attended a Ranger orientation meeting. In one day he went from not knowing what a Ranger was to being one. On his first patrol, a raving lunatic punched him in the face. When Seadog didn't punch back, he was promoted to Ranger shift leader. When Seadog tells me this story three years after it happened, I realize that I was there. As cops were wrestling the struggling and yelling man into the back of a car, the cop keeping the perimeter *actually said,* "Move along, there's nothing to see here."

Seadog doesn't talk about letting people burn their own cars—that kind of old-school idea might not even occur to him—but he does tell me, "If someone wants to be a fire-walker, it's their choice. Let them be a fire-walker. When they decide the coals are too hot, I'll take them to medical. But for me to jump in and try to stop them, that's interfering with their right to the experience." But he will allow them to make informed choices, perhaps stepping in to tell them just how hot *hot* coals are. Some might appreciate the advice; others might want to say Fuck off ranger!

There is a supposed tenet of social interaction at Burning Man that says you can do whatever you want (within the laws of the United States and the state of Nevada!) except interfere with another person's direct experience. Sounds reasonable, but...

Every action out there, if it's worth a damn, has the possibility—usually the hope—of "interfering" with someone else's direct experience, in that it dreams of *affecting* it. It's only when a negative value judgment is put on that effect that it becomes "interference." It-is true, as Larry Harvey observed to me once, that letting unstated notions of "cool" define justice within a tight circle of friends can be a problem. Without specific standards, just an understanding that we are all a team here, the clan can have a hard time dispensing objective justice to its own. Larry likes to tell a story about how someone once fired off a gun so close to Dan Miller's ear that he damaged Dan's hearing— but since they were both insiders in a small community, everyone tolerated an antisocial act for which a stranger would have been strung up.

Someone tells me an amusing story regarding the impossible ambiguity of the "No interference with direct experience" rule. She was on her way to a sunrise reunion with some old friends—a yearly ritual—and with typical Burner whimsy began banging a gong while wandering through a camp, until an aggravated Irishman tackled her and confiscated the gong. She was interfering with his experience—of sleep.

Her husband entered the fray. The Irishman had to realize, he yelled, that he wasn't at home in the Marina, and you can't expect to-sleep out here, and *he* was interfering with *their* direct experience of the morning gong ritual. It seemed as if applying generic Burning Man law couldn't settle this. (The Irishman did calm down and admit that, hey, it's Burning Man; he can sleep later.) Humans in Black Rock must decide for themselves how they are going to get along, and sloganeering is no substitute for, as Larry Harvey might say, direct experience. The end result tends to be a very property-rights-based liberty, where anything that isn't directly and physically damaging someone else's person or property is (if often reluctantly) tolerated.

Danger Ranger isn't really an active Black Rock Ranger anymore. Despite being one of the original three "owners" of Burning Man, Michael Michael has taken on a circumscribed role these days. He's still one of the partners on the board of the LLC, but with no specific responsibilities. He acts as ambassador, freelance troubleshooter, and "director of genetic programming"—his official title—responsible on a big-think level for, in inchoate and undetectable ways, "guiding the event into the future."

His thoughts on the Meaning of It All are thus worth considering. Michael sometimes intimates he is from the future, that he's some Terminator-like visitor on a mission to change the present in order to guarantee a healthy tomorrow. He is classically futique, speculating about a nanotech-driven future when the problem of production has been solved at the atomic level, when we have tiny little machines at our service that can literally construct any physical object we need at almost no cost.

Burning Man places us firmly in an artificial world of perfect abundance. The reason we don't need commerce out there is that we are supposed to have already brought (and bought) with us everything we need to survive and thrive. With all those material needs taken care of, Burning Man makes us learn how to live, love, create, and relate in a space where we have nothing but leisure on our hands. This-could be of great relevance in preparing for that very possible future—a world beyond scarcity, beyond labor for anything other than creativity and joy. It's an attractive and fascinating vision of what Burning Man might really be all about. But there are, as any time traveler knows, an infinite number of potential futures, new ones created with each choice every one of us makes. Who knows which one Burning Man will lead to?

I think it might be "Danger Ranger" who is from the future, anyway. Michael Michael often talks in more prosaic terms, with a shorter time horizon. Politically, he tells me he sees the event potentially fitting comfortably into Nevada's future. As a pioneer in legalized gambling and prostitution, Nevada's comparative advantage could well turn out to be marketing itself as a pioneering free market in experience.

"I see the possibility that someday, like prostitution, some types of drugs may be allowed as a special experience, and Burning Man could lead the way in providing a safe, healthy environment that wouldn't be harmful to [larger] society or culture, a place where people can experience different altered states of consciousness," explains Michael. In his mind, Burning Man represents a beta model of a planetary community—one with values, standards, and experiences that, because the city explodes and scatters yearly, have spread all over the globe. (Ain't that American?) "There are things that go on here that would probably not be allowed in downtown Reno, but at the same time, we erase all traces of ourselves and clean up the land. I haven't seen Reno or Vegas do a disappearing act." (Burners are also apt to make invidious—but telling and true—comparisons between big street parties like Reno's Hot August Nights, with their destructive and violent behavior and mass arrests, and Black Rock's mostly harmless playfulness.)

Michael sometimes hints that, in Burning Man terms, he is slowly disappearing. He sees that the Machine is running with or without him, and intimates that he might just return to whence he came, his mission here completed. This sort of future mystic talk I generally find charming—it adds a bit of zest to one's life to have an acquaintance who is an actual visitor from the Magical World of Tomorrow.

In more recent years, Michael hasn't necessarily even spent much time in Black Rock City during the event, falling back on the oldtimer's love for the week leading up to gate opening and the week after as the true quill, the time when the real magic occurs in a more intimate setting. A city of thirty thousand crawling with cops is not Danger Ranger's ideal environment in which to work.

But there are more important issues at stake than his personal feelings. He sees Black Rock City as a manifestation of a powerful group mind. "I now dedicate myself to and have incorporated myself into part of a much larger whole," says Michael. "For an individual to say that I can't shoot off my fireworks, or fire a gun right outside my tent, or can't do anything else, is a limited personal vision. Now, this doesn't invalidate their needs or make them less true. It could be the event is not fulfilling their individual needs. We will lose a few."

Those new rules Michael refers to were all instituted in the name of safety. Some original desert Cacophonists don't go to Burning Man anymore, not so much because they resent the rules but because they are unhappy with the reason the rules are there: because Burning Man's ever-growing population makes it impossible to actually trust everyone around you. The organizers worry about safety, of course, for obvious and admirable human feelings of responsibility for the people they invited to the party, as well as legal liability. Safety is especially tricky in a Burning Man context because the nature of the event invites and demands behaviors that are not "safe" by most normal standards—fire play, amateur constructions with no building codes imposed, the attempt to live in a place prone to nearly one-hundred-mile-per-hour winds and dust storms.

Sure, safety first and all. But, as Michael asks, what are the real reasons we seek safety? Why are we so concerned with prolonging our lives? "To what end and for how many years? What about quality of life? What is being alive? What is living? There's a chance you may die at Burning Man, but you will never be more alive."

Chapter Eleven

LEAVE NO TRACE

Black Rock City is, at its grandest, a mixture of civilization and magic. Of all the bedrocks of a civilized polity, refuse disposal is the aspect that is both most vital to our well-being and the biggest pain in the ass to cope with by ourselves. And one of the most impressive, least explicable acts of magic is the vanishing act. Members of Burning Man's Department of Public Works (DPW) have become masters of that act of civilization and that act of magic.

One of DPW's most die-hard members is a man known as the Dark Angel of Black Rock City. He's got smoothly muscled cocoa-butter skin, wispy, poetically thin facial hair on a strongly structured but preternaturally youthful face that exudes a sweet strength. And even with that nickname, he's not, strangely enough, any kind of pretentious ass—he's easygoing, mocks the world gently but lovingly, and falls back on D.A. as an everyday name.

When D.A. talks about Burning Man and how it changed his life, he structures the story artfully, like a myth of self-discovery or a superhero's origin story. The bedroom of his Golden Gate Park–area apartment has posters by modern superhero mythologizer Alex Ross and some of D.A.'s own art, which looks like covers of unpublished issues of *The Sandman*.

Sitting cross-legged on his bedroom floor, both of us starting on our first beers of the afternoon, he lays out the myth. "I wasn't always the Dark Angel of Black Rock City. In 1996, I was a graphic designer at a small company in New Jersey. I had been between jobs and could have taken either this job in New York City or this small little graphic design job in New Jersey, and something—I don't know what—told me to take the job in New Jersey, even though I was sick of Jersey. I was going through a breakup and was a little distraught and not sure where I was going with my life. I was twenty-four.

"This was the heyday of the dot-com boom, and at the job they'd circulate magazines for us to keep up with. It was the days when you-still had to pay, like, forty dollars an hour to be on AOL, and we were making little buttons for screens on the great new frontier, the Internet.

"And one day an issue of *Wired* landed on my desk. I looked at it, and I'll never forget it. There was this beautiful girl on the cover with her arms spread out and her eyes closed, and she just seemed to be in this wonderful state and behind her was this thing on fire that later became known to me as the Burning Man.

"I remember just staring at the cover, thinking, *Oh my God, what is-this?* It read: 'Greetings from Burning Man, the New American Holiday.' I was like, *What?* but I kept looking and connecting with that woman. Not like, *Oh, she is so beautiful*—which she was!—but something else that was radiating out of her that I was totally picking up that I hadn't felt before or hadn't understood, and I was experiencing it vicariously through her.

"And then I opened the magazine, and there was this red guy and this blue naked girl and then this regular naked girl, as opposed to being blue *and* naked, and they were just all smiles, especially the red guy in this crazy—I don't even know what kind of outfit you'd call it—and he had his thumbs up, like, *Life is good!*

"And that was so what I wanted to hear. *Oh my God, these people are* happy, *what the hell is this?* And I opened up the next page, and there was some ceremony with fire and all sorts of people—there were children and senior citizens and people in costume and people in nothing—and everybody makes a big deal about nudity and I thought it was just fantastic that everybody was walking around like it was completely normal. I'm trying to read the article, but my eyes just kept returning to the pictures. I kept seeing in my mind this arrow blinking into the pictures saying 'You are here! You are here!'

"And I heard this voice inside myself—I know this sounds a little hokey-pokey, especially coming from New Jersey—but I heard this voice that seemed really familiar, but I hadn't heard it since who knows when, saying 'You must do this!' I could have answered any number of ways, like *maybe, I don't know, I can't afford it, I don't know anything about the desert, that looks kind of weird.* But I said yes. I said yes. I closed my eyes in a firm yes. I listened to this part of me and trusted it and said, *I am going.*"

And so he did. That *Wired* story gave off the vibe that costumery might be appropriate, so he visited a costume shop in Greenwich Village. He was tempted by twenty-dollar plastic wings—more his price range—but the clerk sold him on the lovely hundred-dollar ones made from real black feathers. "The salesman, who was a great actor in the role of a person selling costumes at this Greenwich Village shop, was playing the trickster role with me. He said, 'It's like this, do you want people to just say hi or do you want them to say, *"Hi there!"* ' And my ego went, 'Hmm, *hi there!* sounds good,' and I-went for it. I bought them. Couldn't afford them. Charged them; I still had credit cards back then. In fact, I think I charged that whole trip."

D.A. flew to Reno with a friend who insisted on tagging along. In his Reno hotel he was confronted with TV news reports—this was Burning Man '97—explaining the ongoing contretemps between Burning Man and Washoe County and the cops, and raising the question of whether Burning Man would happen at all. "I'm like, 'Fuck you it's not happening!' And I'm cursing God. Not that I had ever been praying to him, but I was cursing him now. I became really afraid of having to spend a week in Reno. I'm not there for Reno; I'm there for Burning Man. I'm there to experience the New American Holiday! More than that—I'm there to experience what that girl [was] feeling when she was dancing on that *Wired* cover, to reach that state of exaltation."

He arrived on the Hualapai with his friend and ditched him rather quickly. This was something he had to experience alone. "I didn't want any ties to my past to inhibit me. You know, this person knows me a certain way. He knows I might be shy about certain things, might have hang-ups about certain things. But if this person wasn't in my sight, there was nothing to hold me to that—just me confronting me, and there was nothing to hold me to any previous identity. There is nobody here who knows you. Those issues don't exist. Step forward! Step through the goddamn door! So that's what I-did."

D.A. began strolling around, "just smiling and learning to be there in this place where people look each other in the eyes, where it's like, hey, hello, whereas coming from the East Coast, if they look you in the eye it's because they are sizing you up as some kind of threat, or if you're not a threat, you're prey. I immediately had to deactivate that; no no no, let's not take any of that out here. We left that in Jersey."

He saw some things for the first time there. He saw a naked fire-spinner, as fresh and ever-renewing and compelling as a shifting fire itself. She was nude, beautiful, and on display, doing something quite dangerous, yet still safe. "I realized she was protected by all of us, and I was starting to understand what community meant out there."

Wandering alone through Black Rock City, he picked up his new name. On more than one occasion during his wanderings, because of his wings, strangers would address him as a "dark angel." Then his new playa identity was challenged. As he was walking by a camp that was engaged in a huge group meeting, three lovely young girls rushed out to gently accost him. The whole group was staring at him. At his wings. They were the crew of Pepe Ozan's opera, which featured a character that really would come to life if she had wings as lovely and detailed and real as those sported by the Dark Angel.

The wings had *become* D.A. by this point. "I was still learning to trust. I wanted to help, but I was haunted by the thought *If I give them out, will I never see them again?*" He met Rebecca, who was to play the part of the Raven and would don his wings. D.A. was also asked to join the opera crew—"naked blue boy number forty-eight" is how he remembers his role. "So there I am stripping down, and now I'm naked and being painted blue and not by myself. And not necessarily by the opposite sex. I was in this factory line of people painting and being painted." He joined the opera crew, loved it, and of course got his wings back. Or, perhaps, finally earned them.

In '97, the people still raised the Man. He was elevated to his place by a group of citizens gathering and pulling on a rope—anyone who came by could join in—umbilically connecting themselves to the event's central ritual. Nowadays, the best you can do is form a huge spectating circle around an enormous crane that dangles the Man unmoored and alone in the sky and deposits him atop whatever monolith he's standing on that year.

Instead of standing on the perimeter of a closely guarded circle through which one cannot walk without a preprinted laminate, a new-comer could still just grab a torch from Crimson Rose and dance and cavort around the Man and *be* the ceremony instead of just watching it. (Nowadays, Crimson has gathered a national cabal of fire-spinners from around the country, called the Fire Conclave, to form the squad of hundreds of fire-wraiths that beautifully encircle the Man as he burns.) So D.A. grabbed a torch, and "it was just so powerful—you're looking at everybody else, and it's like, *Yeah, this is our connection, this is what we do, this is who we are. This is the part of us that comes out here. We are bringing it to life.*"

D.A. appointed himself guardian angel for a young man pushing his father around the Burn circle in a wheelchair. They were having trouble wending their way safely through, kept clipping people in front of them. "I took the place of the people being clipped and created a visual boundary for them with my wings. I created space enough so that this kid could easily push his father around, and I kept turning around and waving him on behind me and—it felt good.

"Then the crowd had filtered out enough so he could go on on his own, and I stepped aside and gestured for him to pass and he took my hand and just said, 'Thank you, thank you.' And I'm just like, 'You're welcome, enjoy.' He went on his way, and I was just glowing. And this girl taps me on the shoulder and kisses me and says, 'Thank you, I saw that, that was very beautiful,' and then she runs off. And I thought, *Wow, this place is great! You do good things around here and you get rewarded for it.* But that wasn't the reason for doing it. It just happened, and you don't live in a bubble and everything you do creates something. We have an effect on our environment; we create ripples and splashes." Burning Man, instant Karma machine.

He went on to live a night he remembers so well he can tell me nearly every detail of it six years later. He protected a sculpture—a powerful metal man kneeling on the ground, head thrown back in an apparent agonized scream, wrapped delicately in paper by his creator for a wraithlike burn—from the Vegematic's pyromaniacal rampage; then he joined that pyromaniacal rampage, and the night went on and on. In those days, when the Man still burned on Sunday night, his going down was the signal that this was all we had, this compressed night of anything goes. When the sun rose, it was over, and we had to have done everything we needed to do, everything Burning Man inspired us to, by then.

"I needed this. I needed this more than I have ever needed anything before," was D.A.'s judgment on his first Burning Man. "From the depths of my soul I needed to understand this and to feel this, and it felt like I was melting and it felt great. I returned to Jersey, and people would ask me what happened and I'd tell them there was something there to explore but I can't really say what it is. I can tell you what it is for me, and the simple clichéd image might just be naked and sex and fire, and sure, those things happen, but what I found for myself was so much more powerful and life affirming than anything I could have read or expected. I had found what I was looking for and I still didn't know exactly what it was, but I felt it and it was important and I discovered an aspect of myself that was in me the entire time but just needed a place to be born. That's how the Dark Angel of Black Rock City came to be. I stepped off the playa a completely different person, but it wasn't different as in *something else* but different as in who I truly was.

"People would ask me how it was, and I'd say, 'It's like life. How is life? I don't know. You live in it.'"

The world of Burning Man reached out its tendrils through the phone lines with this curious new communications tool, the Internet. Those wires dragged the Dark Angel in even tighter. He kept getting invitations to parties and events happening in San Francisco—"Flambé lounges and Decompressions and see this person do this and that person do that and swallow this and spin this and see, see, this continuing fabulous spectacle—see Hitler on Ice!"

So he headed west. The Burning Man world going on year-round out there delivered an endless array of wonderment and talented, friendly people creating constant excuses for creative and excessive togetherness. Everyone involved remembers these days—1995 to 1998—as an explosion of activity and a feeling that the Big Thing, that magical effect that Larry could sense even from the beginning, was coalescing, that it was really all happening, that the Burning Man scene, vibe, spirit was changing lives, could change the world. Numerous people in the Burning Man community fondly remember working together on a partially National Endowment for the Arts–funded project called Defenestration, masterminded by their pal Brian Goggin, that transformed an entire earthquake-damaged multistory building on Sixth and Howard into a surrealist art display, with furniture jumping out windows and crawling down the facade.

Such collaborations with the normal world of art funding, like the government or foundations, don't really affect the playa, which is part of Burning Man's charm. At Burning Man, achievements are the result of purely voluntary contributions (no one *makes* you buy a ticket) from and by the community for whom the works are made. No one is exploited, and the artist can know why and for whom he is making his offering.

It's not just the big artists, though, who offer something vital to Black Rock City. D.A. stayed in San Francisco, of course, and stayed as close to Burning Man as he could. Thus, he has for years been part of DPW's clean-up crew, the small gang of men and women who stay for a few weeks after Burning Man is over and pick up every single sign that a city of art-partying humans has haunted the Black Rock at all. He is eager to get to the playa as soon as he can each year, and to stay as late as needed.

"These days I find cleanup to be my favorite part of the event, and when I tell people that, they're like, 'What?!' The notion of cleaning up other people's garbage—we're taught to think of that as the worst kind of chore, but it doesn't suck. It's like practicing Zen. It's better than washing your dishes. We are restoring the playa, and the role of custodian is not a lowly role. It's a thing to be proud of. We're reducing everything back to nothing, and it feels so good."

The cleanup can be harder than you might guess, because for four years straight—a curse broken only in 2003—promptly upon the event's official conclusion on Labor Day, the playa was battered with continuous vicious and blinding wind- and dust storms. The playa is flat, cracked perfection before we all arrive, and our cars and our bikes and our feet crunch it until the surface layer is reduced to a fine powder that drifts with the slightest current. When the winds become fast and strong, the air becomes supersaturated with this dust, and it obscures everything and piles up in ridges and waves around any object it can find to light upon.

Jim Mason wrote an amusingly accurate account of all this for the *L.A. Weekly* after 2002's particularly horrific denouement:

I sat through the dust on Tuesday and Wednesday, watching firsthand from the cab of the crane truck. I watched as everything got buried and generally destroyed. Waves of blinding white alkali scratched over the cab as my truck reeled with each blinding gust. Loading anything was out of the question. Trying to sleep in any vehicle was like trying to nap in a Shop-Vac—running. No one could leave. You couldn't see for more than a couple of feet. It was like being incarcerated, against your will and better judgment, in one of the largest expanses of open horizon in North America...The old-timers will even tell you that, back in the day, the wind blew twice that hard, in both directions, simultaneously, and the dust was actually more like sharpened volcanic pebbles dislodged and propelled from the surrounding mountains. It went right through car paint and blue tarps, chafing the skin to blood...As those who stay late know, the dust storms are key: Each year they create a desert full of front-row seats for a performance in which people you know and respect snap in curious and revealing ways. The Burning Man literature makes claims for the transformative nature of the event. But, in reality, the event is only the necessary prelude for the real show: Eight days of no-sleep, lethal dehydration, substance abuse, unrequited sexual aggression, camp drama, faux-fire warfare and heroic art catastrophes leaves everyone hanging on a thin sliver, ready to deal with the skin-stinging, eye-blinding and breath-preventing reality of a good dust storm. And this is where the real tests begin.

All it takes is about two hours of dust on Tuesday before things start heading south on a screaming pulse jet. Within six hours, I get in my vehicle (if it still runs) and start the camp tour to enjoy the now-real scenes of the apocalypse and the generally accelerating disassembly of humanity.

It is an incomparable combination of the sublime and the horrifying, those dust storms, like you've been teleported to one of those misty mystical dimensions from a *Doctor Strange* comic book, the entire world an indistinct white cloud out to ruin your eyes and sandblast your skin, every object a mystery and a hazard. While it's a fascinating display, it also—really and truly and completely—*sucks* and is the only thing that makes me wish to my heart I could be anywhere else but the Black Rock Playa. But still, if you are shopping for extreme experiences, there's one for your $250 ticket. And there is a certain comedic grace to be found in looking at your neighbor through smeared and filthy goggles, banging matted forehead to matted forehead, and laughing really, really loudly at how ridiculously stupid it is you are living through this—that you wanted it!

It is such storms and their aftermath that truly test the mettle of those proud desert rats, Burning Man's DPW. "Now we're digging tents out," says D.A. "People are abandoning their tents, afraid for their lives in these never-ending dust storms, and in some ways, you don't blame them. They think they are going to die, and who knows, they could. Yeah, there could be a corpse in one of those tents one of these days."

Dust storm or no, people will sometimes just leave big nasty shit behind—that couch whose weight is now three-fourths playa dust with two big burn holes in the cushions. "Yeah, there's sometimes that attitude of *Leave anything behind; DPW will take it.* Yeah, those scum-bags will take your filthy couch, whatever," D.A. gripes.

As D.A. alludes, the DPW has developed a bad reputation. Part of that comes from DPW members' often surly behavior. The DPW doesn't just clean up the city, mind; they also set up what infrastructure exists—roads, signs, shade structures for Center Camp, the café, and official Burning Man organizational camps. D.A. admits that as the builders and first occupiers of Black Rock City, they tend to feel possessive about it.

"When all these people show up in what we feel is our living room and start putting their feet up, we get testy," he explains. "We're still hammering away, and someone's just running around naked on a bike, shouting 'Wooo!' a week before the event even starts. We're all like, 'Fuck you, this is a construction zone! Put some fucking pants on! You'll get that thing shot off by a nail gun.'

"A lot of people are oddly afraid of us. I like being approachable. I don't like promoting fear. But if certain people approach a DPW guy and say, 'You guys did a great job' and get a 'Fuck you!' back, they should know exactly what to do with that. 'Right on! Fuck you too!' A *fuck you* is a *fuck you* to some. To some it can be a term of endearment. Some people *want* to hear it. 'Fuck you!'—now you're speaking my language!"

The official DPW story line for the last few years has been that the gig is getting more locked down, more professional. They're phasing out beer as a management tool, and their ranch will no longer be a last-ditch summer home for the country's most feral construction workers. (The DPW's work begins on the ranch months before they are permitted by the BLM to start setting up on the playa.) DPW's two top officers for the past six years are both no longer involved in managing it after 2003's event.

"Work hard, play hard" is the usual explanation you'll get for why DPW workers sometimes seem out of control. "That's what people want out of DPW anyway," Doyle, a four-year DPW vet from Minneapolis, an old Hard Times Bike Club associate, tells me. "If you're rude to [people at Burning Man], they love it. It's your job to be the funny asshole. You earn it by working your ass off and cleaning up after the huge party. But I think it's just the environment out there. Even the locals are fucking nuts—people shooting at each other all the time."

So DPW has fun with its rowdy image, especially during the absurdist yearly parade of its fleet of alternately ferocious and pathetically crumbling vehicles. One DPW member told me, glowing with pride, that he could tell people were *sincerely afraid* of him and his DPW buddies as they glowered and shouted at them at 2003's parade.

During that parade, D.A. jumped from one moving car to another, and when his foot hit a windshield, he cracked it. Oh well, only one thing to do: A squad of big DPW men just *swarmed* the car, bashing glass and carriage and doing a crusher's worth of damage in minutes. They cleaned up the mess promptly. That's the DPW paradigm in a nutshell—do whatever crazy thing you want, but clean up your mess.

The characteristic call of a DPW member is "Give us your beer! We built this city!" A bartender at Aaron Muszalski's Dice and Duck bars got so tired of hearing that line from DPW guys that he made a little sign that he'd wave, Warner Brothers–cartoon style, if a DPWer laid it on him at the bar:...ON ROCK 'N' ROLL. Still, Aaron recognizes that "DPW [workers] endure such fucked-up shit for [minimal] compensation that that sense of pride, that myth, becomes their pay: being able to say that."

They do work hard. During setup, DPW pounds in ten thousand T-stakes by hand, builds and installs more than two thousand signs, drags out thirty-eight miles of roads, and builds a café covering nearly a half acre. They do it all pretty damn fast and with great precision— the roads fall in perfectly calculated arcs from the central point where the Man stands. That is where the first spike is laid in the city as building begins each August. It is an impressive feat, and the esprit de corps valuing toughness and comedic aggression is probably vital to the way it works, bringing nuclear physicists side by side with squatters to make Black Rock City come and go in temperatures that can range over 50 degrees in twenty-four hours and hit as high, I am told, as 120 in the shade. (There may be some tough-guy exaggeration in this.)

Larry Harvey tells me in a post–2003 event conversation that the punk vibe that's the inheritance of Minneapolis's Hard Times Bike Club, who made up Burning Man's first real clean-up crew under Chicken John back in '97 and '98, won't necessarily be welcome at the DPW ranch any longer. It will mean a serious change to Burning Man's culture—which was so wide-open, so inviting, it had room for every type, from the hall monitor to the bad seed, and promised that getting things done was more important than how you looked or acted when you did it.

Burning Man asks a lot of its DPW, whose members are living in isolation in what, as I hope you've gathered by now, can be a very unpleasant place. They become more like true natives of Nevada's Great Basin. The West is wild; something about the weird, wide spaces drives people to all sorts of mental and experiential edges, where it seems every fight could break out in either gunplay or sloppy drunk hugging.

Living in this environment has created, as several DPW workers explain to me, a genuine culture, distinct from the ground up, the very thing Larry Harvey is always nattering on about: unique folkways and methods, games and gags, and even a set of absurdist folk songs rooted in their experience building an instant city with rough-hewn comrades in a place no human has any business being.

But after years of this, it seems as if there's too much opportunity for bad liability problems, and some of DPW's public recklessness and hostility has begun to wear on those responsible for Burning Man's public image. There are lots of fights; things get broken; it just isn't the face Burning Man is interested in projecting any longer. Their old style was summed up by Seth Malice as "a badass elitist specially trained lean mean paramilitary homeless machine" and almost "a militia—when you're done doing all this work for free, we can go out to the shooting range and blow the shit out of junk! Plus, it gives you the right to hate everyone that goes to Burning Man!"

"We are becoming more professional," notes D.A. "And I have mixed feelings about that. We're getting better at what we do. But if they were to try to hire 'professional' people, I doubt that these professionals could handle what we deal with. You have to understand what it is we are doing here. They might just look at it as building things—'I know how to build, no problem.' Me, I'm not a skilled builder. But I am desert-ready and grounded and stable and reliable, and I understand the event and the psychology of the people who go and who work it and who have decisions to make."

There are special things to keep in mind at the DPW ranch, now known as Black Rock Station: the scorpions, the plywood that might go flying through the air and at your head with an unexpected gust of wind, and the fact that someone might be testing some sort of mobile flamethrower around the next turn.

No one wants to hurt him- or herself—probably—but working for Burning Man is certainly not (yet) up to OSHA standards. Some DPW members note that it isn't uncommon to have to gently remind people, hey, should you be welding next to that tank of gasoline or smoking while pumping that gas? (Kimric Smythe remembers with a headache the year DPW took that year's supply of pyro for the Man and, for safekeeping, *welded* it inside a steel container.) I'm told that once there was a gas leak near the DPW commissary, and the warning sign consisted of a dry-erase board with the legend "Hey you—no smokee!" with a scrawled cartoon of a big mushroom cloud.

Burning Man pays DPW crew members varying per diems (though some are pure volunteers), feeds them, and sponsors a beer blowout once a week. After hours, most of them want to be left alone to play as hard as they work. One DPW man who calls himself Dr. Fuckoffsky tells me that once he's signed a paper relieving the organization of liability for his health and life, as Burning Man requires, then for fuck's sake let him have Roman candle fights with his buddies while they drive heavy equipment that they may not be fully trained to operate toward each other!

It sounds ridiculous, but Fuckoffsky has a sober point of some political and social interest: The more responsibility for people's actions you take away from them—including the very basic one of making sensible decisions about what sort of rowdy play is safe, or at least safe enough for them—the less likely they will be able to make those decisions intelligently. Fuckoffsky radically believes in radical self-reliance. And he regrets that the Burning Man he loved is, in his eyes, slowly whittling away at what is supposed to be one of its central principles with the very existence of the Black Rock Rangers.

The fact that this specialized cabal exists with a mandate to handle conflict resolution, says Fuckoffsky, reduces people's *individual* need to enforce justice and community norms and settle conflicts and help one another when they are hurt or lost. Suddenly all that is someone else's job. (The best Rangers, of course, don't want to hear your problem until you've exhausted every reasonable possibility for solving it yourself.)

It's infantilizing, he insists, and he thinks Burning Man can and should be a genuine social experiment where we all, as individuals or freely formed groups, take care of *all* of our own shit—from garbage to conflicts to our own safety. As artist Michael Christian said to me, "Part of the order in the apparent chaos of Burning Man used to be that if someone caught on fire, there would be five people around to put him out. An awareness would kick in that you had to watch out for your friends. But when you get police and fire services, you get people used to not having to watch out for themselves and are docile, and if they catch on fire, the feeling is, Where is the fire department to put me out?"

Taking care of your own shit is the heart of the DPW message and mission. Tony Perez, known as Coyote, the clean-up chief, is inspired by how much cleaning up after itself the Burning Man community does. Through years of getting the message out through Burning Man's newsletters, Web site, and the concerned voices of fellow citizens, he's convinced Burning Man has got thirty thousand mostly well-off Americans doing a more serious job of minding their own shit than any other institution around. If the citizens were perfect at it, there wouldn't need to be a clean-up crew; but if the citizens weren't damn good, the clean-up crew could not possibly get the playa clean enough in a month to satisfy the BLM inspection.

I visit Coyote during the last week of cleanup in 2003. There's around five DPW men and women out where the city used to be, wandering around and picking up whatever they find at a "hot spot"— in this case, a rave campsite. The playa is just for them again, them and the bright blue sky and curving mountains. They are listening, these tough rowdy desert rats, to Cat Stevens's *Tea for the Tillerman* on a boom box. When I note this, eyes raised, to D.A., he stares back without missing a beat and says, "OK, how much do you want?"

Coyote tells me how DPW is getting better and better at returning the playa to its natural, pristine state, and helping win some local respect at the same time. "Most of the locals are crusty sorts, ranchers who came out here to get away from all the madness, and here comes the madness right in their backyard. Most of them are pretty tolerant, but they didn't always have much respect for us. They don't understand too much about piercings and colored hair and wild art pieces. But they do understand a fence that goes up in two days and miles of desert cleaned up in a month."

I spend the afternoon working out there with Coyote and his crew. The task is indeed satisfying: You know what you have to do and you do it, and the results are instant and tangible as your water jug or drink cup fills with debris—wood chips, screws, beads, plastic googly eyes. Sometimes, Coyote tells me, the trash can tell an interesting story. He can tell where a playa bar was—a circle of pistachio shells marks each stool, and a couple of feet in front of the stools is a smashed lime, a wine cork, and some cocktail straws—the space behind the bar itself. And then a few yards away and back is some burned incense and candle wax, a champagne cork, and a condom wrapper. "Yes, we're getting the whole picture now," Coyote says.

Coyote proudly shows me one of the makeshift technologies they've developed to bust up the dunes that grow around any object after dust storms—a frame with fencing inside it, weighted down with tires, dragged behind a big truck. They try not to take any playa dirt away with the garbage, so they do a fair amount of ground breaking followed by sifting for solid objects.

But other than that, it's pretty straightforward: They have to walk over every single inch within the city's fence and pick up everything and anything they see. The BLM comes out after a month or so and selects three areas in the encampment, chosen at random by a computer, each area 1,000 feet by 150 feet. A team of BLM and Burning Man workers walks the area and picks up every single thing still there.-As long as those things, when set down, don't cover more than five square feet of area, then Burning Man has met its clean-up obligation.

After this year's event, Dave Cooper, the BLM's manager for the Black Rock Desert National Conservation Area, announced in a press release that "Black Rock City LLC has once again exceeded BLM's cleanup standards and expectations. The organization not only practices good public land use ethics, it also teaches this ethic to all participants at the event each year. This makes Burning Man the largest 'Leave No Trace' event in the world."

"Leave no trace" is of course a dream, a consummation devoutly to be wished, not a reality. As Chris Campbell says, "Our impact is eternal" would be a more apt and consciousness-raising slogan. The Burning Man trash fence is only about four feet high, and things can and will fly over it, away, and down the open playa where they are no longer Burning Man's legal concern.

And every trace taken from the playa is deposited somewhere else: landfills in Reno or elsewhere. There is no way, truly, to eliminate any trace of our civilization; there is something indulgent in Burning Man's encouraging the notion that sweeping everything away from this one playa is an ecological triumph. Humans do make a mark on the world; this is our glory. The best we can do is be as conscious and deliberate about that mark as we can—know what we are doing, and why, and mind where the traces land.

Traces of Burning Man, as per Larry Harvey's original vision, have indeed begun to spread around the country, the world. Larry and his crew and the tens of thousands who show up have mastered the art of building, occupying, and cleaning up Black Rock City. Now it's time for the next step.

Chapter Twelve

"BEYOND THE VALLEY OF THE GROOVY"

In 2003, the Washoe County Commission denied Burning Man the necessary permits to work on its property at Black Rock Station, embroiling Burning Man in Byzantine Great Basin political machinations and possible lawsuits over zoning that are unresolved as of yet, though the operation at Black Rock Station is running as usual for now. Pershing County also began making noise about demanding its own county "event permit"—which would mean yet another yearly payout. There's always some petty or serious business problem to deal with, Larry says. Running Burning Man is more than a full-time job.-But still, he and his team have mostly figured out this Burning Man–in-the-desert thing.

They even had a good chunk of money left over after 2003, Larry tells me, which is unusual. They no longer allow every member of the LLC to sign checks, so the finances aren't as chaotic as they used to be. They are even beginning to advertise for job openings, instead of simply checking to see which one of their friends currently needs work. One ex-employee referred to the Burning Man LLC as the Make-A-Wish Foundation, since any pal could get any job he wanted, whether he had any demonstrated capacity for it or not.

Burning Man is a dicey business proposition at best, merely on liability grounds—throwing a fire-arts festival in a dangerous desert with a crowd of people not operating under their best judgment might seem an insurance nightmare. What keeps insurance affordable, Larry thinks, is that "[the] community generally doesn't sue us. People go out there and sustain injuries that normally they would probably sue for. Like, 'I got drunk and got up there on the flying starfish and jumped off and broke my leg, and hey, my suffering alone is worth…' But out there, they are more likely to say, 'Well, it's Burning Man, and I'm part of the community and what would my friends say?' Our community serves us well. And anyway, if our lawyers were just to say to a jury, 'They went to Burning Man,' it would be like, 'Oh…'" A young lady did die in 2003, for the first time within the event's perimeter during its official length, after being run over by an art car. There have been a handful of deaths related to-the event over the years since Michael Furey was killed, whether on-the 447 to or from the event, or as a result of injuries sustained during the festival. (The most curious was the death of conspiracy researcher Jim Keith in 1999 after a fall off a mere three-foot-high stage at Burning Man. His knee was injured, and he died in the resulting surgery back in Reno.)

As many observers close to the organization note, Burning Man's saving grace has never been the management style or the genius of anyone on the LLC. It has come from the amazing pull that the idea and the experience of Burning Man have on people. The essence of Burning Man, that thing that makes it work, is a joint, decentralized creation of thirty thousand people, not of Larry Harvey, John Law, any single artist of gargantuan absurdities, the DPW who "built this city!" or any other singular claimant.

The experience's power summons forth a gracious outpouring of volunteer labor to help run the high-ticket-price event (a ticket price that even the volunteers themselves, in most cases, have to pay). Burning Man's volunteer database contains around two thousand names—close to 10 percent of the entire population of the city. And when you consider that anyone who builds an interesting theme camp or works on a piece of attractive art is also essentially volunteering to create the ambience that makes someone eager to buy a ticket to Burning Man, a remarkable percentage of people at Burning Man are contributing directly to the success of its business model, even beyond being paying customers. So many people are working for the business without pay that failure, not success, would be the true miracle.

The business model, such as it is, is "sustained on enthusiasm and forgiveness," Jim Mason says. "And lots of drugs and sex, too. You can't discount that. It's a frontier situation—you get into the middle of a desert, and you start to believe bullshit that you shouldn't believe. It's very important that the event is held out in Black Rock. The isolation is important. So people go out there and lose track, both willfully and unconsciously, of other responsibilities, and they are willing to have a great time of excessive play and excessive work."

So, what do you do after your decision to build a little scrap-skeleton and burn it on the beach transmogrifies over the course of less than two decades into a nearly $6 million culture business, selling that most ephemeral of commodities, community, and gathering tens of thousands of people at hundreds of dollars a head to perhaps the most unpleasant, punishing environment imaginable?

Larry Harvey is serious about changing the world with this and has been from the beginning, when even uttering that thought seemed absurd. With the current number of devotees, and their enthusiasm, their energy, and their dedication to the idea of Burning Man, it sounds less ridiculous.

Now it's time to franchise.

Larry rejects that language, of course; to him, the new plan they are embarking on is more along Freemasonic lines (an interconnected system of lodges of fellow world-changing conspirators) than the McDonald's model (a worldwide squad of cookie-cutter duplicates).

For several years now, Burning Man enthusiasts have been throwing smaller Burning Man–style events in their own towns, from Texas to Maryland to Hawaii to Arizona. They find some out-of-the-way land, usually private; gather, celebrate, make things (usually not on as grand a scale as at Burning Man), usually burn something as a central ritual. To the people organizing such events, known as "regional burns," these attempts to reproduce aspects of the experience that so energized them, to pass that gift on to others who, for whatever reason, might never make it to the Black Rock Desert, are extremely valuable. (That desert itself is home throughout the summer to smaller gatherings of Burners, some consciously trying to re-create the more intimate and unregulated aura of the early days of Burning Man.)

I've been to the biggest of these regional burns, Austin Flipside, for three years straight, and while it's a blast and I have a great time, I've found it lacking in awe and transformation—mostly because of the pleasant, comforting environment. It happens in a grassy meadow, with a swimable stream running through and an outdoor swimming pool, and a handful of actual toilets in addition to Porta-Johns. I think Larry underestimates the importance of the setting when considering why the Burning Man experience grips people so. It adds a sense of adventure, the sense of crisis that Larry has elsewhere recognized as key to community. It doesn't come from kumbaya, he has said; it comes from a unified, joint struggle to survive.

The world of Burning Man has over the years been riven by conflicts and bitterness, and most of them come down not to disagreements over facts but to assumptions about motives. One could spin Burning Man's desire to seed lots of similar events—events with which it will have some sort of partner relationship, with advice and counsel and assistance going out and money, it is hoped, coming back in—as Larry does, as an example of the restless, adventurous spirit of the Burning Man LLC. This experience is so valuable and potentially life-changing it would be niggardly to restrict it to those few foolhardy enough to venture to the grim wastelands of Nevada.

You could also, less charitably, interpret it as basic corporate empire building, that weird desire to never settle back and just do what you do well but to always expand, the impulse that creates new diet caffeine-free vanilla Coke or Disney's California Adventure. Or you could construe it as a desire to run to the head of the crowd and take control of a movement that will go on with or without the further actions of the people currently putting on the show.

It's always a pleasure to bitch about other people's motives, but charity and reason compel us to remember that when it comes to the secret engines driving another's soul, we are only interpreting the pings and rumbles—we can't really get under the hood and take a look-see.

Larry is particularly proud of one unusual aspect of the LLC's corporate structure: "I got the group without any demur to sign an agreement that annihilated equity. We are more a *not*profit than a non-profit." If anyone leaves the LLC, the payoff—the full value of his or her "ownership" of Burning Man—is $20,000. "I originally proposed five thousand, but our attorney said, 'Larry, be real, that's ridiculous. The extra fifteen thousand would be enough to live for half a year.'" It is a sacrifice—the board members are not that young, and they have deliberately not made any preparations for retirement. But this lack of equity is a public sign that they do not intend to take this product of the larger community and profit from it. The only way they can get anything substantial from their "ownership" of Burning Man is to continue working for their salary.

Larry suggests to the regionals: "Be like us. Form an LLC. Annihilate equity. Work by consensus. Then be part of a network with us and you can get help. But not necessarily some of the help you want. I've been listening to them. They say things like, 'Couldn't the big Org get us insurance?' No. For two reasons. First, this big Org isn't going to take responsibility for events that we don't organize. That's insane. Second, we don't want needy children expecting someone else to do everything. It's not hard to get insurance. All you have to do is be really conscientious. And I want you to be really conscientious. We don't want you to be like children expecting someone else to be responsible. If you are like that, then you aren't like us. Those challenges turned us into what we are."

As to the precise mechanisms by which this Burning Man vibe, spirit, movement, call it what you will, define it as you are able, will grow and conquer, Larry understands it's too soon to know and in wisdom impossible to predict. "It's like Black Rock City itself: you create just enough of a framework to let things happen. When you cross that line [into overplanning], you destroy the thing you are trying to create. Culture itself is a spontaneously occurring phenomenon that will happen like any growing thing in certain contexts."

On the matter of precisely what he is trying to achieve—exactly how and into what Burning Man can change the world—Larry can be maddeningly elusive. It's not because he has a hidden agenda that he's too cagey to lay out for the world's judgment just yet, until his power base is secured. (At least I don't *think* that's it.) I suspect it's more innocent and human than that. It's because he himself doesn't know yet. What is the nub of the thing, the secret heart of the Man? We all, all of us who have been through it, can agree that the experience has the power, the tendency, the promise to energize and excite and change and improve people like no other mechanism we've come across. It sparks the passion that leads some to work for the LLC, some to build the biggest thing they can imagine, me to write a book about the event and what happens there.

But no one can agree on what the real secret of the technology is. The people who actually work for the company seem perfectly happy to not have any idea what it is, even as they launch plans to spread it somehow, anyhow.

When I ask exactly how Larry intends to sell this more grandiose vision of the Burning Man Project—beyond just the event in the Black Rock Desert—his answers are exploratory, uncertain. "Well, we have to go beyond the valley of the groovy," he begins. To convince people of the vital cultural importance of supporting the larger Burning Man Project, "we have to begin with the perception that social capital is being spent. We are in crisis; the communal basis for culture has been eroded terribly. That's why there is so little good art. We are all so drastically isolated in our consuming worlds, the basis for civic life and identity is being destroyed. You can see by any measure. Walk outside and look at what's on the street. It's a political crisis—a spiritual crisis if you want to look at it. And the Third World is emulating us. We can decide where history goes. We can have an effect on-a prodigious scale. We can be a movement for the twenty-first century."

He pauses here, which he doesn't do that often. (I've been in three-hour-plus conversations with Larry in which I asked around three questions.) Remember the Doubting Larry on Haight Street in the autumn of love? He's still here.

"I know every raver you ever met said they were going to change the world. The hippies said they were going to change the world. But we're a little different. One novelty I will claim is that we are the first bohemian-based countercultural movement that ever came along that

transcended the limits of a 'scene.' We went civic. We went aboveground. We engaged the world on a scale that not even the Paris Com-
mune did. If we do it right, we can contribute…" What? He never
finishes that last sentence.

I offer up to Larry the notion that it is interesting that he's planning
a social revolutionary movement that is not about fighting authority but is dedicated to working with it. It's not about fighting the
power in bloody hand-to-hand combat but merely about offering up
experiments and possibilities for new ways to live. A very Popperian
revolution, just plugging ahead and generating conjectures and refu-
tations galore. Can we create a temporary anarchist community in
which everyone uses motor vehicles to their heart's content? That,
Larry thinks, has been refuted by experience. Every other change in
the constitution of Black Rock City, every new wave of rules that
pisses off the anarchists, has similarly been a reaction, in Larry's mind,
to circumstances. He insists they don't come at things from an ideological direction, that all their ideas arise from their direct experience
building the desert civilization.

One night, very, very late, in his kitchen, Larry began to muse,
shapelessly, with no specifics, that there must be—mustn't there?—
some political applications, political implications, of this little experiment of his.

I can only chuckle nervously. "I hope not, Larry."

Any political value I saw in Burning Man always had to do with
its avoidance of politics as I see it—the game of some people telling
other people what to do. Burning Man to me was about liberty and
ordered anarchy, the inherent strength and possible joys of a civilization in which all the "government" you need can be purchased in
a freely chosen market. The amenities of civilization—road grading
and signage, plumbing of a sort, electricity for those lucky enough to
be within extension-cord distance of Burning Man's official generator-
powered grid, dispute enforcement (without violence)—were supplied for the price of a ticket by a municipal body that we all joyfully
and consciously chose to pledge fealty to. It was—and in many ways
still is—an anarchocapitalist vision to make Murray Rothbard, author

of the modern anarchist classic *For a New Liberty,* proud. People gathered together and made a world that they loved, and the forces of actual government—the men with guns—were nothing but unwanted intruders who forced their way, as is their wont, into our party.

Larry doesn't see what Burning Man is about in such an individualist framework. He tells me about Neolithic times, when, he says, the entire culture seemed united by one central idea. You can tell by their architecture, he insists. He wants to bring back that original vision of human history, to re-create that sense of total community he sees in ancient man. This is radical, in its core meaning of returning to the root. But he wants to combine this ancient vision of community with the individualist glories of the modern West. He *sees* something that I don't quite see, yet. No one does, and that is to his advantage. (I don't think he sees it altogether clearly, but it's a huge, if dim, shape filling his vision as he gazes toward the future.)

As Larry once told me, "I think there are political and economic interests that, if they understood where Burning Man really could go,-would fight us. But I don't think it will dawn on them until it's too-late. We are very studiously nonpolitical. I think the age of ideology is-over. How do you get ideological solidarity if you don't have communal or cultural solidarity? All you end up with is another niche market.

"But now the idea is that we want people inspired by what happens at Burning Man to go home, not to create a refuge from the world...see, we make a model of the world, a model of civilization, temporary but striking. We want them to go home and reform their towns and cities and apply any lessons they learned to where they really live instead of seeing it as a chance to escape that world."

But what are those lessons? Live on an alkali salt flat with no electricity and no plumbing? Larry gave some hints as to what he thinks the message might be with something he did in 2003. For the first time in Burning Man's modern history, he specifically invited an existing performance group to come and do its regular show. Burning Man partially funded the trip and built a special stage at the foot of the Man itself to accommodate them.

Most interestingly and most unusually, the performance was essentially political agitprop. A lot of lines were crossed with this move, lines that had been of some importance to Burning Man's identity. It used to deliberately mean nothing, stand for nothing, except the widest abstract concepts directly related to being an arts festival in the desert: self-reliance, creativity, immediate experience.

Now, it seemed, Burning Man meant being against chain stores.

The Reverend Billy Talen and his Church of Stop Shopping made their Burning Man debut on Wednesday of the 2003 festival. Billy Talen was a former theatrical director from San Francisco specializing in monologues when a mentor, Sidney Lanier (cousin to Tennessee Williams), convinced him he would do well to hijack the power of the image of the evangelical preacher toward the service of questioning some aspects of big modern consumerism—pointing out that Starbucks' and Wal-Mart's success means death to many smaller businesses and that Mickey Mouse is the Antichrist (for reasons that, even after the show, are still not entirely clear).

The message of the show is confused. Its name clearly overreaches even its own intent. To actually "stop shopping"—to remove yourself entirely from the division of labor—is such a radical move for this culture (and, frankly, a stupid one—you've never known from nasty, brutish, and short until you leave every human to atomistically meet all his needs himself without trading with other humans, which is all shopping is), one the reverend and his own crew clearly don't live up to, that using the name and not meaning it seems a bit of a deliberate outrage.

At his most radical, his actual message seems to be, *Think hard before consuming*—and in your consuming, try hard to support the unique, the local, as opposed to huge monoculture chains. This is fine, though not the type of art Burning Man has typically funded. At the end of his presentation on the soul-freshening powers of not shopping at big chains, the show featured a peroration about the bravery of Rachel Corrie, a Burner who was run over by a bulldozer driven by an Israeli soldier. Now, mourning Rachel Corrie does not *necessarily* mean you are taking sides in the incredibly messy Israeli-Palestinian conflict, but it almost inevitably sounds like you are unless you are very careful, which the Church of Stop Shopping wasn't.

It was all very curious and forced, and at the foot of the glowing Man, it seemed, and I hate to say this, like a sacrilege of sorts. It felt to me as strange as seeing an ad or hearing a commercial pitch at the foot of the Man would have. It took me years to realize it—I was not initially open to this idea—but Larry is right, it does clear your head to live for a week or so in a community not bombarded by commercial messages. But I ended up finding this advertisement for a political view just as jarring. Ah well, it's not *my* Man, and Larry was more than pleased about Billy's presence.

It was Billy's first time at Burning Man, and he instantly, and cornily, adapted—changing his standard evangelical "Hallelujah!" to-"Burnelujah!" and "Praise be!" to "Praise BE-yond!" (the year's art-theme being "Beyond Belief"). One doubtlessly addled young Burner apparently had trouble getting the irony in Billy's presentation and physically attacked him within the first minute of his first performance. Billy figures the attacker mistook him for an actual Jimmy Swaggart–type. Despite that inauspicious beginning, Billy thought everything went well and loved getting to do his show at Burning Man.

Billy's wife and stage manager, Savitri Durkee, was less impressed than Billy had been. "I was against coming to begin with," she told me one typically bright, dry, hot afternoon toward the end of 2003, sitting underneath Billy and his crew's very sturdily constructed shade canopy. "I had a feeling it wasn't the most important demographic for us to talk to, that these were people who probably feel that they are liberals, right? I mean that pejoratively. They are pretty sure they are living the right lives and are really the hardest group to change. They think that they are radical if they recycle and vote for the liberal candidate. So it's a gift economy? People spend a thousand bucks the day before they get here so we get to have the sentimental value of not using money, but people are spending more money, consuming more, than they normally would to come here. It's just humans once again coming to an environment where there is no place for humans and subverting it into a human place. I resent that as an environmentalist. It's another kind of colonialism."

While she admits to some random delight at the creativity and good feelings on display, her enjoyment was tempered by "the large political emergency we have. I don't have much time to feel good about humanity right now. We have a lot of work we have to do. We all need to be political right now."

Larry seems to agree, and that could mean a huge change for Burning Man, or at least for the way he positions it. (As he realizes, the meaning of Burning Man is largely created by what people bring from themselves to the experience, not by anything he's ever done—whether it be burning a Man in the first place or buying plane tickets for Rev. Billy.) In one of our last conversations for this book, he confessed that he was finally ready—as Larry Harvey, though, not as the director of the Burning Man Project—to send out an e-mail advising San Francisco Burners who he thought should be mayor of San Francisco, and to insist that all his colleagues had to vote.

What I'm picking up from Larry's new dispensation struck me as antithetical to what I originally found interesting about Burning Man—that it offered a seeking and celebration of creative expression and liberated experience as a key to brain change and a means to search for what one might call the sacred. There are times, though, when Larry and I are feeling the same things. "We are beings, created things," Larry tells me. "We're the products of genetic mutation, and we're infinitely variable. The world presents itself to us as an artifact with slots to fill. But everyone's gifts are unique and not necessarily apparent to the [people themselves] unless some circumstance calls them forth. The whole story of my progress," he surmises, "might seem blind and hapless. But there was from the beginning a sense of something real in me and the idea that it had to have a home out there somewhere. Intuitively, blindly, as chance allowed, I moved in that direction even if it didn't make any sense by the world's standards. The human world is like a flowery meadow, and the individual is like a weed—each one different. A weed is simply an unwanted plant. It's a human category. There's no such plant as a weed. But the human world is more and more a monoculture. Farmer Jones wants corn and everything else is a weed, and if you can't get with the corn program, Buster, then get your thistle ass out of here! That's the problem everyone faces."

As he looks around at Burning Man, Larry sees lots of weeds essaying things with no apparent practical purpose. "It's weeds, but it's *their* weeds. Who knows what that leads to? Maybe nothing. But unless people are given that opportunity they will never find out. If their judgments are always governed by the world's standards, they might never find that one thing they are brilliant at, that they were born to-do, and that's the greatest tragedy of all—the quiet desperation Thoreau wrote of. That just means that they never discovered what they were meant to do with the transcendent faith that they were meant to do that something. And that's been the moral of my life."

There's a lot I could argue with Larry about, but not that. He sees the world a lot more darkly than I do. And the strange thing is, Burning Man is a big part of the reason I don't see the world as darkly as he does. Larry seems obsessed with the notion that there is something inherently rotten about vaguely capitalist modernity, seeing (as so many people have managed to see all through human history) his own time as uniquely decadent and doomed.

Despite Larry's grim attitude about the world, the modern West by any metric has spread unprecedented wealth and opportunity to almost staggering numbers of people, and in fact, trends on many important measures of well-being—health, wealth, longevity, even the environment—are on the upswing. The particular turn this modern wealth has taken—the commodification represented by the likes of Wal-Mart that so aggravates Larry and Billy—might not be to his taste, but rather than being diametrically opposed to each other, as he thinks, both Burning Man and Wal-Mart come from the same roots. They are both fruits of the same system of market freedom (a system Larry is too wise to openly reject, but regularly insults) that creates the wealth that allows for Wal-Marts to flourish but also allows thirty thousand people to have the resources and time to go to a harsh nothing and build a glorious monument to human will (often using resources purchased at a Wal-Mart): a city, come and gone, dedicated to pure play and pure creativity and human beings doing what they wish, joyfully.

What I want to tell Larry, when he riffs on the horrors of modernity, is that the very existence of Burning Man is a glowing, exploding neon sign pointing to the reality that the contemporary crisis is not as serious and inescapable as Larry Harvey tries to make it, as Savitri Durkee sees it. We have options—never before in the history of the human race have there been as many options and as many means of enjoying them as we in the heavily commercialized, commodified West know. One of those options is to create an intentional community like Burning Man to avoid the aspects of this world we might not like or, at least, would enjoy a vacation from. It's a magnificent experiment, and those who carp that it's all a big lie because they sell tickets are really missing the point.

But Larry talks his communitarian, fashionably doom-mongering talk, a talk that—he doesn't seem to realize—is insulting to almost everyone in the culture. "People don't know the difference between the marketplace and democracy because they've been debauched by fifty years of advertising. I very much think that Black Rock City has political relevance. If it doesn't, gosh, what is it?"

This book, I hope, provides some answers to that question. It's a place for human beings to live vividly free lives and have—as Larry used to recognize—*experiences* that are fundamental, unconditional, marvelous, and worth a thousand lectures on why one ought not to shop at Wal-Mart.

Larry likes to link Burning Man to the sacred, though he can't be any more specific about what that means to him than *being*. But he's glad he's created a forum, finally, where he can publicly play with the idea of the sacred and invite thirty thousand other people to play along. Even in 1990, when Burning Man first moved to the desert, this was his preoccupation, but "there wasn't one person in the world prepared to walk down this path with me. Nobody. Not my partners. When I gave a lecture about the meaning of Burning Man at the College of Arts and Crafts in town, I talked about the sacred, and John [Law] got disgusted and walked out because he's allergic to talking about sacred things."

Larry likes to complain about what he saw as John Law's romantic bad-boyism and underground fetishism, which to Larry's mind would lock out too many people from the Burning Man experience. I can't help feeling that attaching a political message that's explicitly anti-consumerism to Burning Man has the same risks. If you want a world without Wal-Mart, and the people keep insisting on shopping at Wal-Mart...every Utopian vision depends on exclusion, the exclusion of the type of person who wants the kind of world that you don't. Larry has been admirably true to the doctrine of nonexclusion throughout Burning Man's history, insisting it was about nothing more than coming together to create and share an experience. As a nine-year Burner, I would be remiss in my dedication to the city I love to not announce that taking the gift of Black Rock City and making it into yet another vehicle to tell people where they ought to shop seems like a wrong turn to me. After all, isn't that what advertising itself is all about?

Where Burning Man goes from here is anyone's guess—though I am confident it will have more to do with the spontaneous decisions of the tens of thousands who attend than it will with Larry's particular beliefs. As long as the Man goes back to the desert and becomes an excuse for the community to gather and for the people to do what they most wish to do, the Man's death—his eternally recurring death—will not have been in vain.

However political or nonpolitical Burning Man remains, art is still being put forward as Burning Man's best ambassador to the world. The new regionals network is only one arm of Burning Man's world-conquest plans. The other is the Black Rock Arts Foundation (BRAF), founded in 2001. BRAF is a nonprofit art foundation whose mission is to fund Burning Man–style art not at the event itself—that funding still comes out of the for-profit LLC's budget—but in communities around the world.

Interactive is the buzzword for Burning Man–style art, defined by BRAF's Jessica Bobier as "art that blurs the line between artists and audience, with collaboration in the creation or the experience of the piece. Art that requires the action of a participant to complete the piece. It represents an opportunity for people to come together and incites them to interact with one another, whether directly because they are needed to make something happen or just something so exciting it makes people gather, brings them together." It fits in smoothly with the old Burning Man dispensation: art that creates community, art that gives you an opportunity to have an experience other than spectating.

BRAF is starting slowly—it has only distributed around thirty-five thousand dollars in its first three years of existence. But its ideas are already accomplishing more than its money. Charlie Smith is going to do what BRAF has in mind, whether BRAF pays for it or not. Now that the fire is lit, now that the idea is in his heart, it doesn't matter much whether Burning Man helps, hinders, or just gets out of the way. After building Hearth with Syd, Charlie kept making more, smaller hollow metal sculptures that could be filled with wood and burned, sculptures of many different shapes, on wheels so they could be rolled, some that rocked back and forth, many with lovely filigreed shapes cut thinly in their sides so the orange-red light shone through the glow of the hot metal. Charlie now plans to spend most of every year taking his metal fire cauldrons out to the world, to the people who have to fill them with wood to make them burn and breathe and live, because he thinks it's the right thing to do. For him, after Burning Man, it's the *only* thing to do.

I've seen Charlie's mobile fire cauldrons doing their work in environments outside the playa—on a hill in Atlanta overlooking its densely lit downtown, in a sweet meadow outside Austin, Texas—and they *work:* direct experience, everyone's hands on the splintering wood, with the sound of the wood's impact against the metal hitting the chest, the heat washing over the face, a cleansing burn. The people are making the fire. They are making it grow.

It's a mystery to me—I really cannot tell you why this happens, even define what it is—but I've seen it. The act of getting together around a piece of human art, and working together to make it do something new, is an experience that many have never had before. It bathes a person—it has bathed me, I've seen it bathe others—with something, a radiation beyond heat and light. Admiring other people's work, becoming part of it, is to see what a human being can do, and to see him doing it with an intensity and certainty that is as unconditional, as Larry might say, as anything in the physical world— that is to see how life can be and should be.

Chris Radcliffe had a rough year at Burning Man in 2003, returning for the first time since 2000. He managed the rare feat of haranguing Burning Man into giving him a refund check, claiming that Larry had promised him a free pass at the gate that wasn't there. The decision was apparently between giving him his money back and tossing him out, as a result of his verbally assaulting one of their funded artists and holding a generator hostage over a money dispute. "I'm still a prince of that city," says Radcliffe. "They give me everything I want and never fuck with me no matter what outrage I pull. I always seem to get a free pass. You can't hate people who give you that kind of freedom. But it's hard for me to love them sometimes." Radcliffe, like many old-timers (and some merely attracted to the dream of the older, freer Burning Man), thinks something essential in the experience has been killed by the way it is now regulated.

"Now that we've locked it down so much, my big question is: Why not just do it in the parking lot of Eastmont Mall in Oakland? I'm sure we could get the area fire department to let us burn our effigy, and it would be a hell of a lot easier to get to."

As many complaints as he has, if you get Radcliffe talking about Burning Man long enough, he will remember that he loved it once. "I think we were the twentieth-century version of the French belle epoque, that era that launched what we think of as modern art. I live in fear and loathing that I'm not gonna get my hands on the wheel again. That I might have already experienced the peak of my life. I walk around trying to change people's lives, trying to give them the power of taking their living into their own hands. It's not enough to observe. You have to know that when you need to, you can take control. Sure enough, the day is coming when you have to make a choice, and you'll need some experience and confidence that you can-live through it or you'll never have the balls. I'm not going to run into another Burning Man in my life. I don't think any of us ever will. But I hope I can carry what I learned out of it and inculcate into other people's brains that you can do whatever you want and survive-it. That you are more than just you. That's the best thing they gave me."

WE ALL DID THE RIGHT THING

Chicken John has a lot of stories. He's a Burning Man prodigal. He's one of many who were attracted to this party for its absurd freedom. He ran transportation and cleanup for Burning Man in 1998, and then it rained and the cleanup didn't work out on schedule, and then he wasn't working for Burning Man anymore. He would still go, though, most years, even if he'd said he probably wouldn't.

Chicken talks in long bursts that aren't so much a conversation, or even a speech, as a *routine*. During a five-hour drive up the I-5 from Los Angeles to San Francisco in his junkyard-rescued '75 GMC crew cab pickup—which makes noises so constant and disturbing that it-reduces his constant companion, Dammit the Wonder Dog, to a quivering shell-shocked vet—he talks continuously the whole way about the mysteries of Burning Man.

"If you have only three seconds to explain it, the most you can say is, it is literally *saving people's lives.*

"If you have a few minutes, you can go into *how* it's saving people's lives and how it's the most fun thing on the planet you could ever do with your time.

"If you have twenty minutes, you could add how it's single-handedly responsible for changing the face of the earth and history as we know-it.

"But if you have thirty-five minutes, it becomes like the most disgusting, awful fuck-in-the-ass without a reach-around bastardization and the exclamation point at the end of the word *sellout* and a disgusting experiment in how far people will go to debase and disgrace themselves in pathetic social climbing.

"And if you have two hours, well, then—it must be stopped! The impact on the environment and on this small town and these people following it with this blind faith, a cult, disgusting, sucking money out of a healthy art scene and leaving it awful, and spreading disease and danger, and it's a miracle hundreds aren't burned to death…"But when you can explain it for two or three days, write an entire book about it, you can show the negative in comedic context while still postulating the positive. But please remember: The Burning Man arts festival is like taking a VW bug with ten thousand miles on it from 1956 that's been abandoned in a garage with no humidity, in perfect condition, and getting it tuned up and then building a catapult out of thousands of pieces of wood formed from felling old-growth trees by hand with an ax, whittling the pins and releases, and taking two years and three million dollars to take that catapult and send this perfect VW bug into orbit just so this guy with money can stand and listen to this perfectly tuned VW bug fly through the air and smash against the fucking ground just because he can."

The funny thing is, while you might think Burning Man is saving your life, from an "objective outside perspective" (say, your mom), it might appear as if it's ruining it. I heard a tale of a trio of women who were out there together, and each decided to leave her husband. People go to a campout in the desert and are compelled to quit their office jobs. It happens. It happens a lot. Regardless of whether an outsider—even one as well-meaning as old mom—thinks it was the right thing to do, this much is true: You saw a possibility for yourself, a choice that you might not have seen before. And you took it. The world is wider.

I'm talking with Kal Spelletich about the pretension in the Burning Man community that it is providing a fresh, unprecedented way for people to live. He isn't so sure. "How can human interaction be new? It's as old as rocks. What's new about it, maybe, is that they put you in-this extreme, horrific environment where you can't even think straight. And you are trying to collaborate on a big art piece, maybe that's new, or the fact that everyone is irrational and wasted and doped up, great, now let's try and work together! So maybe that is a new twist on an old theme."

A minute or so later, as we continue our talk on the back porch of a crowded Potrero Hill café, even Kal, hardened and cynical-cool, relents. He admits that he does find himself helping strangers at Burning Man, more than he would have expected to. "Why do you start doing that out there?" he asks me, and himself. "Something happens. You're out of the city; you're in this imitation fantasy city. A lot of the other rules and regulations fall away, and suddenly you're more helpful. It's true. I've seen it happen to me. People will come up to me the next year and say, 'Hey, man, you helped me weld my bike last year, and I've been looking for you and here's a twelve-pack—I was hoping you'd be here.' That's cool. That's what I miss about not being there, the big hugs and 'how's it going, man, good to see ya.' And the unique art. Yes, I miss that. I miss that."

Larry Harvey: "Burning Man is an alternative to so many things in the world that I hate, so let's change it—why not? Let's create something. I believe it can be done. I mean, it's a great city, Black Rock City, but if you hang around the city and never leave it, you'll get bored. It's the same old city. I want it to mean more, to be a type of a greater thing, greater and more meaningful because in that greater form it's affecting the lives of millions. There are things out there that need to be changed. I want to create that real change, not just have Burning Man be a celebratory event. I don't want to go down in countercultural history. I could give a damn about countercultural history, and I certainly don't want to be 'Americana'!"

Rev. Al Ridenour: "I always assumed it would end in a few years, either in some glorious spectacular disaster such that from mere association we'd all become famous, or from some pathetic squelching of the event from the powers that be. I'm quite surprised it grew like it did. I can imagine in the near future people will start to assume

Black Rock City is always out there, with the Man burning just being this old municipal ritual that the town fathers have done since time immemorial, and then it's time for the potato sack races! Seeing the Man will be like seeing a Christmas tree, a yearly thing, like, oh, that end-of-summer smell is in the air, let's go to a rave at Black Rock City."

Marian Goodell: "I realized people with nice apartments and great track jobs were leaving them [after going to Burning Man]. I went through a mini–nervous breakdown in, I think, spring 2001. Larry and I went away for Christmas, and my brain hit overload. I ended up with severe headaches and had trouble functioning. I couldn't process information. It was surreal. I felt like I was on an acid trip for six weeks, and I'd never taken acid. One of the things going through my head [laughs]…was that I was overstimulating people, giving them too many choices, and I was actually ruining people's lives by open-ing-their minds up to this colorful existence. The only solution, the only way to heal myself, was to go work for the Visa corporation in a cubicle. It was fucking twisted.

"I told Michael about it at one point. He kinda scared me. He said, 'We're all going crazy.' That really fucked me up for a while. I had to tell myself some of us are going crazy faster than others. I remember him rubbing my back; I was crying as I walked out of a meeting, tears rolling down my face quietly. I said, 'Michael, I've done something wrong. I'm ruining people's lives. This is just wrong. I need to work someplace with white walls where things are really plain.'"

Chris Radcliffe: "You don't need to go to Puerto Vallarta and lay on the beach and eat fish on a stick and drink frozen daiquiris and read Jacqueline Susann novels. You can have a primary experience of exis-tence instead of something processed and fed back to you. Someone once said to me, if you're being entertained, you're not having any fun. And that's perfectly right. What we were doing was a very primary thing. We went out there with no expectation of success in anything, and every time the winds howled through and tore our shit apart we'd pick it up and do it again. It's not like, the movie's over, time to go home. It was a constant process. To be involved in that is to *live your life.* It wasn't so much important, the thing that we were doing—it was important that we were *doing something.*"

Most critics of Burning Man don't take it on its own terms. They merely complain about such things as the ticket cost and the fact that there are cops and that the whole place is full of fucking poseurs whose pleasures and expressions are stupid and lame and why don't they realize it and go back to their fucking desk jobs? Withering contempt always wins any argument, of course. You want to assert something is valuable? Fuck no, it's not! Naked computer programmers on a bike are worthless! OK.

It can get dark and unsettling, sitting in Larry Harvey's dank kitchen blinking long hard blinks against the haze of endless cigarettes. "Burning Man might prevent what all of us imagine will happen in that alternate future involving lakes of blood," says Larry. "Terrible things. The center won't hold; things will come apart. Mass society doesn't work after a certain point. Marx may have been wrong, but he was onto something. [In the end] it has to be about something more than individual liberty. It has to be about a radical unification, something much greater that holds us together. You can have both! They don't interfere with each other. All I'm trying to do [with that year's art theme, "Beyond Belief"] is imbue people with the idea, and they can articulate it and absorb it in their own way, that this is a spiritual thing, that the ritual act has a deeper meaning that transcends their conscious selves."

But he is quick to follow that with a mention of one of the bits of Burma Shave–style signage that traditionally marks the passage from the Burning Man gate into the city proper: "Burning Man is a self-service cult. Wash your own brain."

He is sure in his atheist soul of one thing: Spirituality doesn't have to have anything to do with a deity. "A huge gaseous vertebrate—it's all vanity and anthropocentric wish fulfillment. It's childish. You don't need any of that baggage. You simply need to experience and to share that with others and be carried away in the same sense we were carried away on the beach in 1986. And if people are compelled by it, they will begin to talk to one another about experiences that they'd normally blush to confess to."

There are no clear pecuniary or obviously self-serving motives to why people destroy themselves to the extent they do to make Burning Man happen, or to pull off outrageous stunts there. We are, at long last, human, *homo faber, homo ludens,* creators of meaning, and when our secret hearts pursue longings farther than our minds and words can reach, we will improvise provisionary meanings that satisfy us as long as we can feel, somewhere, somehow, that we are on the right track.

It didn't start as an art festival. It didn't really start as anything but an act and an excuse to gather. "What is art, you know?" muses Michael Michael on the meaning of this train he's riding. "Why art at Burning Man? What is this art thing? There's something much larger here. Art is a vehicle, a symptom of something bigger occurring. It's spreading-beyond the desert, beyond the playa. It's a way of being, of thinking, to change a person: That's the real story, the real thing that's happening."

The change—that knowledge within that you no longer have to be and think and act as you have previously been and thought and acted if you don't wish to—is a mystery, and Burning Man has no monopoly on the technology of generating it. It can come in an instant like a thief in the night, like Christ, or after years of difficult discipline, like those spent with a yogi master, but what's important is that it can happen and that the technologies of change exist and Burning Man is very, very good at reminding people of that.

Erik Davis: "I don't know if it can be a political movement. It is better seen as a cultural movement. It's a bunch of individuals starting to act in a way people in retrospect may see as in concert. The effect of Burning Man is to bring thirty thousand creative individuals in close contact and send them back into the world subtly deformed or transformed. Should we even be asking more of Burning Man than that? There is a sense that the political situation is dire, and people want a ready-made solution and I'm not sure it's Burning Man's job to be that. I'm a little conflicted myself. I don't want it to just be a psychedelic Mardi Gras. But I don't want it to be the next Scientology."

Flash: "You can read all sorts of heavy things into it, but it was nothing heavy at all. Let's go out to the desert and fuck up—propane stuff blowing up, everyone had guns, skeet golf, all the fun stuff. No doubt about it, girls love fire and nudity."

Once, Tyler Hanson was driving into Burning Man and saw a guy, a normal-looking guy in normal clothes, struggling mightily with an air pump, trying to inflate a mattress. He could see the guy wasn't used to doing such things and was having a very hard time.

Tyler thought about how he had spent all summer preparing to build and execute a huge art project and had just driven across the country with piles of metal that had to be put together, and he decided that he must suppress the initial little sneer he felt coming on when comparing the significance of his own contribution to that of this guy who *couldn't even blow up an air mattress* and realized that this person's struggle with the air mattress was as significant as all the work he did and saw that beyond his ego, what really is the difference between him, a guy who worked his ass off on huge public art, and someone who just showed up with a backpack?

"In the fullness, you need all of them together. Maybe that loser who showed up with nothing and ate borrowed noodles had the time of his life, and you can never take anything away from that person." At the end of this story he is ecstatic, seeing the vision of this imperfect perfect society in which everyone has his place and everyone has an equal chance of achieving grace and glory. The Way! The Burning Man Way!

Larry Harvey: "Religion as an organizer of the masses should frighten us."

It's Burning Man '98, the dawning of the first official day of the event. Philip Bonham and I have walked the streets of the city all night, until everyone else dropped away; we had talked through everything we had in our hearts, and then we were silent and he kept crouching in his flowing red kimono, trying to light his rolled cigarette in an increasingly strong but unthreatening breeze. We both stopped and noticed—a good forty-five minutes before we would normally have noticed—that the darkness on the eastern horizon was beginning to seep into a lighter blue with extraordinary subtlety. And then all of Black Rock City began tintinnabulating, the winds stirring unseen chimes all around us and it was all really too much.

We have heard the chimes at dawn, my brother.

Even Chicken John—the most hardnosed punk rocker imaginable, a man who is capable of hours-long rants on the awful disgusting worthlessness of Burning Man, a man who fondly remembers his dead boss GG Allin (the original shock-punk who assaulted and threw shit at his audiences and sang songs like "Bite It You Scum," "You Hate Me–&

I Hate You," and "Eat My Shit")—even Chicken John has a Burning Man Experience.

It was 1996, his second year working for the event, under the tutelage of John Law. It was a loosely structured working situation— "We were all equals under John Law, and no one is John Law's equal." He was on his way bringing needed supplies to the early crew members who were mapping and building the city out in the middle of the Black Rock Playa.

"The truck had broken down. I was stuck in Truckee Meadows. It didn't get fixed until the morning, and I got there as soon as I could, but I was really late. It took me more than three days from leaving San Francisco, and I hadn't showered or changed my clothes and the truck rattled and bounced so much it fucked up my kidneys and I had urinated in my pants. The sun was already low in the sky over the mountains, one of those usual magical Black Rock sunsets. I'm tired as a dog and frantic and filthy and beaten and feeling awful that I had let everyone down because I was so late, [certain] that they'd be really pissed off at me. I mean, *the truck broke down,* but maybe they wouldn't believe me. 'Oh, Chicken, you're such a con man.' They might just think I'm lying and I'm lazy. And I knew they needed the lumber and supplies I was carrying to build the city, and now it was already almost dark and I was lost and couldn't find the encampment fifteen miles out in the middle of nothing.

"I didn't know where they were, so I just went driving off into the open playa, which is the stupidest thing I could possibly have done. But miraculously, I finally found it. And as I pulled up, everyone from the camp ran up to the truck. Everyone was dropping their hammers and running to where I was, and I saw the faces of these people like…and I didn't know most of them. But when I saw them and how they reacted it was…the most magical feeling I ever had in my entire life. I never felt such a feeling of *belonging.* It was like I had died and was approaching heaven with my beat-up truck full of…*life.*

"I had the car in neutral and was coasting with the window down, and I got out and stood on the running board and everyone is waving and jumping. Someone I didn't know said something to me. They said,

'Welcome home, Chicken.' And they *meant* it. Everyone was cheering, like just because I was here now everything was going to be OK. They were all *genuinely happy* to see me. And a woman gave me a long hug and a kiss on the neck, not like a sexual come-on, but like, you're a good boy and I'm a woman and it will make you feel good to feel this. I would have done anything to have that warm feeling again. Which is why I kept working with the event.

"But that warm feeling was gone, never to be had again. Oh, the event gave me other feelings, other quality emotional treats to be…*exploited*. But that moment of me pulling up in that truck, that's what-life is supposed to be about. And I know that one day after some fourteen-year-old shoots me in the stomach on the street, just as some rite of passage to get into the gang, this stupid, pointless thing—and I'm lying in an ambulance on the way to the hospital knowing I'm going to die—I'll think about that moment, and about what it's like to go-home.

"'Welcome home, Chicken.'"

The Man is burning, 2003. A few days of some heavy gossip and grumpy friends and complaints, and this person finked on this obliga-tion and this one's a power-hungry bitch and when the hell can we get out of here? And my head was a little too filled with the things people had to say about one another.

The Man going off was a little screwed up, like it usually is, and some neon was out and an arm fell but finally it all happened. And while the detonation of the Man himself was perhaps no great feat, nothing close to the greatest thing I'd ever seen, it did what it was supposed to do, really all it was ever supposed to do: gather the crowd, the city, the people, give us a reason that we could pretend made sense to come together. And to make things. And to talk. And to make each other laugh. And to celebrate. To get a chance to try something new and feel encouraged in doing so. And I started to realize it was very, very old-fashioned: If you had a big project to work on out there—and I always make sure that I do—you worked all morning, and took a break when the noonday heat was at its worst, and then worked through the afternoon and it all felt so…agricultural, except that the ground I stood on was as barren as it could be. It-was a good rhythm to live in, that's all, a good, sweet, fulfilling, renewing pattern to life: work with your friends all day and celebrate with them at night. Neo-tribalism, indeed.

So I looked at the Man coated in his nimbus of fire, going away, and I remembered a little wisdom from the old days: Why do we burn the Man? If we didn't, we couldn't build him to burn him again next year. And then we wouldn't have the excuse for us all to be here—us, feeling like something bigger and more than just a bunch of strangers and friends—and I realized that this was able to happen, this moment, because whatever it took for us to be here, whatever it took for the city to be as full of charm and delights as it was, we all did it—we all did the right thing. We showed up when we needed to, we swung the hammers, we carried the water, we were brave when courage was required, and every single one of us was an integral part of the strange machine that makes experience that brought us here to witness the Man bursting out with his lights lights lights and he fell and it all worked because we all did the right thing and here we are!

The world is a desert. It's up to us to fill it in.

Acknowledgments

My first thanks must go to the people who allowed me to formally interview them, or who provided me with written reminiscences, about their experiences and observations regarding Burning Man, both on and off the record, named and nameless. Here are the named ones: Justin Atwood (Jarico Reese), John Perry Barlow, Scott Beale, Mike Bilbo (BLM), William Binzen, Stephen Black, Harrod Blank, Jessica Bobier (the Nurse), John Bogard, Joanne Bond, Amacker Bullwinkle, Robert Burke, Chris Campbell, Steven Carthy, Michael Christian, Peter Christian, D.A. (DPW), Dan Das Mann, Erik Davis, Chris DeMonterey, Peter Doty, Doyle (DPW), Harley Dubois, Savitri Durkee, Matthew Ebert (Metric, DPW), Garth Elliott, Kevin Evans, Joe Fenton (Boggman, Black Rock Rangers), Jenne Giles, Wally Glenn, Susan Glover, Marian Goodell (Maid Marian), Andie Grace (Action Girl), Mary Grauberger, Tyler Hanson, Christina Harbridge, Larry Harvey, Steve Heck, Karie Henderson, Duane Hoover (Big Bear, Black Rock Rangers), Michael Hopkins (Flash), Jerry James, Jewelz Cody (Department of Mutant Vehicles), Bill Kennedy, Syd Klinge, Robert Kozinets, Holly Kreuter, Christine Kristen (LadyBee), Vanessa Kuemmerle, John Law, Leonardo, Jennifer Linx (Kamakhya Devi), Candace Locklear, Longpig (Black Rock Rangers), Seth Malice, Stuart Mangrum, Jim Mason, Kevin Mathieu, Mateo, Michael Michael (Danger Ranger), Greg Miller (Seadog, Black Rock Rangers), Steve Mobia, Sergeant Dan Murphy (Pershing County), Aaron Muszalski, Leo Nash, Lisa Nigro, George Paap, Andy Pector, Mark Perez, Tony Perez (Coyote, DPW), Mark Pesce, Nancy Phelps, Richard Pocklington, Jeremy Porter (Cypher, Black Rock Rangers), Mr. Potato (DPW), Chris Radcliffe, Steven Raspa, Randy Reader (BLM), Red, Terry Reed (BLM), Charles Reeve, Howard Rheingold, Austin Richards (Dr. Megavolt), Al Ridenour (Rev. Al), John Rinaldi (Chicken John), Christian Ristow, Will Roger, Crimson Rose, Danielle Schasse, Rosanna Scimeca, P. Segal, Pam Seidenmann, Jim Shaw,

Lanny Shay (Longshot, Black Rock Rangers), Sheriff Ron Skinner (Pershing County), Charlie Smith, Bill Smythe, Kimric Smythe, Kal Spelletich, Vera St. John, Loella Sweet (Mama Lola), Rev. Billy Talen, Gary Taylor (Rockstar), Jeff Thomas (Dr. Fuckoffsky, DPW), Judge Philip Thomas, Jaime Thompson (BLM), Brad Wieners, Cary Wostal (BLM), JoLynne Worley (BLM).

I also must express my gratitude to the various artists and camps that I have worked with and lived with and who have made my nine Burning Mans so memorable. Too many to name all of them, but all the artists allowed me to hold up small roles in great projects with some dignity, and for that I can never thank them enough. Some of them are thanked in the formal interview list above; some more whom I could not neglect among the people I camped with and worked with at Burning Man include Darby Romeo, Philip Bonham, Doron Klein, Zeffron, Dan Tartre, Donya, Suzanne Johnson, Joe Martin (Joe Joe the Clown), and Marlene Kryza. Margaret Griffis took me to my first few Burning Mans and was marvelously supportive in getting this project off the ground.

Jim Graham (Ronjon) of the Burning Man media team was as helpful and encouraging as he was able; Epiphany Stardust graciously offered needed leads and introductions in Austin; Eduardo Vera and Carol Hayman gave kind guidance when it was needed in Mexico; Andrea Rich granted me a forbearance that passeth all understanding; Gollocks got me to pray at an opportune moment; Barry Malzberg, one of my heroes, sent me an e-mail of encouragement whose importance to me he could not have guessed; and Silke Tudor saved my life one night.

Burning Man is indeed a consuming fire. Many friends who cared quite a bit less than I did tolerated long hours of talk about Burning Man and its meaning, and the agonies and ecstasies of writing about it. I thank especially for their patience and friendship Kip Haugan, Carl Liss, Phil Lollar, Sara Rimensnyder, Joyce Slaton, Daniel Browning Smith, and Beth Zonderman.

The residents of a warehouse on Army Street in San Francisco put up with my presence for months while I researched this book. I'd like to thank for their patient hospitality John Rinaldi, the Emmy Award–winning Anna Fitch, Dammit the Wonder Dog, Kelek Stevenson, Freddie Price, Simone Davalos, Paul DeJong, and everyone else who had to wait a little longer for the toilet because of me.

The Odeon Bar in San Francisco, where Valencia meets Mission, is the best place outside the playa to meet important people and have useful discussions relating to the world of Burning Man. I thank its staff, proprietors, and patrons for more than a hundred hours of drunken insight. Scott Beale's Laughing Squid events list (www.laughingsquid. org) is the best means to keep up with the weird art scenes in the Bay Area that both feed into and are fed from Burning Man, and I'd like to thank him for all the effort to keep that grand public resource alive.

My colleagues at *Reason* magazine helped support this book during its buildup and execution. I thank Mike Alissi, Barbara Burch, Charles Paul Freund, Nick Gillespie, David Nott, Sara Rimensnyder, Jacob Sullum, and Jesse Walker for all the advice and encouragement as this wended its way from idea to book. Then-editor Virginia Postrel first gave me the go-ahead to write about Burning Man and its curious relationship with government authorities for *Reason* in 1999. Current editor Nick Gillespie helped convince me that that article would make the germ for a good book and granted me a sabbatical from my daily duties to write it. Kerry Howley, *Reason's* 2003 summer intern, was of enormous help with interview transcriptions and digging up needed clips and information.

There are dozens more acquaintances and strangers who told me interesting tales or observations about Burning Man on the fly, or simply lived out their Burning Man moments with me—many whose names I never even knew. I'd like to thank them all for participating in my act of spectatorship.

Thanks to my agent, William Clark, and my editor, Claire Smith, for believing in the project and shepherding its way to reality. They granted me what a sometimes panicked author needed most: space and time. They nobly bore what must have sometimes seemed a maddening uncertainty. Claire's sensitive intelligence regarding the subject matter and the written word was of immeasurable help in making this-book as good as it is, and any remaining faults are my own. The skilled ministrations of copyeditor Shannon Langone also helped make this a better book.

My family has, of course, been a vital contributor to whatever ability I have to do anything at all, much less write a book. My parents, Frank and Helene Doherty, were always marvelously supportive in allowing me to follow my interests wherever they led, and nothing I've ever accomplished would have been possible but for them. My brother, Jim, sister-in-law, Beth, and nephew, Gram, are a constant inspiration and support.

Angela Izzo-Peppe married me at what must have seemed an awkward moment for her, during the middle of researching and writing this book, just because I needed it. I thank her, and now that this is all over we can have that honeymoon you deserve.

INDEX

About the Author

Brian Doherty is a senior editor at *Reason* magazine, a monthly of politics and culture. He has written for dozens of publications, ranging from the *Washington Post* to *USA Today* to Salon.com, and his work has been anthologized in many books. He lives in Los Angeles and has attended Burning Man for the past nine years.